THE DEVIL AS MUSE

MCI

The Making of the Christian Imagination

Stephen Prickett
general editor

OTHER BOOKS IN THIS SERIES

Rowan Williams, *Dostoevsky*
Kevin J. Gardner, *Betjeman*

THE DEVIL AS MUSE

Blake, Byron, and the Adversary

Fred Parker

BAYLOR UNIVERSITY PRESS

© 2011 by Baylor University Press
Waco, Texas 76798-7363

Jacket Design by Cynthia Dunne, Blue Farm Graphics
Cover Image: *Dr. Faustus in Counsel with the Devil*, from Gent's 1648 translation
    of "Dr. Faustus" by Christopher Marlowe (1564–1593) from a collection
    of chapbooks on esoterica (woodcut). Used by permission of Bridgeman
    Art Library.

Interior Image: BLAKE: ANGELS, 1795. The Good and Evil Angels strug-
    gling for Possession of a Child. Watercolor by William Blake, 1795. Used
    by permission of the Granger Collection, New York.

Library of Congress Cataloging-in-Publication Data

Parker, G. F. (Graham Frederick), 1956-
  The devil as muse : Blake, Byron, and the adversary / Fred Parker.
    p. cm. -- (Making of the Christian imagination)
  Includes bibliographical references and index.
  ISBN 978-1-60258-269-9 (hardback : alk. paper)
  1. Blake, William, 1757-1827--Characters--Devil. 2. Byron, George Gordon
Byron, Baron, 1788-1824--Characters--Devil. 3. Mann, Thomas, 1875-1955.
Doktor Faustus. 4. Devil in literature. 5. Artists in literature. 6. Opposi-
tion, Theory of, in literature. 7. Creative ability in literature. 8. Imagina-
tion--Religious aspects--Christianity. 9. Creation (Literary, artistic, etc.)-
-Religious aspects--Christianity. I. Title. II. Title: Blake, Byron, and the
adversary.
  PR4148.D48P37 2011
  821'.7--dc22

                          2010020205

Printed in the United States of America on acid-free paper with a minimum
of 30% pcw recycled content.

For Matthew, Imogen, and Rosie

and for Jan, as ever

For the serpent was wiser than any of the animals that were in Paradise. . . . But the creator cursed the serpent, and called him devil. And he said, "Behold, Adam has become like one of us, knowing evil and good."

—The gnostic *Testimony of Truth*

Is this the sense of belief in the Devil: that not everything that comes to us as an inspiration comes from what is good?

—Ludwig Wittgenstein, *Culture and Value*

The stranger and enemy, we've seen him in the mirror.

—George Seferis, "Mythistorema"

Contents

Acknowledgments

The discussion of Bulgakov's *The Master and Margarita* in chapter 5 owes much to the stimulus given by participants at the 2009 Trialogue Conference: Literature, Psychotherapy, Spirituality; I am grateful to all those present on that occasion. I would also like to thank Tony Howe, for getting me to read Byron with fresh eyes, and Stephen Prickett, for his generous and most undiabolical support and encouragement.

Notes on References

Quotations from the Bible are taken from the King James Version.

Quotations from *Paradise Lost* are taken from John Milton, *Paradise Lost*, ed. Gordon Teskey (New York: Norton, 2005).

Quotations from Blake's poetry are taken from *Blake: The Complete Poems*, ed. W. H. Stevenson, 3rd ed. (Harlow: Pearson/Longman, 2007). For the longer works, the page reference is followed by a reference to plate and line number.

Quotations from Byron's poetry are taken from *Byron: The Complete Poetical Works*, ed. Jerome McGann, 7 vols. (Oxford: Oxford University Press, 1980–1993). Quotations from Byron's *Don Juan* are referenced with canto and stanza number.

References to Goethe's *Faust* are to the edition by Erich Trunz (Munich: C. H. Beck, 1972); translations are my own except where otherwise indicated.

For Mann's *Doctor Faustus* I have preferred the old and somewhat free Lowe-Porter translation. References are therefore to Thomas Mann, *Doctor Faustus: The Life of the German Composer Adrian Leverkühn as Told by a Friend*, trans. H. T. Lowe-Porter (Harmondsworth: Penguin, 1968). I have sometimes altered the translation to bring it closer to the German; this is indicated on each occasion in the notes.

I

PROLOGUE
Kierkegaard, *Don Giovanni*, and *Doctor Faustus*
The Artist as Faust

Shortly before his death, Keats wrote Shelley a letter of friendly criticism. He had just received Shelley's tragedy, *The Cenci*:

> There is only one part of it I am judge of; the Poetry, and dramatic effect, which by many spirits now a days is considered the mammon. A modern work it is said must have a purpose, which may be the God—*an artist* must serve Mammon—he must have "self concentration" selfishness perhaps. You I am sure will forgive me for sincerely remarking that you might curb your magnanimity and be more of an artist, and "load every rift" of your subject with ore.[1]

To be "more of an artist" is, it seems, to turn away from ethical purpose. If Shelley curbed his "magnanimity," that greatness of soul which for Aristotle gathers together all the virtues, he could better develop the quality that the artist needs: "self concentration," which is "selfishness perhaps." For an artist must serve Mammon. Keats is suggesting that Shelley could work more intensively at making his poems into rich and beautiful things, and that to do so will involve a profound indifference to, perhaps even violation of, ethical considerations. It is Spenser's house of Mammon that is "with rich metal loaded every rift"; it stands next to the gate of hell.[2] "The poetical Character," Keats wrote to his friend Woodhouse, "has as much delight in conceiving an Iago as an Imogen. What shocks the virtuous philosopher, delights the chameleon poet."[3] In that formulation, the emphasis falls on inclusiveness: evil as well as good, Iago as well as Imogen, the opposite principles brought into a kind of equivalence by the chiming of the names. But even there, Keats recognizes an antagonist perspective, that of the virtuous philosopher, which this inclusiveness stands over against; and the advice to Shelley implies something fundamental about the creativity of the artist and what it must exclude or deny. "No man can serve two masters," says Jesus in the Sermon on the Mount, "for either he will hate the one, and love the other; or else he will hold to the one, and despise the other. Ye cannot serve God and mammon." (Matt 6:24). Mammon is there the antagonist principle to God: it also becomes, as any reader of Milton knows, the name of a devil.

This book explores the notion of a radical tension between the ethical and the aesthetic—the virtuous philosopher and the chameleon poet—through the idea of the Devil as Muse, whereby the creative artist is seen as diabolically sponsored or inspired. Its central figures are Blake and Byron. "The very grandest Poetry is Immoral the Grandest characters Wicked. Very Satan," wrote Blake polemically in the margin of a moralizing commentary on Dante. "Cunning & Morality are not Poetry but Philosophy the Poet is Independent & Wicked the Philosopher is Dependent & Good."[4] Much of Blake's own poetry can be read as an intensive working out of the implications of his statement that Milton was a true poet and of the Devil's party. Byron's genius was widely perceived by his contemporaries as satanic, a perception he was not greatly inclined to contradict. His poetry engages intimately not only with Milton's Satan, as has often been noticed, but also with the other great Devil of European literature, Goethe's Mephistopheles, the mocking nihilist "who always denies." Byron embodied the figure of the Devil's-party poet more influentially than any other writer and gave that idea cogency throughout Europe.

The Devil has many titles. The emphasis in this study falls on the Adversary, the supreme figure of *opposition*, in a multiple sense: as the opponent of God; as the accuser, who brings the knowledge of good and evil, that divisive polarity which structures most ethical thought; and as the figure who tells us that our habits of reflective consciousness, with the opposition of mind to world which they presuppose, are alienated, fallen, the mark of our exile from the garden. To think how the Devil might function as the Muse will be to explore how artistic creation works with and through such oppositions, to reconceive or remake them in a more open relationship, at once fruitful and dangerous. Blake's assertion in *The Marriage of Heaven and Hell* that "Opposition is true Friendship" and Byron's self-description in *Don Juan* as "born for opposition"[5] are phrases which can bring together the way they write with their engagement with the Adversary.

But I want first to set up some of the terms of this discussion by looking at a twentieth-century novel: Thomas Mann's *Doctor Faustus.* In this modern version of the Faust legend, the Faust figure is an artist. Adrian Leverkühn is a modernist composer who searches for a way to break through the dead end of self-consciousness which afflicts modern music as it afflicts all modern art. Only through his liaison with the Devil can he achieve this and be empowered to compose great, if darkly terrible, music.

When the Devil comes to him, Leverkühn is reading the essay on *Don Giovanni* which comes in the first part of Kierkegaard's *Either/ Or.* It is helpful to dwell for a moment on this work, since it points the meaning of the Devil's offer; one might almost say that it causes the Devil to appear. *Either/Or* presents itself as two sets of writings, written by two persons from radically opposing points of view. The writings in the first part, by A, celebrate the "aesthetic" way of life, lived in sensuous immediacy; the papers include a piece on the skill of "living artistically" and for the moment, moving between one's roles and interests by a "rotation method" that never falls into commitment. Only thus can one escape the boredom that waits universally on constancy.[6] The second volume contains two enormous letters written by one Judge William in response to A. This writer shows little interest in the arts and characterizes the "poet-existence" as an unhappy one; against the "aesthetic" he affirms the "ethical," a life of reflection, choice, and commitment, exemplified by marriage, extended through time. Here again is Keats' opposition between the chameleon poet and the virtuous philosopher, but given with a fullness on both sides that would seem to compel reflection and choice: either/or. And yet not so, for the aesthetic is sovereign within its own domain, where the immediacy with which life is really felt and lived overwhelms reflection, along with the oppositions generated by reflection and the sense of meaningful choices which they suggest.

It is in those terms that A celebrates Mozart's opera, as the supreme expression of the erotic power of sensuous immediacy. This is the essence of the aesthetic, although it is a power that only music possesses in the highest degree. Music suspends or transcends reflection, which can never grasp the immediate, and outgoes the capacities of language, which can never entirely shake off its obligations of reference and representation. "Reflection is implicit in language, and therefore language cannot express the immediate. Reflection is fatal to the immediate, and therefore it is impossible for language to express the musical."[7] This immediacy is expressed in Giovanni's love of women—instantaneous, infinitely repeated, never diminished, knowing nothing of individuals, the medium and expression of an irresistible, amoral energy. "He desires total femininity in every woman . . . all the finite differences vanish for him. . . . This power, this force, cannot be expressed in words; only music can give us a notion of it; for reflection and thought it is inexpressible."[8]

Such music is *daemonic*, A asserts, and his language allows for a moment the sense of connection with a necessary opposite, which is both excluded and implied. Music must be understood as "a Christian art or, more correctly, as the art Christianity posits in excluding it from itself, as the medium for that which Christianity excludes from itself and thereby posits. In other words, music is the demonic."[9]

Now, enter the Devil—who declares that he knows what Leverkühn is reading,

> a book by the Christian in love with aesthetics. He knew and understood my particular relation to this beautiful art—the most Christian of all arts, he finds—but Christian with a negative sign, of course: introduced and developed by Christianity indeed, but then rejected and banned as a demonic kingdom—so there you are. A highly theological business, music—the way sin is, the way I am. The passion of that Christian for music is true passion, and as such knowledge and corruption in one. For there is true passion only in the ambiguous and ironic.[10]

Notice how the Devil's sardonic, but not inaccurate, description of Kierkegaard as "the Christian in love with aesthetics" brings with it an idea of corruption (*Verfallenheit*) very appropriate to the Devil, but which is entirely absent from the essay on *Don Giovanni*. *Either/Or* is structured upon absolute opposition; the aesthetic and the ethical are distinct, incommensurable realms, so that even the Judge's insistence that A choose between them has meaning only on one side of the boundary. (It seems unlikely that the Judge, a staunch advocate of marriage, could ever hear the music of *Don Giovanni* well enough to qualify as its critic.) But the Devil wickedly collapses the absoluteness of this opposition by reminding us that Kierkegaard is the author of both parts and could not have written so appreciatively about *Don Giovanni* without being "in love with" that which, as a Christian, he must oppose. This kind of love, this special liaison between opposites which deals therefore in "the ambiguous and ironic," brings with it the possibility of corruption.

We can take this as our cue for thinking more generally about the role of the Devil. He is the Adversary, the figure of absolute opposition, whom we must oppose—but who nevertheless, in texts and encounters like these, tempts with desire, with our secret, but now half-acknowledged, attraction to the other side. Throughout his long dialogue with the Devil, Leverkühn is sullen, resistant, rude, antagonistic; he wishes his visitor would leave, insists that he hold his tongue—yet all the time, the Devil rejoins, he is longing to hear more. "I will not let my mouth be stopped by your shamefast ungraciousness; I know that you are but suppressing your emotions, you are listening to me with as much pleasure as the maid to the whisperer in church."[11] The Devil's power of temptation is a version of the power of the seducer, as John Berger describes it in his own novel on the theme of Don Giovanni:

> The stranger who desires you and convinces you it is truly you in all your particularity whom he desires, brings a message from all that you might be, to you as you actually are. Impatience to receive that message will be almost as strong as your sense of life itself. The desire to know oneself passes curiosity. But he must be a stranger, for the better you, that you actually are, know him, and likewise the better he knows you, the less he can reveal to you of your unknown but possible self. He must be a stranger. But equally he must be mysteriously intimate with you, for otherwise instead of revealing your unknown self, he simply represents all those who are unknowable to you and for whom you are unknowable. The intimate and the stranger.[12]

The Devil's gift—a corruption which is also inspiration—is figured and literalized in Mann's novel as syphilis. Leverkühn grows up with no apparent interest in sexual relationships; his passion is only for his studies and for his music; his detachment from the flesh appears as an aspect of his intellectual distinction, his austere, intense purity of aspiration. But at the age of 20, this austerely intellectual young man is drawn to encounter the pleasure of the flesh in a form most opposite to his own temperament and values. Arriving in an unfamiliar town, he finds himself introduced into a brothel by what seems like the merest accident. He leaves the place almost at once, but not before one of the women has brushed his cheek with her arm. A year later he seeks out that one particular woman, "whose mark he bore,"[13] and—although she warns him explicitly against her syphilitic condition—sleeps with her. He then returns to his musical studies, never to see her again.

It was this act, the deliberate contraction of syphilis, which constitutes the Faustian pact; when the Devil visits Leverkühn, some few years later, it is simply to expound the state of affairs that already exists between them. The working of the infection within Leverkühn's brain will stimulate his creativity to an extraordinary degree, making possible the artistic breakthrough which he desires. Until the disease reaches its final phase and his mind collapses, he has a fixed period of time—twenty-four years, the Devil proposes, the period granted to Faustus in the sixteenth-century legend—in which to develop his powers and compose his masterpiece.

This does not mean that the Devil is nothing more than a metaphor for the effects of syphilis. True, Mann so arranges the narrative that we know of the Devil's visit only through Leverkühn's report. That he might be a hallucination induced by the early stages of the disease is a thought that occurs to Leverkühn himself, and which he urges upon his visitor. But the Devil has a powerful reply:

> Your tendency, my friend, to inquire after the objective, the so-called truth, to question as worthless the subjective, pure experience: that is truly petty bourgeois, you ought to overcome it. As you see me, so I exist to you. What serves it to ask whether I really am? Is not "really" what works, is not truth experience and feeling? What uplifts you, what increases your feeling of power and might and domination, damn it, that is the truth—and were it ten times a lie when looked at from the moral angle. This is what I think:

that an untruth of a kind that enhances power holds its own against any ineffectively virtuous truth. And I mean too that creative, genius-giving disease, disease that rides on high horse over all hindrances, and springs with drunken daring from peak to peak, is a thousand times dearer to life than plodding healthiness.[14]

The Devil's argument here strongly evokes Nietzsche, both in the attack on the criterion of "so-called truth" and in the celebration of power; I shall return to that shortly. The more immediate point is that although familiar with the notion of his own "untruth," at home to irony and skepticism, not remotely "Gothic" or uncanny, the Devil is not diminished. He is a real power acting on and within the mind, as real as the effects of syphilis, and what is more to the point, as real as the powers of *genius*—a word that, in its origin, connotes a daimon outside the conscious mind and will. The Devil answers to Leverkühn's artistic genius; he is called out by his exceptional potential and offers himself—like syphilis, through syphilis—as the means to the fulfillment of genius. The Devil himself makes this clear:

Really gifted. That is what we recognized betimes and why from early on we had an eye on you—we saw that your case was quite definitely worth the trouble, that it was a case of the most favourable situation, whereof with only a little of our fire lighted under it, only a little heating, elation, intoxication, something brilliant could be brought out.[15]

What is this case, that the Devil identifies as so favorable? From his school days, Leverkühn possessed a mind of extraordinary distinction, with powers of comprehension and assimilation in all fields of intellect that amounted to genius. But—like Goethe's Faust—in mastering academic fields he rapidly exhausted their interest. His high power of intellect is associated with a certain coldness and detachment, an attitude of mockery, a propensity for ironic laughter; we hear of a characteristic "smile with closed lips, not unfriendly, yet mocking, and with that gesture of turning away."[16] His power of mind, it is suggested, is such as to penetrate to the absurdity or the emptiness of things. This detached, mocking intelligence extends in particular to the forms of culture and of art: "Why does almost everything seem to me like its own parody? Why must I think that almost all, no, all the methods and conventions of art today *are good for parody only*?"[17]

The force of this judgment is supported by the novel's wider presentation of German cultural life in the period around the First World War, as well as by considerations voiced by the Devil specifically with regard to music. Traditional forms, traditional tonalities, are grounded in a more or less bourgeois humanism whose day is done; they are played out, cliché; and those who would evade the modern condition by cultivating earlier modes—"those seeking asylum in the modes of folklore and neo-classicism"—merely persuade themselves that, in the Devil's words, "the tedious has become interesting, because the interesting has begun to grow tedious."[18] Meanwhile the practitioners of the new music who understand this are no better able to compose with sincerity, but are confined to the mere solving of technical puzzles, or to work that betrays "effort and distaste."[19] "It is all up with the once blindingly valid conventions, which guaranteed the freedom of play," the Devil explains;[20] the necessity of critique makes for artistic sterility. What the Devil holds out to Leverkühn—through the "elation" and "intoxication" attendant on the progress of his syphilis—is release from such critical consciousness, a radiant "unreflectiveness," the "rapture" of a true inspiration. Only such rapture will permit the return to the primeval sources of music's power. This will be "genuine inspiration," the Devil insists,

> blissful, ravishing, beyond all doubt, filled with belief, where there is no choice, no tinkering, no possible improvement; where all is as a sacred mandate, a visitation received by the possessed one with faltering and stumbling step, with shudders of awe from head to foot, with tears of joy blinding his eyes: no, that is not possible with God, who leaves the understanding too much to do. It comes but from the Devil, the true master and giver of such rapture.[21]

Such rapture is the Devil's version of that extraordinary, "demonic" immediacy which Kierkegaard's A found in *Don Giovanni* and held up as the perfect, the ultimate form of aesthetic experience.

The Devil is emphatic that he always performs what he promises, and Leverkühn does indeed go on, before his twenty-four years are up, to achieve the kind of artistic breakthrough that the Devil speaks of. His two last compositions are described by the book's narrator in some detail, and from those descriptions we can feel both the attraction and the dangerousness of what is liberated in him by the Devil, by syphilis, and by his genius. These works effectively reject humanist culture in the way they go back, in both formal and thematic ways, to the late medieval period, the time of Luther and of the historical Faust. Leverkühn's penultimate masterpiece, his *Apocalypse*, takes as its subject the end of the world and the terror of the Last Judgment. It is rejected by many of its audience as a "barbaric" work—the "barbaric" being what culture perceives as its opposite. Yet we are given to understand that the work does not so much *oppose* humanist culture as undo the very oppositions out of which culture constructs itself. In an earlier conversation Leverkühn had resisted the proposition that the alternative to culture is barbarism:

> "Permit me," said he. "After all, barbarism is the opposite of culture only within the order of thought which culture gives us. Outside of this order of thought the opposite may be something quite different or no opposite at all."[22]

At which his interlocutor, half-jokingly, crossed himself. In Leverkühn's late music, the "barbaric" quality is reinforced, not mitigated, by the "bloodless intellectuality"of its twelve-tone serialism,[23] a mode which (as Mann presents it) subjects the composer's will to an arbitrary, non-human discipline. In such music, at once barbaric and bloodless, oppositions that seemed absolute blur and dissolve. Vocal and orchestral parts, "symbols of the human and the material world . . . merge into each other," with an effect that the narrator finds "oppressive, dangerous, malignant," yet also fascinating and compelling.[24] Struggling to describe the effect the music makes upon him, he declares that no one can follow him who has not "experienced in his very soul how near aestheticism and barbarism are to each other: aestheticism as the herald of barbarism."[25]

More crucially, the *Apocalypse* is said to achieve its own musical marriage of heaven and hell. The first part of the music concludes by evoking a terrible, hellish laughter: "beginning with the chuckle of a single voice and rapidly gaining ground, embracing choir and orchestra, frightfully swelling in rhythmic upheavals and contrary motions to a *fortissimo tutti,* an howling, piping, whinnying salvo, the mocking, exulting laughter of the Pit." The second part then opens with what would seem an absolute contrast: a chorus of children accompanied by a chamber orchestra, who make "a piece of cosmic music of the spheres, icily clear, glassily transparent, of brittle dissonances indeed, but withal of an . . . inaccessibly unearthly and alien beauty of sound, filling the heart with longing without hope." But at the level of deep musical structure, this heavenly music can be recognized as "the devil's laughter all over again. . . . The passages of horror just before heard are given, indeed, to the indescribable children's chorus at quite a different pitch, and in changed orchestration and rhythms; but in the searing, susurrant tones of spheres and angels there is not one note which does not occur, with rigid correspondence, in the hellish laughter."[26] In this correspondence lies "the deepest secret of this music, which is a secret of identity."[27] Whether that secret identity of heaven and hell is matter for celebration or dismay is left equivocal; an analyst of Leverkühn's music could equally well say that the mocking laughter is transformed into heavenly beauty or that the mocking laughter underlies heavenly beauty. What is, though, clearly suggested is that Leverkühn's artistic breakthrough in composing such a masterpiece depends on breaking through to the realm of the equivocal: where boundaries between opposing states are broken down, and connections between them are made in a manner both disturbing and immensely energizing.

This is the more striking, of course, in that the Apocalypse, as recounted in the book of Revelation, would seem to be the point in time when all ambiguities are resolved and the world divided absolutely and forever between the saved and the damned. But that theology is resisted in this music, which seemingly reaches beyond the opposition of good to evil. "Beyond good and evil" is the site of that amoral life force which inspires Nietzsche's vision, and Leverkühn's "barbaric" music aligns itself with Nietzsche's references to music as potentially the most Dionysiac of the arts, expressive of the flux and the energies of life at a level far below the forms of modern civilization, morality, and rationality, with the potential to overwhelm those relatively superficial cultural modes. I have already noted how the Devil's dismissal of the criterion of objective truth, and affirmation of whatever "enhances power," are given in unmistakably Nietzschean terms. Leverkühn is also associated with Nietzsche in other ways. The brothel episode directly echoes an incident in Nietzsche's biography; Nietzsche's collapse into madness was attributed to syphilis, and it was said that in his madness Nietzsche claimed to have contracted the infection deliberately. Like Nietzsche, Leverkühn finds the traditions of Western intellectual culture to be played out and bankrupt, and the music of the *Apocalypse* seems to parallel Nietzsche's view that the morality which opposes good to evil is a fabrication that can and should be dispensed with. And like Nietzsche again, Leverkühn is not content with negative critique alone but urgently seeks some newly authentic and vital mode of affirmation.[28]

Nietzsche's readers have been much exercised by the way that Nietzsche presents himself as both moralist and anti-moralist at once—as the evangelist, in fact, of anti-morality. Does his philosophy here fall into self-contradiction? Or is such contradiction comprehended and resolved in his profound and brilliant ironies? Or does he disdain the demand for logical consistency as the refuge of the weak mind that clings to a life-constraining rationality? Or is it only pseudo-morality that he exposes and rejects, so that "beyond good and evil" is really a rhetorical provocation? These are the questions that must be asked of any writer who commends the Devil's party. (Certainly they can all be asked equally of Blake.) But one different way of addressing the conundrum goes like this: we can say of Nietzsche what the Devil says of Kierkegaard, that he is in love with aesthetics, and when Nietzsche commends the life of realized energy, the life that acts fearlessly according to instinct, including the untrammelled exercise of the instinctual will to power, what he really has in view is an aesthetic quality, a quality, one might say, of style. In his essay on Nietzsche, Mann spoke of his "heroic aestheticism," compared him to Oscar Wilde, and described him as

> the most uncompromisingly perfect aesthete in the history of thought. His major premise, which contains within itself his Dionysiac pessimism—namely, that life can be justified only as an aesthetic phenomenon—applies exactly to himself, to his life, his thinking, and his writing.[29]

The life of mastery commended by Nietzsche makes most sense if one thinks of the mastery expressed in the artist's sureness of touch and confidence of line, indifferent to moral considerations, caught up and possessed by the process of making art—like the "self concentration" or "selfishness perhaps" which Keats commended to Shelley.

Whether or not this line of thought is a helpful cue for reading Nietzsche, it is clear that in *Doctor Faustus* Mann interprets Nietzsche's vision in terms of the condition of the artist. The unquestioning, instinctive confidence in living which Nietzsche desiderates translates as the rapt immediacy in composition which the Devil promises Leverkühn, and which he achieves in sublime degree, we are told, in his last work. This is a choral symphony, titled *The Lamentation of Dr Faustus*. The *Lamentation* is described as a marvellous achievement that achieves the crucial "breakthrough" from the sterile cerebral self-consciousness of modernity into a mode of pure expression. The work expresses that fullness of being that Nietzsche's writing aspires to, realized in the "Dionysiac" power and rapture of the consummately musical work of art. And, as in the *Apocalypse*, which had suggested the "identity of the most blest with the most accurst,"[30] this again involves the blurring or undoing of oppositions, and specifically of the boundary between good and evil. This strong sense of the ambiguous, where opposites are revealed as coexistent or interdependent, is encoded in the structure of the *Lamentation*, whose twelve-note serialism is anchored to the twelve syllables (in German) of Faustus' last words: "For I die as a good and as a bad Christian." The musical setting of this radically ambiguous statement supplies the thematic material basic to the whole work; it thereby speaks of a deep interdependence that underlies all its variousness, so that the interpenetration of opposites which marked Leverkühn's earlier work "has now become all-embracing."[31]

This ambiguity attaches itself to the work at every level. It is a masterpiece, a breakthrough in modern music, a supreme aesthetic success—while being at the same time a work of the utmost desolation, in which Leverkühn means to deny and "take back" all that is affirmative in the choral symphony of Beethoven. Does the artistic success—the success in expression, in lamentation—redeem, does it even weigh against, the desolation which it expresses? The question is mirrored by Leverkühn's choice of subject: the lamentation of Faustus. With that choice, Leverkühn confesses the diabolical source of his art, aligning his life and artistic career with that of the Faust of legend: a damned soul, and one who, at the end, knows himself to be such, and laments the fact. In the old sixteenth-century Faustbook, at the end of the twenty-four years of power granted him by the Devil, Faustus calls his acquaintance around him and confesses his dreadful transgression; he is taken the same night. Twenty-four years after his contraction of syphilis, Leverkühn invites his acquaintance to listen to extracts from his new work, the *Lamentation*; with his mind on fire, he addresses them in sixteenth-century German, accuses himself of crimes (murder and incest) in a way that is almost entirely delusional, and, on striking the opening chord of the work, collapses into the insanity associated with the final stage of syphilis. He survives in an infantile condition (like Nietzsche again) for another decade.

This horrific climax to the book may sound like an expression of pure dismay at what is daemonic in the pact of artistic genius—and so, at one level, it is. But that dismay, that desolation, was itself sublimely expressed by Leverkühn in the *Lamentation*. It would seem to be the condition of artistic excellence, as well as, in this work, its subject. His power to lament his association with the Devil is a power which the Devil has conferred upon him. The full horror of the pact lies in the way we must see it as both good and bad. The sense of radical ambiguity is picked up in the way that Faustus dies "as a good and as a bad Christian": this riddling phrase implies that his horror at his damnable sin might also be the contrition that could save him, or could have saved him. Leverkühn raises precisely this possibility in his conversation with the Devil. May not the very intensity of his despair, "the rocklike firm conviction of the sinner that he has done too grossly for even the Everlasting Goodness to be able to forgive his sin," be the truest contrition, the most irresistibly attractive to grace? By this route he may escape the Devil after all. But the Devil is unconcerned:

> HE: "You are a sly dog! And where will the likes of you get the single-mindedness, the naïve recklessness of despair, which would be the premise for this sinful way to salvation? Is it not plain to you that the conscious speculation on the charm which great guilt exercises on Goodness makes the act of mercy to the uttermost impossible to it?"[32]

"Conscious speculation" is the problem, for the Christian as for the artist. Theologically, such "speculation" taints his contrition with self-interest and self-consciousness, so that it cannot be wholehearted. Or, in psychological terms, his reflective consciousness—and the Devil is no less himself for being, in his encounter with Leverkühn, precisely the voice of that reflective consciousness—means that he can never be truly carried away, never truly lost in the sincerity of feeling. In the old Faustbook the anguished Faustus tries, on his last evening, to pray for forgiveness, but he cannot, for he thinks that he has gone too far to be forgiven.[33] Leverkühn, in his last semi-lucid moments, tells those around him that his endless speculations that the depth of his sin might be his salvation, mean that he is damned indeed—just as the Devil foretold:

> I carried on an atrocious competition with the Goodness above, which were more inexhaustible, it or my speculation—so ye see that I am damned, and there is no pity for me, because I destroy all and every beforehand by speculation.[34]

The only release from alienating "speculation" for Leverkühn personally is the collapse of his sanity. At this moment his mind is breaking indeed—as the Devil comes for him, as the syphilis floods his brain—and what has been "speculation" and ice-cool casuistry is turning before our eyes into a state of hallucinatory vividness, of burning certainty. What he has earlier in the book employed as *parody*—of sixteenth-century German, the idiom of Luther and of Faustus—here becomes *identification*, an idiom which Leverkühn can no longer put aside; he stands, now, where Faustus stood—and can do no otherwise. He spends the remaining years of his life in an infantile condition, "the most docile of children," cared for by his mother, without memory of the past.[35]

Yet the artwork, the *Lamentation*, achieves its own kind of release from reflective consciousness. It is said to deconstruct or render ambiguous or move beyond those oppositions with which the reflective consciousness constructs the world. We are told by the narrator that it is written, for once, without any element of parody: this being one great mark of its power, its having broken through the constraints which render most art trivial. The Devil had declared the traditional playfulness of art intolerable in the face of the modern critical consciousness of human suffering:

> Only the non-fictional is still permissible, undistorted by play, the undisguised and untransfigured expression of suffering in its actual moment. Its

impotence and extremity are so ingrained that no seeming play with them is any longer allowed.[36]

The Devil here bears a distinct resemblance to Theodor Adorno, the philosopher of aesthetics and stringent critic of contemporary culture; it is relevant to think of Adorno's assertions that "to write poetry after Auschwitz is barbaric" and that "all post-Auschwitz culture, including its urgent critique, is garbage."[37] Mann's narrator, appalled, hears of the opening of the concentration camps as he comes to the tragic climax of Leverkühn's story.[38] But *The Lamentation of Doctor Faustus,* as purely expressive lament, at once personal confession and achieved work of art, would seem to escape these strictures on the "fictional." The Devil as Muse keeps his promises, it would seem. The utter desolation of Leverkühn's final work, "undistorted by play" (*nicht verspielt*), escapes or transforms the alienated consciousness from which it emerges.

The great paradox here is that, in his meeting with Leverkühn, the Devil is the very incarnation of a heightened reflective consciousness: mocking, critical, knowing, alien yet familiar, almost indistinguishable from a projection of Leverkühn's own thoughts. Yet reflective consciousness is what the Devil offers to release the artist from. This speaks in one way of a dangerous duplicity, in another of a fruitful ambiguity. After his encounter with the Devil, Leverkühn expresses his interest in Heinrich von Kleist's essay on puppet theatre, which advances the paradox that a puppet could, in principle, dance with a grace that a human dancer could never achieve. This is because of "the damage done by consciousness to the natural grace of a human being," a damage recorded, Kleist's spokesman explains, in the third chapter of Genesis.[39] Leverkühn gives this accurate paraphrase of Kleist's idea:

> The aesthetic, charm, free grace . . . is reserved to the automaton and the god; that is, to the unconscious or an endless consciousness, whereas every reflection lying between nothing and infinity kills grace. The consciousness must, this writer thinks, have gone through an infinity in order that grace find itself again therein; and Adam must eat a second time from the tree of knowledge in order to fall back into the state of innocence.[40]

If it was the Fall that generated the "reflection" which constitutes normal human consciousness, which can also be described as the knowledge of good and evil, this passage envisages something like a second intervention by the Devil as necessary to cancel the effects of the first. Let me recall once more what the Devil offers Leverkühn as a composer: no painful, imperfect process of critical reflection and revision, but instead

> a genuine inspiration, blissful, ravishing, beyond all doubt, filled with belief . . . that is not possible with God, who leaves the understanding too much to do. It comes but from the Devil, the true master and giver of such rapture.

But in the meantime, "every reflection . . . kills grace."

* * *

It would seem, then, that Mann's novel presents a radical dichotomy, an intensified version of Kierkegaard's either/or, with the aesthetic on one side and ethical or critical reflection on the other. The attraction of the aesthetic, delivering us from the implacable opposition of good to evil and from the alienation entailed by reflection, is enormous; but the price it exacts is disturbing.

In the final chapter I shall discuss *Doctor Faustus* further and consider how, as itself a work of art, it seeks to negotiate or overcome that opposition. For the moment I wish just to sketch the beginnings of an answer, by dwelling for a moment on the sexual act which, according to the logic of the novel, is the condition of Leverkühn's artistic achievement. He himself glosses that encounter when, a little time afterward, he attends his sister's wedding. In conversation, he seizes on the phrase "one flesh" as an idea incompatible with sexual love rightly understood.

> Of course, love and sensuality are not to be separated. One best absolves love from the reproach of sensuality by identifying the love element in sensuality itself. The lust after strange flesh means a conquest of previously existing resistances, based on the strangeness of I and You, that which is of the self and that which belongs to the other. The flesh—to keep the Christian terminology—is normally not repulsive only to itself. With strange flesh it will have nothing to do. Now, if all at once the strange becomes the object of desire and lust, then the relation of the I and the You is altered in a way for which sensuality is only an empty word.[41]

The intensity of Leverkühn's phrasing comes, of course, because he is reflecting on his own experience with the prostitute: the emphasis on the "strange flesh" and on the mysteriousness of love arises from the memory of that specific encounter. Nothing could be stranger to the habitually cold, ironic, cerebral Leverkühn than the body—the *infectious* body—of the prostitute; their strange encounter therefore constitutes a paradigm case of love, as he expounds it: the transformation of the normal alienation of self from other, an alienation otherwise so absolute that any connection appears as "repulsive," transgressive, forbidden. "With strange flesh it will have nothing to do." Under the transformation effected though sexual desire, the strangeness of the other does not disappear; it is still a case of "strange flesh," not "one flesh"; but alienation is no longer absolute, "the relation of the I and the You is altered." Leverkühn's willingness to accept infection symbolizes, in drastic form, that "alteration" of which he speaks.

Encounter with otherness is crucial in this conception of passionate love. It is not a unifying passion, like the rapture that blends and unites Tristan and Isolde, which so impressed Nietzsche when he wrote *The Birth of Tragedy.* Nor is it a consuming passion, like the all-subduing desire of Don Giovanni. Its emphasis on an asymmetry in love chimes better with the "Christian in love with aesthetics," as the Devil describes the Kierkegaard who wrote the *Don Giovanni* essay out of a consciousness that modified, without abolishing, the apparently absolute opposition of *Either/Or.* The Devil speaks with some authority here, as the very emblem of otherness who nevertheless tempts us with, or insists upon, intimacy. Here we can return to the question to be explored in the chapters that follow: what has such liaison with the Devil to do with artistic creativity?

It may be helpful to review the issues thus far in schematic form. Aesthetic rapture, pure immediacy, as realized particularly in music—say, the music of *Don Giovanni*—knows nothing of reflective consciousness, ethical consideration; it is "beyond good and evil." The Devil, as we must normally think of him, brought us to that knowledge of good and evil which bars us from any return to the garden; he is the Adversary, the principle of ultimate alterity, that from which we recoil, that with which the self "will have nothing to do." Now, if we could embrace the Devil wholly, so that he were the Adversary no longer, this would dissolve alterity quite away, releasing energies hitherto suppressed or locked down into old antagonisms, and opening the road to those late works of Leverkühn where all oppositions are provisional and "good" and "evil" are found to be merely aspects of the same great dynamic life source. What does it matter that Giovanni abandons the women he loves? What does it matter that Isolde betrays her husband, and Tristan his king? Just listen to the music. It speaks to us, ungainsayably, of an energy beyond the ethical.

But ravishing though this is, it is difficult, or perhaps impossible, to banish reflection indefinitely. Even within these rapturous works of music, that truth can be felt: the stone statue keeps his appointment with Giovanni; the voice of Brangäne warns the lovers that the night is giving way to the day. Moreover, to banish reflection absolutely brings with it a dread at all that this extinction implies. There is a price to be paid for the Devil's gift. When Leverkühn presses the Devil to describe the nature of hell, the Devil replies that it is precisely the nature of hell that it cannot be described, that it lies beneath all that language can bring to consciousness:

> That is the secret delight and security of hell, that it is not to be informed on, that it is protected from speech, that it just is, but cannot be public in the newspaper, be brought by any word to critical knowledge, wherefor precisely the words "subterranean," "cellar," "thick walls," "soundlessness," "forgottenness," "impossibility of rescue," are the poor, weak symbols. One must just be satisfied with symbolism, my good man, when one is speaking of hell, for there everything ends—not only the word that describes and accuses, but everything altogether. . . . Every compassion, every grace, every sparing, every last trace of consideration for the incredulous, imploring objection "that you cannot, you cannot do so unto a soul": it is done, it happens, and indeed without being called by the word to any reckoning; in soundless cellar, far down beneath God's hearing, and happens to all eternity.[42]

Here is the final end of what it is to break away from reflection. If this foretells the collapse of Leverkühn's mind, it also evokes the unspeakable extremities of the Third Reich, against which the narrative of *Doctor Faustus* is set. In the extinction of witness there is a great terror.

But this either/or is not exhaustive. Not on the one hand to resist the Devil as the implacably alien, nor on the other hand to embrace the Devil's party so wholly that the Adversary disappears, but instead to enter into a relationship with the Adversary as the Devil still, alien yet familiar, dangerous yet enabling, on the razor's edge of ambivalence—might that not offer a kind of equivalent to the effect of love as Leverkühn describes it, where the absoluteness of alienation is overcome, but otherness remains, as the very condition for relationship? And does this, Mann's narrative forces us to inquire, have an equivalent in what the artist does?

We shall return to *Doctor Faustus* in the conclusion to this book. In the meantime, I want to consider how far the ideas explored in Mann's extraordinary novel—about the artist and the Devil, about opposition, alterity, and reflective consciousness—can be generalized, with a view to tracing their relevance to the work of Blake and Byron. Blake is a "favorite author" of Leverkühn's,[43] who sets a number of Blake's lyrics to music, including "The Sick Rose." Byron's *Don Juan* is contrasted in Kierkegaard's essay with *Don Giovanni*, its "reflective" mode being taken by A as a foil to the full, daemonic immediacy of Mozart's music. So there are specific connections here with *Doctor Faustus*. But these need not be labored. What will interest us most in these poets is their interest in the Devil.

2

THE DEVIL AND THE POET

The reason Milton wrote in fetters when he wrote of angels and God,
and at liberty when of devils and Hell, is because he was a true poet,
and of the Devil's party without knowing it.

Blake, *The Marriage of Heaven and Hell*

Blake's comment on *Paradise Lost* has the sharpness and smartness of
epigram. Its quick assertiveness may mislead us into supposing too
easily that we have grasped the whole subtlety of Blake's idea. Clearly,
he is making a specific claim about Milton, framed in a way that suits
his own purposes, which needs to be understood in the light of his
own writing and his own complex and creative response to Milton's
Satan—or, if he is right, Satan's Milton. But that claim can only be fully
understood in relation to the implied larger proposition with which it
is linked: the true poet is of the Devil's party. How are we to understand the general significance of this—the idea of a necessary relation
between the Devil and the poet?

At one level, Blake is suggesting that Milton wrote well about
Satan because he was himself a rebel, fundamentally in sympathy with
libertarian, anti-authoritarian values which a certain kind of reader—
conventionally pious, moralistic, politically reactionary—would think
of as wicked. Come the revolution—or the Last Judgment, or a moment
of clear prophetic vision—these libertarian values and attitudes will be

revealed in their true radiance; until then, they must appear to the orthodox as devilish, as satanic. At this level, when Blake speaks of the Devil he is being provocative or ironic, and transparently speaking in code: it is only the repressed or reactionary consciousness that will find these values threatening or evil. The true poet *is* on the side of the angels, when rightly understood.

But although that is part of what Blake means, and perhaps all of what he sometimes means, his proposition cannot be altogether rewritten in those ultimately reassuring terms. It also speaks of some more elemental affinity between the power of poetry—of art more generally—and energies that are irredeemably transgressive and forbidden, energies that know no moral law: the powers of darkness. These energies stand in relation to the conscious rational self rather as, according to some traditions of Christian thought, the Tempter stands in relation to the individual soul: both intimate and other, insinuating and desirable, but dangerous. The notion that such energies are closely linked with poetic creativity is, in one way, as old as Plato, who suggests in the *Ion* that the poet speaks not from knowledge but out of a state of daemonic possession; but it acquired a special currency at the time of Romanticism. It is epitomized in the figure of Byron, whose thrillingly wicked reputation was felt to be intertwined with his genius, as if his powers had been acquired by some Faustian pact that exiled him from the human convention. Or, a little more ambiguously, there is the poet at the end of "Kubla Khan," the poet that Coleridge dares to imagine himself almost becoming, who would sing from "such a deep delight" that

> all should cry, Beware! Beware!
> His flashing eyes, his floating hair!
> Weave a circle round him thrice,
> And close your eyes with holy dread:
> For he on honey-dew hath fed,
> And drunk the milk of Paradise.[1]

These powers would come into being if the poet could revive within himself the music he once heard in a vision: "To such a deep delight 'twould win me." The phrasing hints at a temptation, a transgression. Can such deep delight be lawful? Can it be good to have drunk the milk of paradise? "Beware! Beware!" The crowd is filled with "holy dread"; they dare not meet the poet's eyes; yet still they circle round, fascinated despite themselves, drawn by an irresistible power of attraction. The idea of the artist in liaison with forbidden powers is, in fact, immediately attractive, like all stories that bring the Devil into human affairs; and in that fact, that immediacy of appeal to something in our nature, there already lies a kind of vindication of Blake's idea.

Oppositions

If we take Blake's suggestion seriously, as something more than a mischievous provocation, then the notion of being of the Devil's party becomes trickier to grasp. For if we are to think in terms of parties, the Devil is surely *on the other side*. It seems axiomatic that he cannot be one of us, and we must not be one of his; his party is always the party of the other. Those medieval frescos of hell which depict him as a nightmarish grotesque, chewing endlessly on sinners, eyes glaring—or merely staring?—with a blank ferocity, a terrible absence of expression, may not be among the subtlest representations of him, but they are surely among the most sincere. Here, we feel, is a figure beyond any conceivable relationship, whom we could never begin to understand, or propitiate, or deal with. He is, simply, the Evil One, from whom the Lord's Prayer (according to one way of translating the Greek) asks that we may be delivered. There would seem to be absolute dichotomy here.

Yet we can also turn the idea of the Devil's party the other way. A party is not only, in its apartness, *opposed to*; it is also *a part of*, and to see something as a part is to imagine it as having relation to a whole. Blake thought of the Fall as a fall into division and separation, such that the opposing principles which make up our being—reason and energy, male and female, wrath and pity—exist in a condition of mutual antagonism or alienation. This is expressed in the polarities and formal oppositions out of which he builds much of his poetry: Innocence and Experience, the Lamb and the Tiger, Heaven and Hell, Urizen and Orc. If the idiom is Blakean, the notion of the Fall as division fits very naturally with the traditional story of the Devil: he creates division among the angels, he opposes himself to God, he is outcast from heaven, he effects Adam and Eve's banishment from paradise. Where there was wholeness, he introduces separation. Goethe's Mephistopheles likewise introduces himself to Faust as a *part*, "a part of that power that always wills what is evil, and always effects what is good. I am the Spirit who always denies." Faust picks up the word—"You call yourself a part, yet stand there, whole and entire"—to which Mephistopheles replies,

> Man, in his folly, may suppose himself to be something whole: I am a part of that part which, in the beginning, was everything, a part of the darkness that gave birth to the light—the proud light that competes against its mother night for her old rank and space. (1335–52)

If the Devil is so clearly a part, does this mean he has a part to play in the whole? Can we glimpse here some trace of a *functional* opposition, if not a dialectical progress? This seems to be the implication of Mephistopheles' riddling line, that while willing evil he achieves good. And Blake's polar oppositions are—sometimes—invoked so as to suggest a fundamental interdependency: as in the *marriage* of heaven and hell. The final line of that work sees through opposition to unity—"For everything that lives is holy"—and an earlier section in the work consists of just the single sentence: "Opposition is true Friendship."[2] The true poet might then be of the Devil's party, paradoxically enough, in the service of wholeness; behind the phrase lies the question of the conditions under which otherness becomes comprehensible as opposition, and opposition comprehensible as relationship.

There are resonances here with the way in which literary creativity has been understood as engagement with otherness. Artistic inventiveness, in Derek Attridge's luminously intelligent study, is described as a culture finding "ways of opening itself to the excluded other on which it depends."[3] "The other" here is not primarily a matter of actual marginalized groups or individuals, although it may be triggered by a fresh perception of these. It is a necessarily relational term, for it is a function—a kind of shadow—of the existing culture, of the whole complex of a society's or an individual's suppositions and habits of perception and existing ways of modelling experience. Any such cultural complex involves contradictions and exclusions, and it is out of these that the other arises. It is that which the culture *cannot* realize, unprecedented, singular, and unforeseeable until the moment of invention. Hence we speak of the artist as creative, or in Attridge's preferred term, inventive: yet the artist does not create freely, in a vacuum, but gives form to that which demands to come into existence. The invention of the other thus requires a reconfiguring of the terms of one's own culture, so that the other can make its appearance, can be apprehended and taken into relationship. This is not to say that it can then be fully assimilated. Here Attridge draws a helpful distinction with creative invention in the sciences, which is characteristically once and for all: the culture absorbs the discovery, is changed permanently by it, and moves on. "The artistic invention is strikingly different: . . . it retains its inventiveness as long as it finds a responsive audience, which is to say as long as it is not wholly and permanently accommodated."[4] No matter how successful, how striking and moving a particular performance may be—of a Shakespearean tragedy, say, or a late Beethoven sonata—we are unlikely to feel that the work has yielded itself up to us, that we have been able to take over what it has to give: the next performance we attend retains the possibility of striking us anew. As Ezra Pound briskly put it, "Literature is news that STAYS news."[5] What the artwork characteristically brings into being—by virtue of which it is a creative work of art—is the possibility of "a repeated encounter with alterity,"[6] where the absence of finality, the fact that the other never becomes our own but remains itself, testifies to the fundamental nature of this encounter, where we can neither rest within the boundaries of the familiar nor abolish them altogether.

This way of thinking about art provides us with a rough working model for understanding Blake's bold assertion connecting the Devil with the poet. The Devil is, in a very obvious sense, a supreme case of "the excluded other." Inventive literary artists, according to Attridge, find ways of opening themselves to the other, making encounter possible; the true poet, according to Blake, is of the Devil's party—which goes further than Attridge but along the same line of thought. The idea of being on the Devil's side may, in the end, correspond quite closely with Attridge's observation that in realizing the other the artist's own way of apprehending the world is shaped and changed by it, in an admission of intimacy or rapport. The other that you invent, Attridge persuasively insists, cannot be simply "outside" you. At the same time, the other that is encountered in the enduring work of art is not "wholly and permanently accommodated" but remains itself, and here again the Devil—the eternal Adversary—fits the bill.

This leaves one tremendous difficulty: the ethical. All that Attridge has to say about literature as engaging and realizing the other might sound, formally, like healthy flexibility and growth, a desirable epistemological suppleness; but it becomes a much tougher proposition when rephrased as a matter of engaging and realizing evil. If the Devil can stand for "the excluded other" in any substantial way, then he surely brings with him the connotation of evil: and what does it mean to open oneself to the Evil One? Attridge himself concedes, indeed emphasizes, that "there can be no guarantee that the alterity brought into the world by a particular literary or other artistic work will be beneficial. . . . Since there can be no certainty in opening oneself to the other—certainty being by definition excluded—every such opening is a gamble. I trust the other before I know what the other will bring. It may be the best, it may be the worst."[7]

This pressure on the ethical is something to which we shall repeatedly return. What is already clear is why Blake should have invoked Milton. For to write creatively is to invent an unprecedented way of apprehending the other, Attridge suggests, and it was Milton in *Paradise Lost*, more decisively than anyone else in the history of literature or art, who first reimagined the Evil One in such a way as to make possible full imaginative relations with him. The cry from Blake and Shelley that Milton was on Satan's side is a thesis that, in its crudest form, has been vigorously challenged; yet it stands as a partial interpretation of this undeniable fact: that Milton brought the Devil into being, made him there for us, in a way that the monsters in the medieval frescos, or the malignant demons of the late-medieval imagination, could never be. *That* achievement, Blake suggests to us, epitomizes what it means to be a true poet.

This supreme act of invention by Milton was also, however, an act of recovery. For Satan was not always the Evil One absolutely. The Bible allows us to trace how the conception of the Devil evolved, and a thumbnail sketch of this will help us to appreciate both what Milton is doing with Satan in *Paradise Lost* and more generally what the Devil might have to do with "true poetry."

The Secret History of the Devil

To begin, then, at the beginning: there was no Devil in the garden of Eden. Genesis relates only that Eve was brought to break God's command by a highly intelligent snake, "more subtle than any beast of the field, which the Lord God had made."

> And the serpent said unto the woman, Ye shall not surely die. For God doth know, that in the day ye eat thereof, then your eyes shall be opened, and ye shall be as gods, knowing good and evil. And when the woman saw that the tree was good for food, and that it was pleasant to the eyes, and a tree to be desired to make one wise, she took of the fruit thereof, and did eat.
>
> (Gen 3:1-6)

The identification of the serpent with the Devil was to become a deeply rooted presumption in the Christian tradition. But it is not made anywhere in the Old Testament, nor in the New. There are one or two ambiguous hints of it in apocryphal writings not included in the canon, but it seems to have been first established by Justin Martyr, writing in the middle of the second century A.D. It is not part of the original story, but a retrospective interpretation of that story, an ethical rationalization of an event which is in itself profoundly ambiguous.

The logic of such an interpretation is not hard to understand. The serpent's advice brought humanity into a mode of consciousness, a way of knowing good and evil, that is full of pain and division. Instead of paradise, there is rupture in our harmonious relations with God; there is shame, and sorrow, and anxiety; there is alienation from the processes of nature—pain in labor, for men and women; and we are condemned to die, we become mortal beings. What could be more natural than to attribute this painful change in our state to a force of pure malice, which we can confidently understand as evil, rather than to the more obscure and ambiguous intentions of the serpent, who must seem, on the face of it, to be offering a thing that is genuinely, as Eve thinks, "to be desired"?

What is true of the opening of Genesis is essentially true of the whole of the Old Testament. The Devil, as the great enemy of God and man, is nowhere to be found, although in some of the places we might think to look for him, we can detect the pressures that were to bring him into existence. His prototypes are the angelic figures who act as *satans*—a *satan* being an adversary, one who blocks the path or stands opposite, not necessarily with evil intent. There is, for example, the mysterious being who wrestles against Jacob in Genesis 32, both injuring and blessing him, although there the word *satan* is not used. A clearer example comes in Numbers, where the prophet Balaam is travelling to Balak, the King of Moab. Balak has asked for Balaam's support against the people of Israel: specifically, that he should curse them.

> And God's anger was kindled, because he went: and the angel of the Lord stood in the way for an adversary [*satan*] against him. (Num 22:22)

In acting as a *satan*, the Angel of the Lord is clearly functioning as an extension of God's will. In fact, God has appeared to be in two minds about this journey. In verse 12, when the first embassy from Balak comes to Balaam, God tells him "thou shalt not go with them"; in verse 20, after the second embassy has come to him, God says, "If the men come to call thee, rise up, and go with them," on the strict understanding that he will act only as God shall instruct; but then, when in the next verse he does indeed go with them, "God's anger was kindled, because he went"—as if permission had never been given. As Balaam has throughout expressed unwavering loyalty to God's will, God's anger at this point is unreasonable, and disconcerting. The Angel as *satan* thus has the function of expressing an aspect of God's will in a form sufficiently distanced from God himself to allow for its apparent ambivalence, its negative aspect. When Balaam finally sees the terrible Angel blocking his path, sword in hand, he falls on his face and says, "if it displease thee, I will get me back again," at which the Angel lets him pass, with the injunction (once more) that when he is with Balak, "only the word that I shall speak unto thee, that thou shalt speak" (Num 22:34-35). Balaam here seems to have passed some kind of test, or made the necessary submissive response to the manifest power of the Angel: the *satan* here is both the adversary who blocks the path and a kind of examiner.

With Balaam, the Angel is acting as *satan* only on a particular occasion. In other passages the word has the force of an official job description: the *satan* is seen as man's appointed adversary, working as a kind of public prosecutor within the courts of God. The central example is the exchange that sets in train the book of Job:

> Now there was a day when the sons of God came to present themselves before the Lord, and Satan came also among them. And the Lord said unto Satan, Whence comest thou? Then Satan answered the Lord, and said, From

going to and fro in the earth, and from walking up and down in it. And the
Lord said unto Satan, Hast thou considered my servant Job, that there is
none like him in the earth, a perfect and an upright man, one that feareth
God, and escheweth evil? Then Satan answered the Lord, and said, Doth Job
fear God for nought? Hast thou not made an hedge about him, and about his
house, and about all that he hath on every side? thou hast blessed the work
of his hands, and his substance is increased in the land. But put forth thine
hand now, and touch all that he hath, and he will curse thee to thy face. And
the Lord said unto Satan, Behold, all that he hath is in thy power. (Job 1:6-12)

This Satan is not yet *satanic*. There is no suggestion that he is a fallen
angel. (That too is a much later story, retrospectively read back into
the biblical texts from about the end of the second century A.D.) He is
one of the sons of God; he appears before him from time to time, and
is clearly working for him under license, acting only with God's permission. He is a functionary in the court of heaven; or, put another way, he
embodies an aspect of God's will.

Yet he is more clearly distinct from God than was the Angel who
blocked Balaam's path. Although one of the sons of God, he is also
distinguished from them; unlike the rest, he seems to be acting as a
semi-freelance; and he is acquiring a personality that subsumes his
function—so that "the *satan*," the Adversary, can here also properly
be translated as "Satan," a proper noun. His conversation with God is
delicately poised between the competitive, even antagonistic—as he
challenges God's praise of Job—and the collusive: for it is God himself,
we note, who drops Job's name, as if angling for the response that Satan
gives. "Put forth thine hand," says Satan, but God delegates the task—
"all that he hath is in thy power"—so that the infliction of enormous
and undeserved suffering which follows both is and is not the act of
God. Satan's involvement is, however, invisible to Job, and for the great
majority of the book nothing can assuage his passionate lamentation
and complaint; if he does not quite curse God to his face, he certainly
curses life. As with the serpent in the garden, it is clear what tremendous pressure on the ethical imagination would be relieved if the agent
of this suffering could be identified as the Devil, a force of unequivocal
malice and evil.

The God of Isaiah 45 declares, "I am the Lord, and there is none
else, there is no God beside me. . . . I form the light, and create

darkness: I make peace, and create evil: I the Lord do all these things"
(Isa 45:5-7). This is very much how God manifests himself to Job at
the end, as the God of totality—"there is none else"—whose ways are
therefore beyond comprehension or challenge, and who overwhelms
Job's complaints not with any justification of what has taken place, but
through the sheer tremendousness of his power and presence. "Canst
thou draw out leviathan with an hook?" (Job 41:1) is one kind of answer
to the problem of evil: asserting a reality that is beyond all conceptual-
izations of good and evil. But at the start of Job it is not quite the case
that "there is none else": there is also Satan. What this does is to allow
us to conceptualize the darker, painful aspects of God's government
under a form distinguishable from God, yet not absolutely outside or
hostile to what he ordains for humanity.

One can see how this figure of Satan offers the ethical imagination
a certain scope for maneuver, a certain relief from ambivalence (how
could God do this?) in ambiguity (was it really God who did it?). Certain revisions of Old Testament passages have come down to us which
nicely illustrate this dynamic. The idea that God commanded Abraham
to sacrifice his only son was sufficiently problematic to the author of
Jubilees for him to introduce the figure of Mastema (a version of Satan)
to suggest this experiment to God, precisely as Satan suggests to God
the persecution of Job. Jubilees was not, in the end, included in the
canon, but something similar can be seen in Chronicles, an abridge-
ment of the books of Samuel and Kings. In Samuel we are told that
"the anger of the Lord was kindled against Israel, and he moved David
against them to say, Go, number Israel and Judah" (2 Sam 24:1). Such
census taking is, however, a sin, as David recognizes after the event, and
God punishes the sin by the death of 70,000 Israelites through pesti-
lence. When the author of Chronicles came to this passage, he softened
it to the extent of making Satan, not God, the instigator to sin. "Satan
stood up against Israel, and provoked David to number Israel. . . . And
God was displeased with this thing; therefore he smote Israel" (1 Chr
21:1, 6). The inciting to sin is part of Satan's testing and tempting function, under God; he is, one might say, here nothing more than a double
or surrogate for the darker aspect of God's will; but by introducing him
as a quasi-independent agent, the author mitigates what was, in Samuel,
ethically problematic or unintelligible in God's behavior.

The Old Testament *satan* never splits off from God altogether to become a force of unequivocal evil. It is true that he can be a distinctly unattractive figure. To act as prosecutor is never likely to be popular, and sometimes, as we have seen, Satan behaves also as an *agent provocateur*. There can also be a sense that he performs his duties with unseemly zeal. In Zechariah, the prophet relates his vision of Joshua come to judgment:

> Then he showed me Joshua the high priest standing before the angel of the Lord, and Satan standing at his right hand to resist him. And the Lord said unto Satan, The Lord rebuke thee, O Satan; even the Lord that hath chosen Jerusalem rebuke thee: Is not this a brand plucked out of the fire? (Zech 3:1-2)

The angel (who seems here to merge with the Lord himself) then replaces Joshua's filthy clothes with clean ones and tells him, "Behold, I have caused thine iniquity to pass from thee" (Zech 3:4). So there was, it seems, some kind of case to answer, some iniquity to be cleansed; Satan's professional readiness to accuse was not malicious; but it was in this case inappropriate, and he is therefore to be rebuked.

In the New Testament, that rebuking rises to a crescendo. Jesus' mission is repeatedly represented as a struggle against Satan, who now has a much higher profile, and in many passages this struggle is portrayed without ambivalence, as a matter of ethical black against white. Paul writes to the Corinthians, "Be ye not unequally yoked together with unbelievers: For what fellowship hath righteousness with unrighteousness? And what communion hath light with darkness? And what concord hath Christ with Belial?" (2 Cor 6:14-15). The reference to Belial, or Beliar in the original, is obscure: it seems to be the name, or one of the names, of an antagonist, or the antagonist, of God; but it is clear in any case how the passage epitomizes the new Pauline sense of a strong spiritual dichotomy. Similarly, the clause in the Lord's Prayer that asks, "Lead us not into temptation, but deliver us from evil" (Matt 6:13), sets itself against the kind of collusion between God and the Adversary that appeared in the book of Job; it petitions against ambiguity. "Deliver us from evil" could equally well be rendered "Deliver us from the Evil One," as noted earlier: in the Greek, the two meanings are indistinguishable. The Devil as we have come to think of him, as a force of unqualified evil with whom we should have as little as possible to do, is coming strongly into being in these New Testament passages.

This makes good sense. What was ambivalent in the God of the Old Testament, or simply beyond the reach of ethical consideration, is now polarized out into the opposites of good and evil. The realization in Christ of a figure of unambiguous goodness, understood to convey the goodness of the divine, generates a divine figure of unqualified evil as its necessary opposite.

Yet even in the New Testament, it can be argued that Satan still retains much of his old identity as official prosecutor and tempter, the divinely *appointed* Adversary of mankind. In his recent "biography" of Satan, Henry Kelly has argued that the prevailing New Testament view is still of a functionary who exercises a delegated power over life on earth. Satan's activity in accusing and convicting as many as may be tempted away from the right path is certainly to be resisted, and he is doomed to fall from power as a result of the coming of Christ: but he is not yet a force of radical evil. Translations of the New Testament that associate Satan with "evil" beg the question, Kelly maintains: for "the Evil One" he would substitute "the harmful one" or "the trouble-some one," as less tendentious versions of the Greek. Satan becomes absolutely *evil*, according to Kelly, only in the postbiblical commentaries of the Church Fathers, when the story of Satan as rebel against God and fallen angel, motivated by envy and pride, is first put together.[8]

With regard to the New Testament, Kelly's argument is in some respects open to challenge. It might seem, for example, that a line is crossed when Jesus, in Luke 10:19, appears to refer to Satan as "the enemy." But the precise moment when Satan first becomes evil, in this absolute sense, can be left for biblical scholars to debate. For my purposes, it is enough to establish that the conception of an unambiguously evil Devil, as traditionally understood to be the enemy of God and man, is a late development. This then gets read back retrospectively into passages, such as the account of the Fall, which in themselves suggest a much more teasing account of the ways of God in which any clear-cut ethical opposition of good against evil can be hard to discern. What this brief outline of the evolution of Satan shows is that the figure of the Devil has, so to speak, a secret history behind him. He emerges from the Church Fathers to face us as a figure of opposition, alienation, and unqualified moral evil—alienated from God, fallen from heaven, the instigator of the Fall, and the malicious enemy of mankind—whereas the secret history speaks of collusion and ambivalence, observes only limited evidence of his malice, and notes that he used to work for the divine administration, and conceivably still does.

What I want to draw from Blake's comment on Milton can now be put as the following suggestion: poetry feels its way back into the processes that produce the Devil in his final, unregenerate form. This is not to say that it necessarily *undoes* those processes. It is a question of *connecting* the Evil One with the ground of ambivalence from which he emerges, without privileging either origin or outcome. The stance of the artist here can be illustrated by contrast with the different lights in which biblical scholars have presented their findings. Kelly draws a clear line between the "Old Biography" of Satan as official prosecutor licensed by God, which he argues is the dominant conception throughout the Bible, and the "New Biography" of Satan as fallen angel, enemy of God, and Evil One, which is how he comes to be interpreted. Kelly regards this later interpretation as a *mistake*, which has skewed our ethical thinking and our understanding of human nature; he would like us to return to the Old Biography in our understanding of the Bible. He is thus a kind of fundamentalist in scholarship, who offers his analysis as undoing the traditional view of the Devil. Jeffrey Burton Russell, on the other hand, would see this as "the genetic fallacy: the notion that the truth of a word—or a concept—is to be found in its earliest form. Rather, historical truth is development through time."[9] His analysis of the trajectory of Satan's representation is broadly similar to Kelly's (though they disagree over the New Testament); but the significant difference is that Russell is more interested in where the trajectory is heading than where it came from. He sees the later stories as developing, not distorting, the earlier; the progressive realization of Satan as the Evil One is phenomenological truth, not historical error.

Blake's true poet, I want to suggest, writes in the space between these contrasting emphases, holding both in view together in a kind of photographic double exposure. Milton is Blake's case in point; let me therefore illustrate this from *Paradise Lost*.

Satan in *Paradise Lost*

Aspects of the secret history were not unknown to Milton. As well as reflecting on his own reading of the Bible, he would have known the Church Fathers' attacks on gnostic heresies which questioned the goodness of the Old Testament God, and he would have been aware of the extreme antinomian views attributed to the sect known as the Ranters, notorious in the early 1650s: some denied the Devil's existence outright, but some, more interestingly, held "that the Devill is the left hand of God, or the back part of God, or the dark part of God . . . and therefore the Devil is not so much in the fault as men think he is."[10] Milton does not, of course, himself subscribe to the secret history but works with the later, received account. Satan set himself against God, fell from heaven, tempted Eve in the form of the serpent. Nevertheless, at crucial moments Milton makes us feel that this account— of Satan as the Evil One—is essentially retrospective. He does this in two interlocking ways. Firstly, he creates a very strong sense of Satan's former glory as radiant archangel. Much of this splendor still adheres to him at the start; what the poem gives us is Satan *becoming* the Evil One, just as the serpent in Genesis, the Old Testament *satan*, and perhaps even the Satan of the New, came to be interpreted as the enemy of God and man.[11]

Secondly, when the poem characterizes Satan as diabolical, Milton regularly makes us feel this as a dynamic act by the retrospective narrator rather than as a simple recognition or identification of what Satan *is*. This can be conveniently illustrated from the question of Satan's name and the ways in which the poem refers to him. To know the name of a devil, Goethe's Faust says to Mephistopheles, is to know what kind of being he really is: whereupon to his repeated question—"What do you call yourself?" "Who are you, then?"— Mephistopheles returns only oblique answers.[12] In *Doctor Faustus*, Leverkühn asks his diabolical visitor four times who he is, but elicits only the mocking permission that he may pick any name he likes: "Choose one yourself, if you would call me by name . . . choose any one you list among the pet names the peasants give me."[13] And in *Paradise Lost*, Satan is not essentially Satan, that is just how we have to think of him:

> Satan (so call him now: his former name
>
> Is heard no more in Heav'n). He of the first
>
> If not the first archangel . . .[14]

Thus Raphael to Adam. Raphael also refers to him as Lucifer but again makes clear that this too is only a way of conceptualizing him: "So call him, brighter once amidst the host | Of angels than that star the stars among" (vii.132–33).[15] Like Adam, we never learn the original name of the Devil. Instead, we must call him by some name or title of our own choosing, which will both express and tend to determine how we regard him, or how we understand his relation to us. Milton refers to him by a variety of titles and epithets, and these cover a considerable range: the Archangel, the Arch-Enemy, the Adversary, the Apostate, the Devil, the Fiend, and the Tempter, as well as, most frequently, that special term to which Raphael introduces Adam: "Satan."

The first of these entitlings comes almost at the very beginning, as the answer to the great question which Milton's whole poem is written to explore:

> say first what cause
>
> Moved our grand parents in that happy state,
>
> Favoured of Heav'n so highly, to fall off
>
> From their Creator and transgress His will
>
> For one restraint, lords of the world besides.
>
> Who first seduced them to that foul revolt? (i.28–33)

The answer is immediate and emphatic:

> Th'infernal Serpent. He it was. (i.34)

This merges the serpent in the garden of Eden with "the great dragon . . . that old serpent, called the Devil" that we hear about in the book of Revelation, who led a war in heaven against Michael and his angels but was cast down into the bottomless pit. This monstrous being—"a great red dragon, having seven heads and ten horns"—will be released for a time, full of "great wrath," to wreak havoc upon earth before the Last Judgment (Rev 9:9, 3, 12). Later in his poem Milton refers again to this passage: the apocalyptic vision of how "the Dragon, put to second rout, | Came furious down to be revenged on men" (iv.3–4) is anticipated by the moment when the Devil, "now first inflamed with rage" (iv.9), comes down to the earth to seek out Eden. Here too the Devil in the garden is seen as, or assimilated to, the enraged serpent-dragon of Revelation.[16]

What kind of answer does this give to Milton's question, or demand, that the Muse tell us the cause of the Fall?—that is to say, that the Muse tell a story which meets the question of why we feel ourselves to be exiles from paradise, radically unhappy beings whose idea of fulfillment is painfully at odds with our actual state, and who have in some obscure way betrayed the possibilities inherent in our creation. This is the question that *Paradise Lost* is written to ask. The immediate answer given here, at this early stage in the poem, is that the great cause is the Devil, conceived of as the infernal serpent, the dragon loosed from hell. Clearly this is only, at best, a very provisional kind of answer: we shall need to know more, to hear the whole story. In one sense, it is hardly an answer at all, for the nature of the Dragon, its motives, its thoughts and feelings, are hardly imaginable. It is not at all like us; it is the dragon, an absolutely alien being. In another sense, however, this makes it rather a good answer—that is, an emotionally satisfying answer—to Milton's great question. Why are we unhappy in this way? It can only be that there is a great force of malice in the world, enraged, implacable, and destructive. It is unintelligible, and so all the more terrifying, yet to know it as unintelligible—to image it as a great many-headed serpent-dragon, for example—brings a measure of relief. It gives form to our distress and, without minimizing its intensity, locates its source outside ourselves, in the utterly nonhuman. "Th'infernal Serpent. He it was": one can feel in the voicing of the line the pleasure of emotional release, the discharge of energy in the act of location and identification.

Although the Devil in *Paradise Lost*, when we meet him, is never monstrous in that way, he is regularly referred to as "the Fiend." Like "th'infernal Serpent," this is a phrase which carries a built-in emotional charge: it is an alienating word, which cannot be voiced without the accent of repudiation. A fiend—and still more, *the* Fiend—is not a being with whom one can establish a relationship, or to whom human measures are appropriate. "So stretched out huge in length the

Arch-Fiend lay | Chained on the burning lake" (i.209–10). Here the effect is grand; but the term is often a diminishing one, showing us the Devil as a distanced figure in a long perspective, which is sometimes predominantly visual, sometimes predominantly ethical. It is visual, for example, when the Devil makes his way through Chaos:

> Into this wild abyss the wary Fiend
> Stood on the brink of hell and looked a while,
> Pond'ring his voyage . . . (ii.917–19)

It is ethical when the Devil presumes to justify his malice to himself:

> So spake the Fiend and with necessity,
> The tyrant's plea, excused his dev'lish deeds. (iv.393–94)

It is both ethical and visual at once when, challenged by Gabriel in paradise, the Devil looks at the scales set out in heaven and there sees his prowess weighed and found wanting:

> The Fiend looked up and knew
> His mounted scale aloft. Nor more, but fled
> Murmuring, and with him fled the shades of night. (iv.1013–15)

At these moments we see the Devil as a figure in a larger landscape, malignant but remote, a force capable of being "placed" and summarized by his title.

Yet we are always aware that this *is* a diminishing perspective, rather as we are when Malcolm refers to the Macbeths at the very end of Shakespeare's play as "this dead butcher and his fiend-like queen." The poetry of *Paradise Lost* dramatizes a dynamic narrative voice: "the Fiend" is not what the Devil is absolutely, but what the poet is felt to call him in particular situations and under the pressure of particular perceptions. The real force of that title comes from the tension in which it exists with other ways of referring to him. Famously and controversially, the Devil is also given a heroic stature, a vital presence and energy, and a psychological inwardness and complexity that are without precedent in earlier poetry or art. In book 1 in particular, though not only there, the Arch-Fiend continually bleeds into the Archangel, as in the great passage where he surveys the massed troops of the rebel angels:

> His form had yet not lost
> All her original brightness nor appeared
> Less than archangel ruined. (i.591–93)

The double negatives strive to do justice to the tension in that extraordinary phrase, "archangel ruined," as does the use of "yet" and "but" in the intricate series of counterbalancings which follow:

> Darkened so, yet shone
> Above them all th'archangel: but his face
> Deep scars of thunder had entrenched and care
> Sat on his faded cheek, but under brows
> Of dauntless courage and consid'rate pride
> Waiting revenge. Cruel his eye, but cast
> Signs of remorse and passion to behold
> The fellows of his crime, the followers rather
> (Far other once beheld in bliss) condemned
> For ever now to have their lot in pain,
> Millions of spirits for his fault amerced
> Of Heav'n and from eternal splendours flung
> For his revolt. Yet faithful how they stood,
> Their glory withered. (i.599–612)

The Archangel is darkened—yet radiant—yet scarred and careworn—yet dauntless in mind—yet vengeful and cruel—yet struck with compassion for his followers whose virtues, like his own, in some sense survive and interpenetrate the withering of their glory. At this sight, the Archangel/Devil is moved by such a powerful complication of feelings that "in spite of scorn, | Tears such as angels weep burst forth" (i.619–20). The reference to angels makes the tears remote, yet also intensifies them. On the one hand, since he was an angel, what he wept were not what we know as tears but rather the strange kind of tears that angels weep (who we may suppose are not much given to passionate grief). At the same time, we respond as if to an intensifying simile: in spite of his fallen and therefore unangelic state, he wept with such intensity, or such purity of compassion, that his tears were like the tears of angels (whose compassionate nature the line presumes we know, or here makes us know). The double effect, which appears to analysis as a contradiction, holds all the tension of "archangel ruined"; at stake is the kind of relation that can be kept open with an alien being, or with an alienated state of being.

In another passage this effect is present in even more concentrated form. The moment comes as the Devil surveys his new environment in hell:

> Is this the region, this the soil, the clime,
> Said then the lost archangel, this the seat
> That we must change for Heav'n, this mournful gloom
> For that celestial light? Be it so . . . (i.242–45)

Said then the lost archangel: the weight of yearning evoked through the long half-line, the utter simplicity of "lost," and the stammering hesitation with which the Archangel struggles to come to terms with the "this" of his surroundings, give the passage a tremendous poignancy. To be lost in this strange place, exposed to this dreadful change: we can sympathize with this. The line reaches out to him. But the line cannot reach him. For "lost" is not only an expressive term, it is also denotative, a term of judgment: "the lost archangel" is lost from heaven, lost to his own angelic nature. The poetry remembers his lost title and restores it for a moment, just as he remembers for a moment all too keenly that lost "celestial light" before stiffening into that heroic acceptance-cum-defiance of his situation—"Be it so"—which, since Milton, we have learned to call *satanic*:

> Farewell happy fields
> Where joy for ever dwells! Hail horrors, hail
> Infernal world! And thou, profoundest Hell,
> Receive thy new possessor, one who brings
> A mind not to be changed by place or time!
> The mind is its own place and in itself
> Can make a Heaven of Hell, a Hell of Heaven.
> What matter where, if I be still the same? . . .
> So Satan spake. (i.249–71)

At the sight of his fallen troops, he wept "in spite of scorn"; here, at the sight of hell, he scorns in spite of pathos. And we stiffen with him as we read, hardening from sympathy into the assertiveness of judgment, from seeing the Devil as the lost Archangel to naming him as Satan, a term of repudiation which marks the gulf between him and us just as sharply as he insists upon the gulf between himself and his surroundings. Yet the movement of the whole passage ensures that within Satan or behind Satan we are also conscious of the lost Archangel, whose name is heard no more.

Milton is aware that *satan* means "adversary," and that it is not originally a proper name but becomes so only through its application to the Devil. When the Devil speaks for the first time, the poem introduces him as "th'Arch-Enemy, | And thence in Heav'n called *Satan*" (i.81–82). Later he is referred to as "the Adversary of God and Man, | Satan" (i.629–30), as well as simply, opposing Michael in the war in heaven, "the Adversary" (vi.282). When Raphael tells Adam to call the fallen Archangel "Satan," he means him to understand that this being is now his enemy; and whenever Milton refers to the Devil as Satan, as he frequently does, he invites us to understand the same thing. These references identify the adversary as the enemy: they see the *satan* as satanic, in line with the traditional Christian interpretation. Yet Milton also holds onto, or feels his way back to, something of the sense we find in the book of Job, that God and Satan are working together, and that the Adversary may not be the enemy absolutely. Although from the most obvious and central point of view the Devil is acting against God and against mankind, we are also allowed to glimpse a perspective in which he is acting very much with God's knowledge and permission if not indeed with God's positive connivance:

> So stretched out huge in length the Arch-Fiend lay
> Chained on the burning lake. Nor ever thence
> Had ris'n or heaved his head but that the will
> And high permission of all-ruling Heav'n
> Left him at large to his own dark designs
> That with reiterated crimes he might
> Heap on himself damnation while he sought
> Evil to others and enraged might see
> How all his malice served but to bring forth
> Infinite goodness, grace, and mercy shown
> On Man by him seduced, but on himself
> Treble confusion, wrath and vengeance poured. (i.209–20)

In this perspective, the "dark designs" of the Adversary are seen to converge with those of God, and although the opposition between the Devil's "malice" and God's "goodness" is strenuously maintained, still we are made aware of an underground connection between them. This convergence is bound to affect how we regard both parties. It is difficult to see God here as a morally attractive figure; in his deliberate permission of acts by which the Devil will heap damnation upon himself and do damage to us, he occupies at this moment almost the same imaginative space as the weird sisters in *Macbeth*, and his "infinite goodness" seems to be intended partly as an instrument of vengeance. Conversely, the perception that it is the Adversary's action which *generates* goodness (albeit against his will) must complicate how we perceive that action. God and Satan are not in collusion, as they are in the book of Job; they hate each other and oppose each other; but Milton brings to the edge of consciousness the thought that things work out *just as if they were in collusion*.[17]

The general principle illustrated here is this: the dualistic way of thinking that separates good from evil, and so brings the Devil into view, becomes poetically alive when, going beyond itself, it calls itself into question, or maintains some consciousness of its own activity—as when it remembers the Devil as the lost Archangel. Such "remembering" may, it is interesting to speculate, retrace the actual processes which brought the Devil into being. In her study of the origin of Satan, Elaine Pagels argues that Satan is always understood to be "the intimate enemy."[18] He is never associated with Israel's external enemies—Babylon, or Rome—but is most characteristically invoked by one Jewish or Christian group against another: stories of Satan spring up as expressions of conflict within the community. Thus the interest in Satan which appears in the apocryphal writings of the second and first centuries B.C. can be linked to conflict between hellenizing Jewish groups and rigorists who resist integration into Hellenistic culture, as expressed in the Maccabean war. And Satan's high level of visibility and activity in the gospels needs to be understood in relation to their date of composition: written close in time to the disastrous Jewish revolt against Rome in 66 A.D., they are in an important sense "wartime literature,"[19] reflecting urgently on the perverse and destructive course into which radical groups had betrayed the Jewish nation. "Those who

asked, 'How could God's own angel become his enemy?' were thus asking, in effect, 'How could one of *us* become one of *them?*'"[20] It is Judas,
not Pilate, who is associated with Satan in the gospels (see John 13:2).

Pagels' hypothesis about Satan as the intimate enemy is not essential to my argument, but it is helpful in thinking about his relation to
creativity. It chimes with the idea that Blake's true poet is energized
precisely by the coexistence of alterity and affinity. Her argument suggests how the trajectory of Satan's larger history—his evolution from
intimate to enemy—might be not just a finding of scholarship but
present in a single moment of experience, where the very strength
with which we identify him as a destructive and alien figure bears witness to our acknowledgment of relation. He *is* the Devil: all the more
so because he was/is of our party. "How could one of *us* become one
of *them?*" would have been a question full of meaning to Milton, composing *Paradise Lost* at a time when God's chosen nation had, as he saw
it, voluntarily sold itself back into subjection. It would have been no
less meaningful to Thomas Mann, writing in exile at the end of the
Second World War and setting *Doctor Faustus* precisely in the context
of Germany's embrace of fascism. Less striking, but still perhaps part
of this pattern, is the creative interest in the Devil shown by those
Romantic poets who held in one sense or another to their radical values while many of those around them betrayed the cause. Byron's most
brilliant portrait of Satan, as we are shortly to see, comes in a poem
that eviscerates the turncoat Robert Southey, ardent republican turned
sycophantic monarchist. This is not to say that those representations
of Satan are political allegory, but rather that the political situations of
those writers involved them in that felt complication or interwoven-
ness of otherness with affinity on which all *interesting* literary representations of the Devil depend, and which—if Blake is right, if Attridge is
right—is the root of literary creativity.

Byron Invokes the Bible

What the Devil presents to us when he finally emerges as the Evil
One may be summed up as two things: moral clarity (the clarity of
dichotomy) and alienation. This is just as Genesis foretold: what we are
given is the knowledge of good and evil, and the sense of exile which
such knowledge brings. Poetry is of the Devil's party in this sense: that

it makes us alive to the secret history that lies behind the Devil, and so makes us alive to the processes that lead to those twin outcomes of moral clarity and of alienation—which come to seem less final, less definitive. Milton's poetry, while accepting the traditional view of Satan as the Evil One, has its own ways of making us feel the forces that bring Satan, thus conceived, into being—an imaginative equivalent of the secret history. But the secret history remains secret: which is why Blake could say that Milton was of the Devil's party without knowing it. It is not until Byron—a more *knowing* poet—that the secret history of the Devil is really brought to light, and brought openly into relation with the demand for moral clarity and the experience of alienation. The two great biblical pressure points in the evolution of the Devil are the early chapters of Genesis and the opening of Job. In a period of just two months in 1821, Byron wrote two works which scandalously drew attention to both.

It was his drama *Cain* that brought the secret history of the Devil most directly into view. Byron uncovers it at its most sensitive point: the Devil's absence from the garden of Eden. Cain, who is yet to kill his brother, asks Lucifer if it is true that he brought Adam and Eve to sin:

CAIN. But didst thou tempt my parents?
LUCIFER.   I?
    Poor clay! what should I tempt them for, or how?
CAIN. They say the serpent was a spirit.
LUCIFER.   Who
    Saith that? It is not written so on high:
    The proud One will not so far falsify,
    Though man's vast fears and little vanity
    Would make him cast upon the spiritual nature
    His own low failing. The snake was the snake—
    No more. (I.i.216–24)

In the preface to the play, Byron firmly reiterated the point:

The reader will recollect that the book of Genesis does not state that Eve was tempted by a demon, but by "the Serpent"; and that only because he was "the most subtil of all the beasts of the field." Whatever interpretation the Rabbins and the Fathers may have put upon this, I take the words as I find them, and reply with Bishop Watson upon similar occasions, when the Fathers were quoted to him, as Moderator in the schools of Cambridge, "Behold the Book!"—holding up the Scripture.[21]

By thus letting the snake out of the bag, Byron gave huge offense. *Cain*, as he later reflected, was the Mont-St.-Jean—the Waterloo—of his Napoleonic literary career. The Lord Chancellor refused to grant it the protection of copyright, because of its dubious character and intent. Hostile reviewers denounced the play as irreligious and destructive and insisted that Byron was simply wrong about the serpent—that the fact that it could talk, or the consequences of its action, or verses elsewhere in the Bible, proved beyond question that it must have been the Devil all the time.[22]

The vigor and the irrationality of these denials suggest how much was felt to be at stake. This can also be glossed by Shelley's unpublished essay on the Devil, composed at about the same time that Byron was writing *Cain*. Shelley observes that the Devil makes no appearance in the earlier books of the Old Testament, and that it is the Christians who "have turned this Serpent into their Devil," a figure "invented or adopted" in a desperate endeavour "to reconcile omnipotence, and benevolence, and equity, in the Author of an Universe where evil and good are inextricably intangled and where the most admirable tendencies to happiness and preservation are for ever baffled by misery and decay." Hence the doctrine of the Devil is "the weak place of the popular religion—the vulnerable belly of the crocodile."[23]

Where Shelley differs from Byron, as he was well aware, is in writing with polemical intent. His critique is intended to expose the Devil as unreal, a mere piece of religious mystification, in an unmasking which will promote the death of the religious crocodile. When Shelley points out that the Devil is an invention, he is not doing so in the spirit in which Attridge talks about the invention of the other: as an invention that brings into view a reality, one which both emerges from and transforms the cultural starting point in the newly apprehended relationship. The Devil in Byron's *Cain*, however, is such an invention, and does not conform to Shelley's purposes. For here, the removal of the devil mask is performed by Lucifer himself. The Devil is re-imagined, his relation to God and to man is reconfigured, but he by no means evaporates. Lucifer certainly points out that the demonizing of the snake is a very human piece of scapegoating, the product of "man's vast fears and little vanity." But his conversation with Cain—his enlightening of Cain—will end with the killing of Abel, the bringing of sin and death into the world. It thus comes to look curiously like the temptation in the garden of Eden as traditionally understood. Baudelaire was to write that the Devil's finest trick is to convince us that he does not exist.[24] In *Cain*, Byron opens the possibility, at least, that the discovery that there was no Devil in the garden of Eden may be the forbidden knowledge of good and evil that reinstates the story of the Fall in something like its traditional form. Against his critics he always maintained that he was writing not against religion but in a religious spirit—not the spirit of contemporary churchmanship, to be sure, but that of *Paradise Lost* in particular, and of the Bible itself. "Behold the Book!" This, although wickedly provocative, was not necessarily disingenuous.

Cain will be further discussed in a later chapter. The point to be made here is that Byron allows Lucifer a nontrivial dramatic reality, while at the same time allowing some of the darkness traditionally associated with the snake as Devil to flow back toward the fundamental source and nature of things. For it was God who was really the Tempter, Lucifer firmly points out, planting "things prohibited within | The reach of beings innocent, and curious | By their own innocence" (I.i.200–202). This suggestion, which meets with no rebuttal in the play, points us back toward the God of Isaiah 45, the one and therefore all-encompassing God, source of good and evil alike. Such a God would appear to be inaccessible to ethical considerations. What troubled Byron's detractors was the perception that Byron was writing in the same way—planting profoundly disturbing thoughts within the reach of innocent and curious readers, without concern for how they might be resolved or accommodated. Moreover, the idea of God as the Tempter, the role traditionally assigned to Satan, along with the moral ambiguity that attaches to Lucifer in the play, made for a blurring of moral clarity, an intermingling of the Adversary with that which he was understood to oppose, which greatly alarmed the self-appointed moral guardians among Byron's readership.

Such intermingling is yet more knowingly evoked in *The Vision of Judgment*, a poem which Byron wrote immediately after *Cain*. This poem responds to a work written by Southey, the poet laureate, on the death of George III the year before. Southey had solemnly related a vision in which he saw the soul of King George triumphantly pass its examination in the afterlife and ascend into heaven. Southey's poem bases itself, therefore, on the eternal dichotomy between salvation and damnation: it is an assertion of moral clarity. Byron's response is a wicked, incisive parody. Without much enthusiasm, the Devil claims the soul of George from the Archangel Michael, pointing to his abysmal political record; witnesses from history are called; but when Southey himself turns up and begins to read from his poem, neither Satan nor Michael can bear to listen to his terrible verse, and in the ensuing chaos George slips unobserved into heaven.

The key passage, though, is not satirical, but records the encounter of Michael and Satan before they get down to business. Byron evokes their eternal conflict, but also recalls the opening of the book of Job.

> He and the sombre, silent Spirit met—
> They knew each other both for good and ill;
> Such was their power, that neither could forget
> His former friend and future foe; but still
> There was a high, immortal, proud regret
> In either's eye, as if 'twere less their will
> Than destiny to make the eternal years
> Their date of war, and their "Champ Clos" the spheres.
>
> But here they were in neutral space: we know
> From Job, that Sathan hath the power to pay
> A heavenly visit thrice a year or so;
> And that "the Sons of God," like those of clay,
> Must keep him company; and we might show,
> From the same book, in how polite a way
> The dialogue is held between the Powers
> Of Good and Evil—but 'twould take up hours. . . .
>
> The spirits were in neutral space, before
> The gate of heaven; like eastern thresholds is
> The place where Death's grand cause is argued o'er,
> And souls despatched to that world or to this;
> And therefore Michael and the other wore
> A civil aspect: though they did not kiss,

> Yet still between his Darkness and his Brightness
> There passed a mutual glance of great politeness. (249–80)

"They knew each other both for good and ill." Such mutual knowing breaks down the absoluteness of opposition, between persons as between ethical principles. Byron sets this encounter in "neutral space," an area of the imagination where the eternal antagonism between good and evil may be suspended, though not abolished. It is the fulcrum point in Satan's history, the moment when he may be encountered as "former friend and future foe." Byron's allusion to Job is facetious, and yet not so, for the rapport between these old enemies has a real correspondence with the rapport between God and Satan in Job. Yet here the moment is more charged, for he is not simply returning to the early conception of Satan, but superimposing that conception upon the later, where Satan has become the eternal enemy, and holding the two together. Byron—who read a chapter in the Bible every day[25]—may also be recalling a passage in the Epistle of Jude, where Satan and Michael likewise dispute what is to become of a leader of his people after his death. Jude is writing against those who "speak evil of dignities," and refers to the model behavior of Michael toward Satan:

> Yet Michael the archangel, when contending with the devil he disputed
> about the body of Moses, durst not bring against him a railing accusation,
> but said, The Lord rebuke thee. (Jude 1:8-9)

Jude echoes Zechariah's vision of the high priest Joshua, quoted earlier, where Satan, although to be rebuked, was still clearly acting as a functionary in the court of God. In Jude that is no longer so clear: Satan is becoming a more unequivocally negative figure, but he is not to be rebuked beyond a certain point. A "railing accusation" would be improper; disparagement of the Devil should only go so far. Byron gives this thought wonderfully vivid life in the "mutual glance of great politeness" that passes between Michael and Satan, well-bred aristocrats that they are, and that links, for a fragile moment, the darkness and the brightness. "The other," crucially, remains itself—"they did not kiss"—and there is in this eternal alienation matter for a great regret, which partly recuperates it: the other remains itself, yet is also not beyond all relationship. Saint Paul's seemingly rhetorical question,

"What communion hath light with darkness? And what concord hath Christ with Belial?" (2 Cor 6:14-15), finds a kind of answer here.

Beyond Good and Evil? Totality and Ambivalence

If the Devil is the Evil One absolutely—the nightmarish sinner-chewing monster of medieval wall painting, or "th'infernal Serpent" that Milton's poem first thinks to title him—then he is absolutely alien to us, and we can only fear him and shun him. In the original Faust legend, the Devil first appears to Faustus in the form of monstrous beasts, and next as a sheet of fire. But he then assumes a human shape (that of a friar), and returns as the articulate, reflective, self-possessed Mephistopheles. This progression expresses a meaningful logic of the imagination. To summon the Devil may be to find that we have conjured or constructed a being with whom we can imagine entering into relation—a being (to put it at its simplest) who is interesting to us, whose own consciousness we are drawn to try to imagine. This can be thought of as a kind of dialectical movement: a repudiation or casting out which brings the Adversary into view, followed by the establishing of some kind of relationship with the being thus formed. When this happens, we begin to engage with what is other or alien, to feel in alienation a paradoxical resonance for ourselves. The act by which Faust summons the Devil—expressing his familiarity with forbidden knowledge, his magician's art—can thus be seen as a parable for the poetic imagination. This can be developed further. What the Devil offers Faust is a great extension of his existing power. To establish a liaison with the Devil is to grow sensitive to intimations of his own connection with God, to move back toward the ground of ambivalence from which he emerges. This process takes the artist back toward the primordial, pre-ethical creativity of Isaiah 45: "I am the Lord, and there is none else. I form the light, and create darkness: I make peace, and create evil: I the Lord do all these things." No wonder if approach to this energy source increases the artist's power. Keats, thinking particularly of Shakespeare, saw the character of the poet as relishing "the dark side of things" as much as "the bright one," since, chameleonlike, it is "every thing and nothing—It has no character. . . . It has as much delight in conceiving an Iago as an Imogen."[26]

Nevertheless, if the Faust myth stands as a parable for the poet, it tells us that such an access of power, such approach to the energies of divinity, is ethically *dangerous*. The previous chapter looked at Thomas Mann's *Doctor Faustus* in this connection; much of Mann's work is concerned with tensions between the aesthetic and the ethical, and I want here briefly to consider one part of *Lotte in Weimar*, which was written a few years before *Doctor Faustus*. This section gives us a lengthy account of Goethe's artistic genius, as perceived by Dr. Riemer, Goethe's personal secretary. I quote from it here for two reasons. The first is that Riemer discusses artistic genius in terms highly relevant to the secret history of the Devil and to the relation between the Devil and the artist. The second is that Mann obliges us to see these reflections on Goethe's genius as bound up with the way that Riemer embodies a certain mode of reflective consciousness.

A little context is necessary. The Lotte of the title was, in her youth, the woman immortalized in Goethe's semifictional, semiautobiographical *Sorrows of Young Werther*. Now, as a respectable elderly widow, she is paying a visit to the Weimar of the great Goethe. She is received in Weimar as a celebrity, an almost sacred figure. Everyone wants to meet Lotte, and urgently to talk to her about Goethe—for they are all, in different ways, troubled or arrested by the presence of Goethe in their lives. This, we are led to see, is because of the pervasive presence of the *artist* in Goethe's relations with others. Charlotte is the natural focus of these concerns because in her personal history she embodies, in the most direct and intimate way, the question of Goethe's relation as artist to the life material on which he draws.

Riemer is one of those who come to see her. He has much to say about Goethe's supreme and unquestionable greatness as an artist, while being gripped by something troubling in its ethical orientation that would seem to be inseparable from its genius. He celebrates Goethe much as Keats celebrates the Shakespearean "poetical character" as the power to be "every thing and nothing." Riemer speaks of this power in the highest terms: he sees it as godlike. But precisely for that reason, he feels—more strongly than Keats—intensely ambivalent toward it: which is also to say that he regards it as inherently ambivalent. It would not be accurate, Riemer says, to describe Goethe as *inspired*.

It is something else, I know not what; something higher, perhaps, let us say. He is illumined. But inspired he is not. Can you imagine the Lord God being that? He is the object of our fervour; but to Him it is of course foreign. One ascribes to Him a peculiar coldness, a destructive equanimity. For what should He feel enthusiasm, on whose side should he stand? For He is the whole, He is His own side, He stands on His side, His attitude is one of all-embracing irony. I am no theologian, my good friend, and no philosopher. But my experience has often led me to speculate upon the relation between, yes, the unity of the All and the Nothing, nihil. And if it is allowable to derive from this sinister word a cult, a system, a mental attitude towards the world, then one may justly go on to equate the all-embracingness and the nihilism. It follows that it is wrong to conceive of God and the Devil as opposed principles; more correctly, the diabolic is only one side—the wrong side, if you like—of the divine. If God is All, then He is also the Devil, and one cannot approach to the godlike without at the same time approaching to the diabolic—so that, in a manner of speaking, heaven looks at you out of one eye, and the hell of the iciest negation and most destructive neutrality out of the other. But whether they lie close together or far apart, it is two eyes, my dear lady, that make up one gaze. So now I ask you: what sort of gaze is that wherein the horrifying contradiction of the two eyes is united? I will tell you, tell you and myself: it is the gaze of absolute art, which is at once absolute love and absolute nihilism and indifference, and implies that horrifying approach to the godlike-diabolic which we call genius.[27]

"Horrifying" is a strong word. Riemer is continually half-withdrawing the idea and then returning to it. He speaks of "the exceptional well-being one feels" in Goethe's presence, yet this is "accompanied withal by some distress, so that at times you cannot sit still in your chair, but would like to run away." He speaks of Goethe's extraordinary tolerance of whatever life presents as something marvellous, yet also something disturbing,

amounting to a most peculiar coldness, a crushing indifference; to the neutrality of absolute art, my dear lady, which always takes its own side and says in the words of the old rhyme: "I care for nobody, no, not I." It amounts, in other words, to an all-embracing irony. While we were driving one day he said to me: "Irony is the grain of salt without which nothing we eat would have any savour." My mouth went open, and not only that, a cold shiver went down my back. For I am not like that man who had to learn how to shiver and shake; I admit that I shiver easily, and here was reason enough. Think what that means: nothing has savour without irony. *Id est* nihilism, that is nihilism itself, the destruction of all feeling save for absolute art—if you can call that feeling.[28]

The all-embracingness of Goethe's being is godlike, Riemer says; like the gods of pagan myth, it gives off a sweet aroma, which is indescribably pleasant to breathe; and yet it precludes not only the ethical, but also "joy," the joy of involvement, of partisanship:

> When we say "a god," we also mean a being not Christian; and in all that I have been describing there is nothing Christian, you may be sure. No faith in anything good in the world, no espousal of the good, no feeling or enthusiasm for it. . . . It is an unbelieving spirit, it has no heart, or rather one which manifests itself only in the form of sympathy, and in a kind of light and casual trifling. Its real essence is an all-embracing scepticism, the scepticism of Proteus. The wonderfully pleasant feeling that we have must not mislead us to believe that joy dwells therein. For joy, unless I am entirely wrong, dwells only in faith and enthusiasm, yes, in taking sides—never, never in mocking irony and destructive indifference.[29]

Riemer's dismay at Goethe's indifference to taking sides suggests why Blake's conception of the poet as of the Devil's party needs to walk the tightrope that it does, insisting on partisanship even while it looks to energies beyond good and evil. Riemer sees in Goethe "the neutrality of absolute art," which, embracing all things indifferently, overcomes the conception of God and the Devil as opposed principles. Such art takes us back to the tremendous, ambivalent divinity of Isaiah 45, source of good and evil alike. But it is very noticeable that Riemer cannot respond to the Goethean all-embracingness (or irony) with a corresponding embracingness or irony of his own. His response, on the contrary, is ethically inflected, and deeply troubled. Goethe's power of vision makes for "nihilism," "mocking irony," "destructive indifference." There is a slide here between Riemer identifying nihilism with the dark side of the artist's vision and his locating it in the coexistence of the brightness and the darkness together. The tolerance of the diabolical is itself seen as diabolical; Goethe's indifference to the ethical, his absolute unconcern with taking sides, provokes in Riemer a response that reinstalls the claims of the ethical, or rather that struggles unhappily to do so.

The historical Riemer gave up his own academic career to work as Goethe's secretary; Riemer in Mann's narrative refers repeatedly to the desirability, yet impossibility, of leaving his employment. Close personal contact with Goethe is represented throughout the novel as problematic, even dangerous; Riemer's fascination with Goethe's sublime indifference, the presence and fullness of his being, seems to have left him obscurely damaged. How deeply his admiration for Goethe has destabilized him is powerfully communicated by his endless oscillations between praise and criticism—to overstate the effect only a little, this worshipper of Goethe's genius would hate him if he dared—and by the tremendous pressure under which his thoughts about Goethe pour out of him, for page after page of text, on the occasion of his meeting with Charlotte. I have needed to quote him at length in order to convey this hectic, overwrought quality in his account. Toward the end of his interview,

> the man appeared wholly exhausted, and no wonder. A person does not talk at such length, all in one burst and with such eloquence and vehemence, on such a theme—so burning to the speaker as this obviously was—without expending himself utterly. He showed signs which Charlotte noticed with apprehension—to use a favourite word of her visitor. She even felt a certain distaste. He was pallid, beads of sweat stood on his brow, his ox-eyed gaze was blind and staring, his mouth was open, his breath came in audible gasps. The expression on his face was like a tragic mask.[30]

What has put Riemer under such terrible strain is the exposure to Goethe's genius, which he both reveres and mistrusts in ways that, being no artist himself, he can scarcely reconcile. There is real substance in the questions he raises about the morality of art and the humanity of the artist—much of what he says overlaps with what Mann writes elsewhere about Goethe—but he also speaks as someone damaged by his fascination with the great man. This, of course, exemplifies the point of his concern: but it also makes him an imperfect witness. Mann makes us see that Riemer is struggling, obsessively, almost pathologically, to conceptualize a power which exceeds and escapes conceptualization, and to establish the moral tendency of a power which is, by his own account, beyond good and evil. The English word (used also in the German, as a foreign term) is exactly right: Riemer is all *apprehension*, giving voice to the reflective consciousness which must stand outside the all-embracingness of art in the fearful attempt to apprehend it.

Here we seem to have two things: the all-embracing vision of the artist, said to be at home with the diabolical, and the reflective consciousness of the witnessing narrative voice, which transmits to us that idea of the artist's vision, but does so with palpable inadequacy and strain. But these do not exhaust the situation, for there are not two elements here but three. As well as the kind of "indifferent," all-embracing art which is being posited, there is also the art of Mann. This is an art grounded in reflective consciousness, as the extracts given are already enough to indicate: it is self-conscious, intellectual, conceptualizing, to a fault; its formal mode is that of realist narrative, accepting the responsibilities of representation, renouncing the immediacies of modernism. It has much in common with the voice of Riemer and shares in his concerns: but through Riemer it reaches beyond him to forge or express a *relation* between the "absolute art" here posited as Goethe's and the reflective consciousness which necessarily stands over against it, on one side.

Reflective Consciousness and the Siege of Contraries

In Genesis, reflective consciousness is associated with the Fall. It could even be said to constitute the Fall. "Your eyes shall be opened, and ye shall be as gods, knowing good and evil," are the serpent's words to Eve; the immediate consequence is a shameful sexual self-consciousness— "they knew that they were naked"—and the expulsion from paradise. It is a myth about loss, and about growing up, and about the link between knowledge and separation. It is a wholly dismaying event, on the face of it: but the thought that the serpent may not have been the Devil restores to the event a deep ambivalence (as, in another way, does the Christian doctrine of the Fortunate Fall).

Something of this deep ambivalence is present also in Blake's dictum about true poetry in its relation to consciousness. Milton "was a true Poet and of the Devils party without knowing it."[31] This can be read in two ways. By one reading, Blake is saying that all true poets are of the Devil's party, as was Milton, although he did not know it. This tends to imply that if Milton had been more fully conscious of his true affiliation, he would have written even better; he would no longer have been "in fetters" when writing of God, for example. But Blake's assertion can also be taken in a different sense: *all true poets are of the Devil's party without knowing it.* By this reading, a certain unselfconsciousness or lowered level of consciousness is essential to true poetry, and knowledge, or reflection, is its enemy. Blake's ambiguity here as to the status of reflective consciousness is not accidental. It chimes with the dual impression often made by his poetic voice, as *both* knowing *and* (in a strong sense) naïve. The sublime visions of this poetic visionary are liable to carry a provocative, canny, streetwise edge; equally, the political and psychological insights of this incisive thinker are liable to be expressed in an idiom that holds knowledge at arm's length from clear conceptualization. In Blakean terms, the issue is of how, and whether, Innocence can coexist with Experience, except as pure contradiction, pure dichotomy, either/or. Knowledge naturally works with oppositions: a thing is so, not so. But if the true poet is one who both does and does not know that they are of the Devil's party (and there is a comparable ambiguity built into the very notion of being *of the Devil's party*, as we have seen), then perhaps such a poet can loosen the opposedness of opposites, and make reflection something other than the instrument of alienation.

In Turgenev's novella *Faust*, innocence and experience come together precisely over the Devil in literature, with an extraordinary and destructive release of energy. The central figure, Vera, is a woman of striking natural grace and innocence. She owes this to the protective upbringing of her formidable mother, who in particular forbade her all contact with poetry and with fiction of any kind. The mother "feared like the devil anything that might affect the imagination," and she rejects poetry's traditional claim to combine the useful and the pleasurable, as decisively as Kierkegaard's Judge William himself could have wished. "I think one has to choose in life in advance: *either* the useful *or* the pleasant, and thus come to a decision once and for all. I too once wanted to combine both the one and the other. It is not possible and it leads to ruin or to vulgarity."[32] The mother believes in either/or, and this leads her, with firm and deliberate logic, to reject all forms of imaginative literature.

But now the mother is dead. The daughter is safely married to an amiable man with no interest in the arts. Their contented marriage is broken open by the arrival of Pavel, who was once half in love with Vera when she was a girl, but was then turned away by the watchful mother. Pavel is the narrator of the story, the writer of the letters to a friend of which it is composed. He is thus, formally, a center of reflective consciousness, and his rootless habit of reflection is associated with a certain weary detachment, a failure of vital energy and purpose, an emptiness of life, as is true of many another nineteenth-century Russian protagonist with Hamlet and Byron as his ancestors. But Pavel is strongly drawn to Vera, and he undertakes her literary education—her imaginative awakening. He begins by reading her his great favorite, a work he once knew by heart: Goethe's *Faust*. She is gripped by the experience, more intensely than he understands. These readings work upon her as a seduction; she falls passionately in love—"What have you done to me!"[33]—but is destroyed by the conflict between her new feelings and the mother-inspired sense of ethical prohibition, rather as Gretchen is destroyed in *Faust*. Pavel survives to resign himself to the thought that Faust had bitterly chafed against: life is "renunciation, constant renunciation—that is its secret meaning, its solution: not the fulfilment of cherished ideas and dreams, no matter how exalted they might be."[34] What is to be renounced, this would seem to suggest, is not only transgressive passion and aspiration, but also imaginative literature, its vehicle and stimulus, as Vera's mother always knew. (In the shadows behind Vera is Dante's Francesca, another victim of dangerous literature, damned forever as a result of reading the story of Lancelot and Guinevere.) Does this mean that *Faust* is to be renounced, that the tendency of his work reveals Goethe to have been of the Devil's party? Yet it is another work of imaginative literature, indeed another *Faust*—Turgenev's—that gives voice to this consciousness in Pavel, and so reaches beyond it.

The ambivalence involved here is caught in an exchange between Pavel and Vera on the figure of Mephistopheles, as Pavel recounts it.

Mephistopheles frightens her not as a devil, but as "something that might be found in anyone". . . Those are her own words. I began to explain to her that we call this "something" reflection; but she didn't understand the word reflection in the German sense: she only knows the French *réflexion* and is

accustomed to thinking it beneficial. Our relationship is astonishing! From
a certain point of view I can say that I have a great influence on her and am,
as it were, educating her; but she too, without noticing it herself, is in many
respects changing me for the better.[35]

Mephistopheles frightens Vera, but "not as a devil." He is not absolutely *other*, but figures something that she can recognize, "that might
be found in anyone." And if she can relate to Mephistopheles, she also
finds herself in a real relationship with Pavel, a relationship of mutual
influence: imaginative literature provides the site, the possibility, of a
transformative connection between her radiant innocence and what
Turgenev conveys to us as Pavel's middle-aged emptiness, his mood of
"uneasy boredom."[36] Such relationship is "astonishing": it involves an
awakening in both parties to the existence of the other that both opens
new horizons and is morally hazardous in ways that Pavel does not yet
suspect. That ambivalence is located by Turgenev in the ambiguity of
"reflection," which has for Vera in its French form a beneficial connotation, while in German (*Bedenken, Nachdenken*) it readily carries a
darker implication. The ambiguity of the word points to the uncertain
ambivalence of Mephistopheles and the kind of nihilistic reflection he
engenders as the spirit of negation who allegedly brings about good
despite himself. Beyond that it points to the ambivalence of Goethe's
art itself—that ambivalence which so disturbs Riemer—in its necessary connection with negation, its familiarity with the Devil.

The key point about the Devil in this context is that he is always
the *Adversary*, the one who stands opposite, or acts in opposition, or
negates, or contradicts. Mephistopheles is the spirit of negation, the
spirit who always denies. What this often means in practice, at least
in the first part of *Faust*, is that through his sardonic reflections he
holds up to Faust a mirror in which all his "Faustian" aspirations to
lose himself in rapture of one kind or another—heroic suicide, communion with nature, passionate love—appear as absurd and tawdry
posturing. Mephistopheles continually threatens to make Faust see
himself through the Devil's eyes; he threatens him with a certain kind
of self-consciousness, which is also self-alienation. *Ich bin der Geist der
stets verneint* (1338). "I am the Spirit who always denies" is the natural
translation, but *Geist* includes the sense of "mind" as well as "spirit."
Mephistopheles is also the mind, the faculty of reflection, in its

negative aspect: *mind, which always denies*. Gretchen shudders at him because she sees that there is nothing in which he *participates*, or with which he sympathizes. He takes *Anteil* in nothing, she says—*Anteil* meaning literally attachment as a part—and in his presence love for another becomes impossible (3488–97). Reflection stands over against that which it reflects, as the metaphor suggests; it can readily be felt as inherently alienated or alienating, as driving into dichotomy the knowing subject and a sharply external objective world—the world in which consciousness finds itself, from which it (therefore) distinguishes itself, and to which it (therefore) opposes itself.

This is, perhaps, a peculiarly Romantic analysis. Hegel's discussion of "the unhappy consciousness" theorizes this in one way, as a state of incomplete development, before the mind raises itself up into full participation in reality. Kierkegaard's aesthete writes feelingly about Hegel's account, recognizing in it the unhappy fate that awaits those who have not learned to live unreflectingly in the present moment.

> All alone, he faces the whole world as the "you" with whom he is in conflict, for all the rest of the world is for him only one person, and this person, this inseparable bothersome friend, is misunderstanding.[37]

Such a description strongly evokes Byron. It applies in particular to *Lara*, and the final canto of *Childe Harold*, and the consciousness of exile—which is also the sense of consciousness *as* exile—that is the ground and starting point of so much of Byron's work. What Hegel figures as imperfectly mature, a phase in a larger process in which alterity will be recuperated, Byron sees as *fallen*. "The Tree of Knowledge is not that of Life," Byron's Manfred bitterly declares (I.i.12), in an expression that links the alienated consciousness of the Byronic hero with the biblical Fall. The knowledge of good and evil is not only knowledge of opposition, but knowledge which opposes.

Behind Manfred's bitterness, of course, stands the great archetype of alienated consciousness, or of self-consciousness as fallen: Milton's Satan. One good reason for finding Satan the most interesting and engaging character in *Paradise Lost* is the impression he gives of *depth*, which we do not get from the other devils, or from God, or from Adam and Eve. Behind what Satan says and the actions he performs, there is always a space for an ulterior consciousness. "The mind is its own place, and in itself I Can make a Heaven of Hell, a Hell of Heaven," as he best knows (i.254–55): and these lines, although intended as an assertion of autonomy, in fact express the grimmer truth of a consciousness that is bound to assert itself *against* its environment. The concomitant of such heroic subjectivity is alienation.

Milton repeatedly makes us understand how Satan's malice is a function of his sensitivity to goodness and beauty. For Satan, the Adversary, perceives goodness with the intensity of one who stands over against it, outside it, opposed to it—and because opposed, excluded—and because excluded, tormented by his exclusion, and urgent to reduce that tormenting sense of difference by destroying the goodness which is its ground. When Satan encounters Eve walking alone in the garden, he is at first overwhelmed by her loveliness:

> Her Heav'nly form
> Angelic but more soft and feminine,
> Her graceful innocence, her every air
> Of gesture or least action overawed
> His malice and with rapine sweet bereaved
> His fierceness of the fierce intent it brought.
> That space the evil one abstracted stood
> From his own evil and for the time remained
> Stupidly good, of enmity disarmed,
> Of guile, of hate, of envy, of revenge.
> But the hot Hell that always in him burns,
> Though in mid-Heav'n, soon ended his delight
> And tortures him now more the more he sees
> Of pleasure not for him ordained. Then soon
> Fierce hate he recollects. (ix.457–71)

The poetry makes us live through the movement of mind which constitutes the Devil: the movement from a kind of rapture, a "rapine sweet" which is also a stupor, a suspension of mind, to an acute consciousness of the other as other which is, instantaneously, hatred of the other, and which is so as a kind of consequence of that capacity for rapture. Hell tortures him "now more the more he sees I Of pleasure not for him ordained."

This is what he elsewhere calls, in a precisely intelligent, all too self-knowing piece of analysis, "the hateful siege of contraries." The phrase comes as he *sees*, but cannot *feel*, the pleasures of the earth:

> With what delight could I have walked thee round
> (If I could joy in aught) sweet interchange
> Of hill and valley, rivers, woods and plains,
> Now land, now sea and shores with forest crowned,
> Rocks, dens, and caves! But I in none of these
> Find place or refuge and the more I see
> Pleasures about me so much more I feel
> Torment within me as from the hateful siege
> Of contraries: all good to me becomes
> Bane, and in Heav'n much worse would be my state. (ix.114–23)

As when before Eve, his alienated consciousness is marked by an emphasis on the visual, on seeing pleasure as opposed to feeling it. Of all the senses, it is sight that most readily suggests or interposes distance and difference between the perceiver and the perceived. What we see is *over there*, unlike what we hear, even, and certainly what we taste, smell, and touch. This is a difference to which it is easy to suppose that a blind poet will be peculiarly attuned. Seeing also readily connotes, in English, knowing and understanding (do you see what I mean?), and carries with it the separation of the perceiving self from the world as object. The knowledge of good and evil, in *Paradise Lost* as in Genesis, is a matter of enhanced eyesight: "your eyes . . . shall perfectly be then | Opened and cleared" (ix.706–8).

This "satanic" mode of consciousness has a very general significance. To this it might be objected that Satan's consciousness is alienated, not because it is consciousness, but because he is Satan, whose state of mind is the *consequence* of his rebellion against God and his fall into hell. But myth, which must tell a story, often places in chronological sequence matters that more truly coexist. Milton recognizes this in the way that he opens his poem; we begin in hell, and Satan's alienated consciousness is our starting point, so that it seems as much the cause as the consequence of his hatred, his envy, and his rebellion. It is where we start, where we have to start. The general significance of what Milton gives us here can be suggested by a comparable passage from Rilke.

In the eighth of the *Duino Elegies*, Rilke contrasts the free participation in being which we can imagine enjoyed by young children and animals with our own adult consciousness of the world, our own way of being in the world—or rather, of not being in the world:

> Never, not for a single day, do *we* have
> before us that pure space into which flowers
> endlessly open. Always there is World
> and never Nowhere without the No: that pure
> unsupervised element which one breathes
> without desire and endlessly *knows*. A child
> may wander there for hours . . .

> This is what fate means: to be opposite,
> to be opposite and nothing else, forever. . . .

> And we: spectators, always, everywhere,
> turned toward the world of objects, never outward.
> It fills us. We arrange it. It breaks down.
> We rearrange it, then break down ourselves.
> Who has twisted us around like this, so that
> no matter what we do, we are in the posture
> of someone going away?[38]

Intrinsic to normal consciousness, consciousness conceived as spectatorship, is separation, opposition, and, potentially, estrangement. For Rilke's conscious adult, like Milton's conscious Satan, there can only be opposition.

The opposite of opposition is a hard thing to conceptualize. Rilke's child can wander in pure space, *into* which flowers endlessly open: neither space nor time interposes the measures of separation. The child would seem to be participant, not spectator. In Satan's envious address to the goodness of the earth, just quoted, it is telling that he should describe the pleasures of earth's landscape as "sweet interchange." Interchange—a blurring or opening up of lines of demarcation and opposition—is precisely that in which the Adversary cannot participate. Paradise is characterized by interchange at every level: but most especially in the intercourse between Adam and Eve, whose sexual love

Milton places so emphatically before the Fall. As they embrace and kiss, so Satan turns away, the anguished voyeur of their mutuality:

> Aside the Devil turned
> For envy, yet with jealous leer malign
> Eyed them askance, and to himself thus plained:
> Sight hateful! sight tormenting! (iv.502–5)

This is the first time in the poem—deep in the fourth book—that Satan is called "the Devil." It is as though this is the moment, this movement of envious turning aside, that defines him as the Devil, or that most clearly shows what it is to be the Devil and how the Devil rises into consciousness in response to the perception of delight as located out-side the perceiving self. What is to be perceived is always *over there*.

But what of *our* consciousness as readers of Milton's poetry? In responding to *Paradise Lost*, do we have to choose (as some critics have chosen) between reading with rapture and reading reflectively? Is it a case, when we read, of either/or? This would be rather like the choice of pastimes open to the more cultured of the fallen angels, between music and philosophy. Some opt for heroic song:

> Their song was partial but the harmony
> (What could it less when spirits immortal sing?)
> Suspended Hell and took with ravishment
> The thronging audience. In discourse more sweet
> (For eloquence the soul, song charms the sense)
> Others apart sat on a hill retired
> In thoughts more elevate and reasoned high
> Of providence, foreknowledge, will and fate,
> Fixed fate, free will, foreknowledge absolute,
> And found no end in wand'ring mazes lost. (ii.552–61)

Each of these groups is "partial," "apart," as if missing the whole. *Paradise Lost* conspicuously offers us both music and reflection. Whether it brings the two together can be disputed; T. S. Eliot wrote that we have to read Milton twice, once for the sound and once for the sense.[39] Yet what the Satan passages characteristically give us as readers of poetry is the movement or interrelation between rapture and reflec-tion, each being made present to us through the other. There is a kind of interchange, although not the "sweet interchange" of paradise. The other is functional here, creatively, dynamically, rather than the occasion of a hateful siege of contraries.[40]

We can glimpse here a model for how a relation with the Devil might figure—might enable—the working of poetry. Put in such general terms, the model is inevitably sketchy, and begs many questions. Let us now test it, and put flesh on its bones, by looking in some detail at Blake and at Byron, before in conclusion returning more briefly to Mann. What does their own work owe to the Devil, and what do we mean by the Devil in each case? "Without Contraries is no progression," wrote Blake in *The Marriage of Heaven and Hell*.[41] How far he was able in his own poetry to make that claim good, we now consider.

3

BLAKE AND THE DEVIL'S PARTY

Let us send to the aid of our honesty whatever we have of devilry in us.

Nietzsche, *Beyond Good and Evil*

Energy and Opposition

The Marriage of Heaven and Hell is the most exuberant, swaggering, and exhilarating of all Blake's works. It was written in or very shortly after 1790, in that apparent dawn of liberty of which Wordsworth wrote that it was bliss to be alive, when the revolution in France still promised to bring in a New Jerusalem on earth. The liberty which Blake proclaims and celebrates is not political only, although it certainly includes the political. It is liberation of the energies of life. Those energies are to be liberated from all doctrines which impose a moralizing division between good and evil on the wholeness of human being. Such doctrines have usurped the powers of reason, claiming for it a false dominion over the energies of the psyche, whose contours reason should rather trace, without seeking to control. Instead, this moralizing reason has misrepresented those energies as evil—has demonized them as the energies of hell.

What could be more fitting, then, than for Blake to challenge this false doctrine by giving the Devil a voice, and allowing that voice to merge with his own?

THE VOICE OF THE DEVIL

All Bibles or sacred codes have been the causes of the following Errors:

1. That man has two real existing principles, viz, a Body and a Soul.

2. That Energy, called Evil, is alone from the body, and the Reason, called Good, is alone from the soul.

3. That God will torment man in Eternity for following his energies.

But the following Contraries to these are true:

1. Man has no Body distinct from his Soul, for that called Body is a portion of Soul discerned by the five senses, the chief inlets of Soul in this age.

2. Energy is the only life and is from the body, and Reason is the bound or outward circumference of Energy.

3. Energy is eternal delight.

Blake then moves to overturn the story which has given us the Devil as the fallen force of evil, in a lightning analysis that brings theology, psychology, and politics brilliantly together:

> Those who restrain desire do so because theirs is weak enough to be restrained; and the restrainer or reason usurps its place and governs the unwilling.
>
> And being restrained it by degrees becomes passive, till it is only the shadow of desire.
>
> The history of this is written in *Paradise Lost*, and the governor (or reason) is called Messiah.
>
> And the original archangel, or possessor of the command of the heavenly host, is called the Devil or Satan, and his children are called Sin and Death.
>
> But in the *Book of Job* Milton's Messiah is called Satan. For this history has been adopted by both parties.
>
> It indeed appeared to Reason as if Desire was cast out; but the Devil's account is that the Messiah fell, and formed a heaven of what he stole from the abyss.[1]

The Bible itself is wiser than the story that has been derived from it. In the book of Job, the reason that presumes to sit in moral judgment, and bring accusations of sin or incipient sin against Job, is called Satan and correctly identified as the enemy of man. Blake here invokes what I have been calling the Bible's secret history of the Devil, which recognizes an element of collusion between Satan and God, and inflects this for his own purposes: what links the Satan of Job with the God of Christian tradition, and with Milton's Messiah who drives Satan and his angels out of heaven, is their presumption of *righteousness*. This emanates merely from their weakness in energetic desire, which is the only life. When Milton transmitted the traditional story from the orthodox point of view, he duly elevated such righteousness as deity, and denigrated the energies of desire as fallen into hell.

But Milton was also a great poet. The poetic imagination, for Blake, is always the expression of energy. The poetry of *Paradise Lost* therefore refutes the story that it tells:

> *Note.* The reason Milton wrote in fetters when he wrote of angels and God, and at liberty when of devils and Hell, is because he was a true poet, and of the Devil's party without knowing it.[2]

And this sense of creativity as joyously diabolical is reinforced at every point by Blake's manner in the *Marriage*: its insouciant brilliance, the shameless freedoms that it takes, the whiplash ironies, the delight in parody and exaggeration, the cascade of formal experiment, its fearlessness of assertion, its play of fantasy, its wicked provocations.

That manner prompts, however, a further question. How seriously does Blake mean us to take his devilry—and how seriously should we take it? Are the *Marriage*'s commendations of energy and instinct, its affirmations of "pride" and "lust" and "wrath," mock-diabolical only, but really imbued with the sense of a larger ethical responsibility? Or do they amount to a posture that is permanently and fundamentally antagonistic to the ethical? Or do they point to a region beyond good and evil, where moral considerations are found to be illusory? These questions, which the *Marriage* so acutely poses, and perhaps poses us with, extend across the whole range of Blake's work. They appear thematic, and could be answered thematically, in terms of Blake's meaning(s) or position(s). But their greatest interest comes when one sees how they interlock with the way Blake writes, and with a certain *parodic* quality in his work—parody that involves a particularly subtle way of being of a "party," of taking one side against another. It is this parodic quality, I want to suggest, that expresses the kind of relationship with the Devil entertained by a "true poet."

"Opposition is true Friendship."[3] Thus declares the *Marriage* in a single freestanding line of text near the end. Let me—for the moment—take that as the cue for addressing the questions just raised, and explore the line of reply which it suggests: through the idea of integration or, more precisely, complementarity. Blake regularly thinks of the Fall as division, a fracturing of our primal unity of being into intellect and emotion, male and female, reason and energy, Urizen and Orc, and all the various dualities and quartets that make up his mythology of the psyche. Returning into Eden will mean comprehending how these polarities and oppositions in our being come together in Eternity in a true unity, in what Blake describes in his later *Milton* as "the severe contentions | Of friendship" (599; 41:32–33). This line of thought implies that when Blake invokes the Devil—the Adversary who can never be a friend—he does so strategically or mischievously, in a provisional spirit. That is to say, he is voicing an unruly transgressiveness as this has been constructed by the organs of repression, and infusing it with such life and warmth as to reveal the construction as paranoid or absurd or life denying. Yes, he can write in the margin of Lavater's *Aphorisms*, "Active Evil is better than Passive Good," allying himself with Milton's Satan: "Evil, be thou my good";[4] but the "evil" Blake espouses in the *Marriage* is understood to carry those silent inverted commas. These are the energies which repression calls evil, and which may under the regime of repression manifest themselves as dangerous or destructive, but which are essentially no such thing. Thus the hell of torment which the censorious angel points out to Blake as his destiny turns into a pastoral idyll as soon as the angel departs. Another such moralizing angel, refuted in conversation by a Blakean devil, embraces the devil in his flame of fire and is "consumed": he is now himself "become a devil" and Blake's "particular friend. We often read the Bible together in its infernal or diabolical sense, which the world shall have if they behave well."[5] By this infernal reading, the Devil is only the Adversary for as long as God holds him down; there really can be a marriage between heaven and hell. In political terms, the fires of rebellion will forge a truly free republic; in psychological terms, desires liberated from inhibition will open the integrated personality to true delights. For as the last line of the *Marriage* declares, in a triumphant return to the language of an avowed spirituality, everything that lives is holy.

Certain of Blake's songs do lend themselves to such a vision, where what is opposite is no longer what is threatening or hostile. When little Lyca gets "lost in desert wild" among the beasts of prey, her anguished parents fear the worst. But encountering her innocence, lions and tigers prove not to be the destructive creatures that her parents supposed; the wild animals are noble spirits that protect and cherish the girl, and lead the parents, fearful no longer, to join them in their "palace" in the wilderness.[6] The pair of poems telling this story—"The Little Girl Lost" and "The Little Girl Found"—were transferred by Blake between *Songs of Innocence* and *Songs of Experience*, as able to move freely between the two opposing states. Or there is the little vagabond, in *Experience*, who imagines the good consequences of bringing the warm human pleasures of the alehouse into what is now the coldness of the church:

> Then the parson might preach and drink and sing,
> And we'd be as happy as birds in the spring;
> And modest dame Lurch, who is always at church,
> Would not have bandy children nor fasting nor birch.
>
> And God, like a father rejoicing to see
> His children as pleasant and happy as he,
> Would have no more quarrel with the Devil or the barrel,
> But kiss him and give him both drink and apparel.[7]

The singing that goes on in this church is indistinguishably sacred and profane. The little vagabond can imagine how God and the Devil might kiss and make up. This is naïve: but the naïvety of a child's imagination penetrates, for Blake, to the truth of things.

However, the child is living in the world of experience—the church is cold, pious dame Lurch behaves callously toward the children in her charge—and the pressure of social realities in *Experience* makes the child's vision seem naïve in a more vulnerable sense. We feel it also as a wishful fantasy, whose very limited power to imagine a transformed world is felt in the diminishing effect of the triplets in the homespun four-beat line. By the time Blake issued *Songs of Experience* in 1794, the revolutionary energies released in France had been found to lead only to terror and bloodshed, while in Britain, now at war, the forces of reaction and repression were firmly in the ascendant. The affirmative confidence of the *Marriage* was something which, at some level, Blake never lost: but its symbolic or imaginative truth was no longer being manifested on the stage of history or of social reality, as it perhaps seemed to be in the magical year of 1790. The vagabond's dream of integration, of a pleasure-loving church in which drinking and praying went harmoniously together, feels tenuous. More certainly real is the present reality of conflict between the church and the alehouse, at a moment when societies for the suppression of vice, and for the reform and regulation of the poor in God-fearing ways, were springing up by the year.[8] And these social pressures are made palpable for us as readers in the friction between the symbolic truth of (the child's) imagination and the immediate social realities which oppose it. Another of the *Songs* that works like this is "The Chimney Sweeper" from *Innocence*, with Tom Dacre's comforting dream of liberation and joy. "Though the morning was cold, Tom was happy and warm; | So if all do their duty, they need not fear harm."[9] In these lines can be heard both the voice of innocence and a parodic voice that mimics establishment complacency. This dual viewpoint expresses the power of the transformative imagination even while it simultaneously marks its limits.

Rebellion's Limits: The Darkening Angel

The tension in Blake's attitude to the energy that flouts moral considerations can be traced in the evolution of one particular figure in the 1790s. In the "Song of Liberty" which concludes the *Marriage*, we hear of the "new-born terror," the "new-born fire," hurled down by the gloomy jealous king, but who brings down with him all the old order. He himself survives unscathed, and as the "son of fire" he "stamps the stony law to dust . . . crying: Empire is no more! And now the lion & wolf shall cease."[10] This figure of revolutionary energy reappears in Blake's longer poems, where he is named as Orc; in Latin, Orcus is one name of the god of the underworld, and Blake's Orc is strongly associated with the Devil. In *America*, the next of these poems to be written, Orc proclaims an extended version of the song of liberty, to the anger and dismay of Albion's Angel, who speaks for the old repressive order of empire. The angel rebukes him:

> Art thou not Orc, who serpent-formed
> Stands at the gate of Enitharmon to devour her children?
> Blasphemous demon, Antichrist, hater of dignities,
> Lover of wild rebellion and transgressor of God's Law,
> Why dost thou come to Angels' eyes in this terrific form? (202; 7:54–58)

This is to identify rebellion with the Devil of Scripture, specifically with the child-devouring dragon of Revelation. (Just so the narrative voice at the start of *Paradise Lost* identified Satan with "th'infernal Serpent," in a similar movement of counter-accusation.) Orc's reply accepts the association with the Devil by linking himself to the serpent in Genesis, but rejects the traditional valuation of the serpent's role.

> The terror answered: "I am Orc, wreathed round the accursed tree.
> The times are ended, shadows pass, the morning 'gins to break." (202; 8:59–60)

This implies a radical revision of the traditional reading of Genesis, or perhaps a return to those early gnostic writers who celebrated the serpent as bringer of knowledge.[11] The poem ends with the liberating fires of Orc burning though the defences of the plague-ridden European powers, to the dismay of priests and monarchs. Orc, "the Demon," is a Devil figure, but his energy is an unequivocally positive force. He is "the terror," but a terror only "to Angels' eyes," to the forces of repression; his fires burn only what is corrupt. This is essentially the same positive revaluation of devilish energy as appears in the *Marriage*, although given in a simpler form, without the *Marriage*'s play of irony: the Orc of *America* is something of a comic-strip hero.

But in subsequent poems he becomes first a diminished and then a more problematic and disturbing figure. In *Europe*, the sequel to *America*, he occupies only a small part of the poem, and his appearance at the conclusion is much less consequential. Blake can find for him only the most perfunctory, wooden, unenergetic verse:

> But terrible Orc, when he beheld the morning in the east,
> Shot from the heights of Enitharmon,
> And in the vineyards of red France appeared the light of his fury.
> The sun glowed fiery red!

> The furious terrors flew around
> On golden chariots raging, with red wheels dropping with blood;
> The lions lash their wrathful tails;
> The tigers couch upon the prey and suck the ruddy tide. (245;14–15:198–205)

This feeble writing, embarrassed by its own rhetoric of vehemence, is painfully inadequate to the contemporary events in France to which it uneasily refers. *There* is indeed the Terror, the mob violence, the purges, the show trials, the guillotine; but this Orc is not remotely terrible. If Blake still feels that he must affirm him as the principle of energy, he is here himself writing "in fetters," as he said Milton wrote of God. Orc's next appearance, in the *Song of Los*, occupies just three lines, although this is still enough to transmit the birth of a new age from Europe to Asia; but in the *Book of Urizen*, written 1793–1794, he is associated more with pain and horror than with triumph. His conception is a fall into further division which makes Eternity shudder; he grows in the womb, horribly, as a worm and a serpent; his birth, "howling," as "the Human shadow," is enough to give the Eternals a paralytic stroke, and to cut Los off from the vision of Eternity; his father bathes him "in springs of sorrow" and chains him down with the "Chain of Jealousy" (268–69; 19:363–68, 20:374, 394). This does not mean that Blake despairs of energy; we get four lines that reassert Orc's revolutionary potential, chained down though he is.

> The dead heard the voice of the child,
> And began to awake from sleep.
> All things heard the voice of the child,
> And began to awake to life. (269; 20:396–99)

But whereas in the *Marriage* the torments of hell were a mirage, the mere projection of the repressive mind, in *Urizen* the anguish associated with diabolical energy and desire is felt as a substantial thing. It is the anguish not just of the old reactionary order, but floods the whole poem. The "jealousy" which chains Orc down has deep roots, and responds to something that appears really monstrous, or dismaying, in his birth. And Orc himself has a smaller part to play in the whole poem; much more of Blake's *poetic* energy is now invested in his antagonist, the principle of repressive and constraining authority, Urizen, under whose "deathful shadow" (269; 20:395) he now lies.

These developments were taken still further sometime after 1797, when Blake gave a much extended account of the same scenario in the *Four Zoas*. The chaining down by the father now comes specifically from his apprehension of an oedipal challenge, and the chain strikes root down to the center of the earth, enmeshing itself in Orc's body which itself becomes "a living chain," so that no imaginable power—including the father's repentance—can free him from it.[12] The "immortal demon" or "howling fiend" is still, at first, an awesome figure. Thousands of "spirits of life"[13] attend upon him; his body seems to contain the whole world; in his rage he defies Urizen, brooding envious over him, with the splendid defiance of Satan in hell or Prometheus on the rock: "my fierce fires are better than thy snows."[14] But Urizen's presence is enough to "weaken [his] divided spirit,"[15] and although he continues to despise and scorn Urizen, he nevertheless becomes the servant of his will. Urizen compels Orc into the form of a serpent and makes him climb up into the Tree of Mystery, "that he [Urizen] might draw all human forms | Into submission to his will."[16] As in Genesis, a female figure is tempted to eat the fruit of the tree, with disastrous consequences; she gives birth to the destructive, blighting figure of Vala, the Shadowy Female; she in turn embraces Orc, tormenting and dividing him with jealousy; he at last breaks his chain, but his rising up seems merely to contribute to the war being waged by Urizen; he "rends" Vala, but this merely increases her cruelty and power; and he is "consumed in his own fires":

> No more remained of Orc but the serpent round the Tree of Mystery.
> The form of Orc was gone; he reared his serpent bulk among
> The stars of Urizen in power, rending the form of life.[17]

Blake never engraved the *Four Zoas*, and we need not assume he was satisfied with the work. But let us pause to consider what he is giving us here, in the characteristically dense and tangled mode of his later works. Orc is still the figure of fiery energy who opposes oppression. But he is no longer the straightforwardly positive force that he once was. His power to act is severely limited; he is weakened by Urizen and brought to serve Urizen's purposes, in what has been identified as "the Orc cycle," where the power of energetic desire "inevitably declines into passive acceptance of impersonal law and external reason."[18]

Orc's net contribution to the whole would seem to be an increase of pain, disintegration, and strife. This degeneration in Orc reflects the course of revolutionary France during the 1790s as it appeared to radical eyes. The high hopes of a true liberation in the early years had given way to the Reign of Terror which in turn gave way to a new imperialism—all the time strengthening, it could well be said, the grip of repression and the appetite for war in England. By the end of the 1790s, Orc could indeed seem to have been working for the cause of Urizen despite himself. The rise of Napoleon would only strengthen the sense that the true form of Orc was gone, and that his serpent bulk was now among the stars of Urizen in power.

If Orc was always associated with revolution, he was associated also, from the start, with the Devil, and his decline during the 1790s brings the Devil down with him. In the *Marriage*, "Hell" is the place of energy and eternal delight, and when "the new-born terror" is cast down as fire from heaven, he "falls" only to triumph. Similarly, in *America*, when Orc identifies himself as the serpent "wreathed round the accursed tree" he is announcing himself as liberator, and nothing in the poem contradicts this. But the description in the *Four Zoas* of Orc as nothing more than "the serpent round the Tree of Mystery" is a much more negative image. It conflates the traditional view of the serpent/Devil in paradise as evil with Blake's consistent imagery of the tree as a great ramifying outgrowth of mystification, often specifically religious, that binds, encloses, and restricts. There is still a good deal of internal tension in this image, for it holds together the traditional religious abhorrence of the Devil with a radical critique of traditional religion. We shall come back to this when we come to Blake's Satan. But what is clear is that the amoral, rebellious energy that Blake associates with the Devil is the site of intense ambivalence: and this goes together with a mode of writing that is enormously more self-interrogating and brooding, more entangled in the crisscrossing ramifications of things, than possessed by the trenchant energy of utterance which marks Blake's earlier work.[19]

This increasing ambivalence concerning the Devil can also be seen in one of Blake's designs. In 1795 he made a series of freestanding color prints, one of which has the title *The Good and Evil Angels*. Set against billowing flames of fire, a naked male figure, his body the same reddish-brown color as the flames, stretches out in vain to seize a young child.

The Good and Evil Angels Struggling for Possession of a Child.
Watercolor by William Blake, 1795.
Used by permission of the Granger Collection, New York.

Chained by the foot, he is prevented by a much lighter-colored figure, who holds the terrified child just out of reach of the darker figure and the flames. Both appear to be airborne, high above the sea. The posture of the muscular dark angel has a superbly balletic quality in the poised energy of his stretching out; the light angel's movement is contrastingly awkward as he twists away, or perhaps shrinks back, with the lines of the terrified child cutting across and neutralizing the lines of power in his own body.

This design closely follows a small illustration in the earlier *Marriage of Heaven and Hell*, filling the plate containing the "Voice of the Devil" section, so that it comes immediately below the declaration "Energy is Eternal Delight." The plate that follows deplores the restraint of desire. The text of the *Marriage* thus prompts us to read the dark fiery angel as the embodiment of energetic desire, and the fair figure, who is female in the *Marriage*, as figuring inhibition or restraint, shrinking fearfully from the flames of eternal delight—although in three of the surviving nine copies of the *Marriage*, the figure of energy is not chained down, so that she is about to be overwhelmed by it.

But in 1795 Blake made one important change to the design of a few years earlier. This was to the head of the dark angel. The face is older—a face of experience—and the eyes are large and blank. The dark angel is now blind. His blindness is reinforced by the way that he is now reaching out *past* the child, into an empty foreground, whereas in the *Marriage* there was a clear space separating them. The effect is to make the dark angel a more genuinely terrible figure, as well as greatly increasing his dominance in the composition. *These* angels can certainly be seen as good and evil in an unironic sense, even though the *Marriage* told us that those terms are merely the names given by "the religious" to reason and energy. For energy now appears as blind. We recall that Orc in the *Four Zoas* is blind to the way that he serves the will of Urizen[20] and that his energy, released, does more harm than good. Or we can turn this observation another way and say that pure energy can never be released to fulfillment. An earlier passage in the *Four Zoas* emphasizes that the chain of jealousy binding Orc can never be removed. Similarly, in Blake's 1795 design the fetter and the blindness reinforce each other in keeping the dark angel from his object of desire. If there were a fetter only, as in *Marriage*, we could imagine that it could be broken: but blindness seems more intimately and permanently part of the self, like the "mind-forged manacles" in "London."[21]

Did Blake, then, begin the 1790s as an enthusiast for the revolutionary potential of energy, only to withdraw or severely modify that confidence, in his own version of the retreat from—or rethinking of—radicalism that can be seen in many of his contemporaries? At some level that is probably right; but my concern here is less to map Blake's changing emphasis over time than to highlight the ambivalence that underlies those changes and to explore the relation between that ambivalence and the artistic achievement.[22] What the events of the 1790s unfolded was a moral ambiguity that was always implicit in Blake's commendation of hell. As a moral *thinker*, Blake may have moved across a spectrum of attitudes to energy, with the pressures of moral insight increasingly challenging and moderating the clean energetic thrust of his writing; but his truest *poetry*, it can be argued, finds ways of gathering up the whole of that spectrum in single moments of ambivalence. The evil angel in Blake's 1795 design remembers, and is still locked in dialogue with, the affirmative potential of the original figure in the *Marriage*; in Milton's phrase, he is not less than archangel ruined; and the complex consciousness which this elicits is at the heart of the design's extraordinary life and power. In particular, it holds the fettered angel tensely separate from his opposite, while inviting us to imagine—with alarm but also with desire—their coming together.

The Eternal Adversary

There is a second way of hearing *The Marriage of Heaven and Hell*. We began by reading its devilry as patently ironic, as looking to realize the complementarity of energy and reason, in a true marriage of heaven and hell. Opposition, in this scenario, is true friendship. But it is also possible to hear the title as ironic, and to read large parts of the *Marriage* as implacably antagonistic. As well as rereading the familiar Bible for its "infernal," complementary sense, Blake speaks also of the very Bible of Hell, which "the world shall have whether they will or no."[23]

The first view would rescue the Devil as having a constructive place in an imaginably different scheme of things. This was how the radical thinker William Godwin wrote about Milton's Satan in 1793:

> Poetical readers have commonly remarked Milton's devil to be a being of considerable virtue. It must be admitted that his energies centered too much in personal regards. But why did he rebel against his maker? It was, as he himself informs us, because he saw no sufficient reason for that extreme inequality of rank and power which the creator assumed. . . . He bore his torments with fortitude, because he disdained to be subdued by despotic power. He sought revenge, because he could not think with tameness of the unexpostulating authority that assumed to dispose of him. How beneficial and illustrious might the temper from which these qualities flowed have proved with a small diversity of situation![24]

It is tempting to imagine Godwin developed this idea from something Blake threw out in conversation. And if Godwin ever looked at the *Marriage*, he may have supposed that he was transmitting the gist of what Blake there says about the Devil, in less paradoxical terms. "With a small diversity of situation"—a shift in perspective, a change in the culture—the Devil can become your particular friend, indeed everyone's friend. The principle which animates him—for Blake, energy; for Godwin, indignation at injustice—should not be demonized, as is usually done, but has only to be recognized as virtue for flowers to bloom in the desert.

But Godwin seems simpleminded next to Blake. Godwin patronizes the Devil, but Blake impersonates him, in a manner authentically dangerous to *any* scenario of virtue. Here are some of the more Nietzschean of the Proverbs of Hell from the *Marriage*:

> Drive your cart and your plough over the bones of the dead.

> The road of excess leads to the palace of wisdom.

> The tigers of wrath are wiser than the horses of instruction.

> Sooner murder an infant in its cradle than nurse unacted desires.

To which can be added this freestanding sentence from later in the work:

> *One Law for the Lion and Ox is Oppression.*[25]

Taken as a whole, the Proverbs of Hell recommend the free expression and realization of the energies of life, without reservation. To a certain kind of liberal, humanist psychology, as to the antinomian strain in dissenting Christianity, this may not seem so very alarming. But with Blake's most trenchant formulations, such as those given above, even the most sympathetic reader is alerted to a strong sense in which they are dangerous or untrue. The dead are not so easily left behind, and if we desecrate their place of burial, they are the more likely to come back to haunt us. The road of excess leads to liver damage. Vehement anger is often uncomprehending. "Sooner murder an infant . . ." cries out to be denied. And one law for the lion and the ox—say, for a Napoleon and a manual laborer—is not oppression but justice.

To register the force of these objections is not, however, to throw the proverbs out. They may be symbolically or psychologically true while being practically dubious or destructive. My objections were all notably unimaginative. At a more symbolic or psychological level, it may be true that the worst thing of all is to *nurse* unacted desires— intimately to nourish desires that one dare not express or perhaps acknowledge, so that they are all the time growing stronger. In a certain symbolic sense, it is very intelligible to desire to live as one imagines a tiger to live, in a single flowing movement of unswerving instinctual execution, rather than to live reflectively and cerebrally, by precepts, between possibilities, in the domesticated and instrumental way of "instruction." But Blake's way of putting these thoughts—as proverbs of hell—insists that we perceive them as paradoxes or *counterstatements* that set up an unresolved tension between two conflicting ways of seeing. (This is unlike normal proverbs, which typically invite the response, "how true!") As one of the other Proverbs of Hell has it, "A fool sees not the same tree that a wise man sees"[26]—leaving us with the difficulty of determining who, then, is really the fool.

For all the holistic tendency of his thought, Blake loves to write as the adversary; counterstatement is fundamental to his poetry. In the *Marriage*, as elsewhere, this is reinforced by the existence of particular texts to which Blake is responding, often parodically. The Proverbs of Hell stand counter to the book of Proverbs in the Bible, perhaps as part of Blake's larger project to produce "the Bible of Hell." The freestanding sentence denouncing one law for the lion and the ox opposes the verse in Isaiah that declares "the lion shall eat straw like the ox" (Isa 11:7); the prophecy of a time of universal peace and community, when the wolf shall live with the lamb, is disputed by the voice from hell (though Isaiah does not speak of law). The passage on the Devil as fallen from heaven offers a corrective to *Paradise Lost* and to the traditional view of the Devil more generally. The *Marriage* in its title and in several specific passages sets itself against the writings of Emmanuel Swedenborg, who related his edifying encounters with angels and devils in a series of works, one of which was called *Heaven and Hell*. And even where Blake has no specific passage in view, the sense of counterstatement is pervasive, as most obviously in the use of the terms "Heaven" and "Hell," "Good" and "Evil" in something like the opposite of their accepted senses.

As an engraver, Blake was trained in the art of inversion, of seeing things the other way round. "Opposition is true Friendship." But in six of the surviving nine copies of the *Marriage*, Blake has deleted that sentence by coloring, obliterating it beneath the dark waters from which his leviathan emerges, as if to withdraw the faith it expresses. This crucial equivocation expresses what is equivocal in the *Marriage* as a whole. If with one voice it speaks of integration, with another voice it rejoices in conflict and division. That second voice insists that energy is forever at war with reason and restraint, and invigoratingly so. The movement beyond good and evil leads not to the understanding that everything that lives is holy, but to the assertion of the Nietzschean will to power. The Proverbs of Hell are offered not as provocations, but in earnest: the true poet is forever of the Devil's party, rejoicing in the energies of an eternal opposition.

Blake's pleasure in counterstatement appears most unmistakably, of course, in the *Songs of Innocence and Experience*. The first copies of *Songs of Innocence* were issued in the year of hope, 1789; *Experience* became the counterpart to *Innocence* in 1794; and although Blake continued to issue *Innocence* as an independent volume, the *Songs of Experience* had always to be bound up with *Innocence*. That is, they were written as poems of opposition, and were only to be understood in those terms. In some of the lyrics in *Experience* that oppositional principle is also expressed within the single poem—nowhere more clearly than in "The Clod and the Pebble":

"Love seeketh not itself to please,
Nor for itself hath any care,
But for another gives its ease
And builds a Heaven in Hell's despair."

So sang a little clod of clay,
Trodden with the cattle's feet;
But a pebble of the brook
Warbled out these metres meet:

"Love seeketh only self to please,
To bind another to its delight,
Joys in another's loss of ease,
And builds a Hell in Heaven's despite."[27]

The understanding of love as self-transcending altruism is followed by the counterstatement that love expresses the self-seeking urge to domination, in what appears to be an absolute opposition. What are we to make of this? We can say that these are two opposite kinds of love, or views of love, that the poem separates out so schematically as to insist that they are irreconcilable. In Pope's *Essay on Man*, "God and Nature" may have "bade Self-love and Social be the same,"[28] but such smooth reconciliation of opposites is not an option here. The poem seems to defy resolution. We may wish to see the pebble's assertions as corrupt or deplorable, but the poem gives us no encouragement in this: the two views are balanced equally—six lines for the clod, six for the pebble—in a formal symmetry that suggests pure contradiction, impasse.[29] Or, if we press the poem harder for some sense of what its poetic voice intends, another reading presents itself, in which the little word "but" gains weight. The pebble is not only juxtaposed to the clod, it is correcting the song of the clod. By moving to and finishing with the pebble, the poem asks and expects that the reader recognize the psychological truthfulness of the pebble's understanding: and such recognition, acknowledging that there is "delight" in dominion over others, is itself a kind of complicity. The hardness of the pebble has, after all, a certain superiority to the softness of the clod, "trodden with the cattle's feet." There is something pebble-like in the impervious self-containment of the entire poem. The pebble's song, unlike the clod's, gets a word of approval: its versification, at least, is "meet." And at the end the pebble takes a trick by redescribing the clod's idealism—building a heaven in hell's despair—in a final line that appropriates and reconfigures the clod's own terms: "builds a Hell in Heaven's despite." This is to invoke Milton's Satan and the pleasure in dominion (over others, over circumstance) which Satan asserts.

> The mind is its own place and in itself
> Can make a Heaven of Hell, a Hell of Heaven. (i.254–55)

Like the *Marriage*, but more disturbingly than the *Marriage*, the poem makes us inward with the Devil's sense of things: for it is surely the Devil's voice that is speaking at the end, relishing the dark pleasures of power, speaking to us of a truth which we might rather not have heard, but which claims from us a kind of assent.

The Trace of Wit

The Marriage of Heaven and Hell is an equivocal work, as we have seen, that speaks to us both of ultimate integration and of endless conflict.

Its ambiguity is at once ethical (is energy really diabolical, yet really a force for good?) and generic (is the work a visionary manifesto or a *jeu d'esprit?*). Not to choose decisively between those readings is to recognize how the *Marriage* flickers brilliantly between them. For all the energy of the line it draws between heaven and hell, its vitality is expressed less in the sharpness of its oppositions than in the ambiguity of how we should take those oppositions—of the tone in which, or the consciousness with which, Blake speaks in the voice of the Devil. It is an ambiguity figured in the fact that most of the surviving copies of the work both do and do not contain the statement "Opposition is true Friendship." This text lies beneath Blake's wash of color as a secret presence, obliterated and inaccessible, withdrawn from consciousness, yet half implied by the intimacy he claims with the powers of hell. In this it is like the secret history of the Devil, which tells that he was once/is really the associate of God, but has been lost to view, obliterated by a polarizing moral consciousness. The equivocation, the flickering sense of ambiguity, is the literary device through which Blake both adopts and half undoes that polarization.

This hint of a consciousness that holds opposites together can be found also in some of the *Songs*. Let me return for a moment to "The Clod and the Pebble." We have seen how that poem presents an absolute opposition, a pure contradiction: and if, restless at this, we seek to resolve that contradiction, it is the pebble's voice that emerges as dominant. This would seem to reinstall opposition in a still more disturbing way: between the force of the poem and common morality. Nevertheless, clod and pebble do have something in common. Neither recognizes the other's perspective; each is sealed within its own stanza. Their views of love also have this in common, that neither view has any place for relationship properly speaking. Either the self is altogether lost in identification with the other, or the other is there only to strengthen and aggrandize the self. Relationship would be *between* self and other, with both in play. Now, the poem itself deals in relationship, and so gets beyond polarity, insofar as it implies an ironic consciousness that has brought clod and pebble together and found in their antagonistic positions a curious symmetry. Although the pebble sings the final stanza and has in an important sense the last word, the poem as a whole could not have been sung by the pebble.

Such consciousness might be described as the play of wit, in the spirit of T. S. Eliot's account: wit, though impossible to define, "involves, probably, a recognition, implicit in the expression of every experience, of other kinds of experience which are possible."[30] It would sound odd, though, to describe "The Clod and the Pebble" as a witty poem. It does not quite carry the consciousness, the site of Eliot's "recognition," which that would imply, although the potential for such consciousness is suggested by certain aspects—the gesture toward fable, the neatness of the symmetry, the aphoristic quality, the faintly arch jingle of "these metres meet," above all the measured disproportion between the lightness and slightness of the form and the weight of the conclusion. We might say that such self-consciousness is there in the poem as a felt absence or secret presence, implied but unvoiced.

Similar reflections are prompted by another of the *Songs of Experience* which explicitly presents itself in terms of an opposition, while pressing the question of its (un)imaginable relation to its contrary.

Tiger, tiger, burning bright
In the forests of the night,
What immortal hand or eye
Could frame thy fearful symmetry?

In what distant deeps or skies
Burnt the fire of thine eyes?
On what wings dare he aspire?
What the hand dare seize the fire?

And what shoulder and what art
Could twist the sinews of thy heart?
And when thy heart began to beat,
What dread hand? And what dread feet?

What the hammer? What the chain?
In what furnace was thy brain?
What the anvil? What dread grasp
Dare its deadly terrors clasp?

When the stars threw down their spears
And watered Heaven with their tears,

Did he smile his work to see?
Did he who made the Lamb make thee?

Tiger, tiger, burning bright
In the forests of the night,
What immortal hand or eye
Dare frame thy fearful symmetry?[31]

This is a much more formidable manifestation of energy than the "tigers wild" who play around the sleeping Lyca in "The Little Girl Lost." This tiger defies all attempts to situate it within a narrative; the threat or challenge it embodies is all the more disturbing for being wholly indeterminate. The poem comes to its climax on the line, "Did he who made the Lamb make thee?"—the key question of the poem, and in a sense the key question of the *Songs* generally. It is a question that both demands and defies an answer. There would seem to be no imaginable synthesis between the God who so loved the world that he sacrificed his only begotten son—the God who both created the innocent lamb and was himself the Lamb of God, overflowing the distinction between Creator and creation—and the "burning" energies embodied in the tiger, which suggest only the most "dread" and terrible creator, insofar as any creator at all can be imagined for such a being. Blake's questions have been variously answered by commentators, and it is not possible even to determine whether they are substantial or rhetorical—whether they are asking urgently about the nature of God, or dismissing any notion of a transcendent Creator. In either case they tear at notions of divinity as the tiger might tear at its prey. Insistently repeated without pausing for reply, they turn from questions into something more like exclamations, addressing themselves only to the tiger, who we can be sure will give no reply. The gesture of would-be rational inquiry is ruthlessly overridden by the rhythm of incantation. The poem can be heard as exulting in its own irrationalism; it seems as much intimate with as appalled by the tiger, whom Blake addresses with the old second-person forms of "thy" and "thee," markers of familiarity—or reverence. There is something willing and collusive in its fixation on this great symbol of burning energy, a manifestation of Blakean Hell if ever there was one, standing superbly indifferent to the need for interpretation and meaning.

After the series of hammerblow questions, the penultimate stanza modulates for a moment into a different key. We are told that at the tiger's emergence, the stars threw down their spears and watered heaven with their tears. This seems to be a broadly positive image: the stars letting their weapons fall ("threw down" *could* mean "hurled down in attack," but this seems not to fit the context) is an image Blake uses elsewhere for the weakness of counter-revolutionary forces when confronting France, and "watering heaven" may make an arid place more fertile (though water often has negative connotations for Blake, and tears are commonly egotistical). So the lines can be read as saying the following: overwhelmed at the sight of the tiger, the stars confessed their weakness as antagonists, and this confession was a desirable thing. However, a degree of uncertainty, and hence anxiety, attaches even to these lines.

When we come to the main clause, the sense of disturbing challenge increases to a maximum, as the terrible questioning returns: "Did he smile his work to see?" The stars were weeping in pity and dismay. Was the Creator likely to be smiling, rather than dismayed also? Or if he smiled, was this a grim smile, the malignant smile of a tigerish God? The line remembers that when the God of Genesis looked upon his work in the creation, he saw that it was good. It asks whether it is possible to see the tiger as good—whether it is possible to envisage, in this case, a marriage between hell and heaven: "Did he who made the Lamb make thee?" The second question, capping the first, brings the poem to its climax on a note of dark triumph, as if the poet knows that this question cannot be answered, or cannot be answered in the affirmative. We have seen how Isaiah's prophecy of the wolf living with the lamb was repudiated in the *Marriage*; Blake's question seems to demand another such repudiation. Opposition is *not* friendship. Symmetry is a fearful, unresolvable thing. And so the poem ends by simply reiterating the presence of the tiger, burning bright, beyond the reach of Blake's questions as it is beyond good and evil.

Thus far, then, "The Tiger" is a poem of pure energy, a devilish poem, superbly indifferent to moral anxiety or concern for integration. But as is true of the *Marriage* and also perhaps "The Clod and the Pebble," the affirmation of energy is shadowed by a trace of wit. For there is a simple answer to the poem's climactic question, although it is easily overlooked. "Did he who made the Lamb make thee?" "The Lamb" here could mean not only the animal and the symbol but also the poem with that title which appears in *Songs of Innocence*, with which *Experience* was always bound up. Blake's unanswerable question can simply be answered yes, if taken to be about poetic making, textual creation. Similarly, the poem's opening question—"What immortal hand or eye | Could frame thy fearful symmetry?" is a terrible and troubling question if we think about God and the creation, but a much easier question if we think about the poem in front of us, which is framed— symmetrically—by the repetition of the opening stanza at the close. Just one word is changed: "could" becomes "dare"—for by the end of the poem it is clear that the thing *could* be done, since Blake has done it. We have, indeed, witnessed the work: the reiterated questioning that fills the poem not only mimics the rhythm of hammering at the tiger's imagined creation, it *is* that hammering, as the tiger is created in the poetic imagination.

Once we become aware of this trace of self-reflexivity—a trace of self-consciousness, a trace of wit—everything is subtly altered. The absolutely oppositional reading is modified. Did he who made the Lamb make thee? Yes, self-evidently. And so, what the poet hath joined, let no god put asunder. The grounds of the joining—the prospects for the marriage—are still opaque to us, and problematic: we feel only that there is a relationship, not purely antagonistic, between lamb and tiger in the consciousness of the poet. That consciousness itself is withdrawn from us. We can speak only of a *trace* of self-consciousness, marked by the trace of something like wit. But that allows us to hear, in the daemonic or exclamatory surges of the poem, in its "dread" quality and in its uses of that word, something that approaches the essentially *relational* mode of parody.

This kind of doubleness can be felt wherever our sense of the Blake who is transported by his imaginative vision, sometimes as a holy fool, sometimes as a tiger of wrath, is shadowed by the sense of another Blake, canny, provocative, and self-aware. This shadowing is most apparent in *The Marriage of Heaven and Hell*. "The Prophets Isaiah and Ezekiel dined with me, and I asked them . . .": the knowing casualness with which Blake makes the outrageous claim, without withdrawing from what is truly extraordinary in the claim, is what makes the effect.

After dinner, "I then asked Ezekiel why he ate dung, and lay so long on his right and left side. He answered, 'The desire of raising other men into a perception of the infinite.'"[32] When Blake wrote that, did he smile his work to see? The shift in tone between the question and the answer would be comical, were any baseline standard of decorum operating. Again, there is a subliminal knowingness, traceable in the alertness to rationalist critique of Scripture, such as Voltaire expressed in the article on Ezekiel in his widely circulated *Philosophical Dictionary*:

> Several critics have been repelled by the Lord's command to him to eat bread made of barley, wheat, and millet, smeared with human excrement, for three hundred and ninety days.
>
> The prophet exclaimed: "Phew! phew! phew! Up to now my soul hasn't been polluted," and the Lord replied: "Very well, instead of human excrement I'll allow you cow dung; you shall knead your bread with cow dung."
>
> Since it isn't customary to eat such jam on one's bread, most men have found these orders unworthy of the divine majesty.[33]

Blake's way of reporting his conversation with Ezekiel on the same subject both incorporates Voltaire's satirical irreverence and annihilates it.

Another good example is the punning names Blake gives to several of his mythological figures, most strikingly to Urizen. There is real weight and power, an authentic sense of the archetypal, in Urizen's brooding presence, both in text and in illustration, where Blake develops a figure of sinister sublimity, vastly bearded and aged, from a classical relief of Jupiter Pluvius. Yet the name of Urizen both contains and conceals at least one pun: your reason. In this latent pun can be glimpsed, behind the awesome figure in the text, a mocking, satirical consciousness, in which the name of the Father would be revealed as nothing more than a play on words, and Urizen himself as merely what Blake calls the authority principle in a different kind of poem: old Nobodaddy. But to bring this consciousness to the surface would destroy the imaginative reality of Urizen—would reduce him, as an object of critique, to the kind of rational abstraction that is itself Urizenic, and destroy moreover the imaginative power of many passages in the prophetic books. The pun remains latent; in all the many places that Blake uses the name, he never supplies the kind of nudge from the context that would activate it. Yet it is still there, beneath the surface.

Blake is primarily a poet of the imagination; from first to last, he referred to himself, and to true poetry, in that way. That he really conversed with Ezekiel, that Urizen really exists, is not in doubt: for Blake holds that the real is the imaginative, and that the measure of reality supplied by Newtonian physics and Lockean empiricism is wholly inadequate. But sometimes, even in Blake's most uncompromising expressions of this principle, we can hear a shadowing consciousness:

> Mental Things are alone Real . . . I assert for My self that I do not behold the Outward Creation & that to me it is hindrance & not Action it is as the Dirt upon my feet No part of Me. What it will be Questiond When the Sun rises do you not see a round Disk of fire somewhat like a Guinea O no no I see an Innumerable company of the Heavenly host crying Holy Holy Holy is the Lord God Almighty.[34]

If this is visionary, it is also, in the way it invokes and replies to a skeptical questioner, provocative and oppositional. Blake is not so caught up by his vision of the angels as to have forgotten how other people see the sun. There is a flash of irony, of sardonic wit, in the way that Blake has his materialistic questioner liken the sun to a *coin*. That "O no no" is alive to "other kinds of experience which are possible," to quote once more Eliot's description of wit. Much of Blake's visionary writing can be seen as an extraordinary mutation of eighteenth-century mock-heroic, which similarly finds its life in the relation between two opposing forms of consciousness. Consider, in *The Rape of the Lock*, Pope's equation of Belinda with the sun:

> Not with more glories, in th'etherial plain,
> The Sun first rises o'er the purpled main,
> Than, issuing forth, the rival of his beams
> Launch'd on the bosom of the silver Thames.

The wit of the writing, conveyed through the mock-heroic expansiveness, recognizes an alternative perspective in which the celestial Belinda appears merely as a self-obsessed young woman who supposes that the world revolves around her—even while, like Blake, it says to such an alternative, "O no no":

> If to her share some female errors fall,
> Look on her face, and you'll forget 'em all.[35]

The effect is distinctly un-Blakean, of course. In the Pope there is the characteristic sense of the one perspective being held against the other, so that the wit is all about holding the balance between the imaginative and the actual, or between the power of art and beauty and the irreducible facts of life. In the passage from Blake the perspective of imaginative vision is offered as pretty much overwhelming the other on contact. Yet precisely in that *offering* there is a momentary, more or less subliminal flash of consciousness.

We can also express this by saying that Blake was not a mad poet in the way that Southey thought he was. Crabb Robinson recorded the account Southey gave of Blake to a gathering at Charles Lamb's.

> Southey had been with Blake & admired both his designs & his poetic talents;
> At the same time that he held him for a decided madman. . . . He showed
> S. a perfectly mad poem called Jerusalem—Oxford Street is in Jerusalem.[36]

This was probably the passage Southey saw:

> There is in Albion a Gate of precious stones and gold
> (Seen only by Emanations, by vegetations viewless)
> Bending across the road of Oxford Street; it from Hyde Park
> To Tyburn's deathful shades admits the wandering souls
> Of multitudes who die from earth. This Gate cannot be found
> By Satan's Watch-fiends, though they search numbering every grain
> Of sand on earth every night, they never find this Gate. (730; 34.55–35.2)

Oxford Street is in *Jerusalem*; and a gateway to another world, perhaps ultimately to Jerusalem, can be seen in Oxford Street. If this is visionary (or mad), it is also a formula for mock-heroic: or in Blake's case, mock-prophetic. For the passage recognizes quite explicitly "other kinds of experience"—the ways of Satan's watch-fiends, who can never find this gate. (One wonders with what consciousness Blake showed this passage to the sober-minded Southey, who reported that Blake "did not seem to expect that he should be believed.")[37] The consciousness in which these two ways of seeing find their *relation* is certainly marginal in *Jerusalem*, and disappears altogether for long passages of the poem; it is never the point of the poem, as it is in the *Dunciad*, when Pope sees the goddess Dulness in the Strand, another London street; but if Blake's engagement with the symbolic imagination is different from

Pope's on the one hand, it differs also from that of Christopher Smart, whose imagination burns away all sense of incongruities:

> Let Shobi rejoice with the Kastrel—blessed be the name JESUS in falconry
> and in the MALL.
> *For I blessed God in St James's Park till I routed all the company.*[38]

This under-consciousness in Blake expresses a kind of doubleness in the self that is crucial to the effect of some of his finest lyrics. In "A Poison Tree" this doubleness is itself, as duplicity, the subject of the poem, and lends itself very naturally to a stance that might easily be called diabolical:

> I was angry with my friend;
> I told my wrath, my wrath did end.
> I was angry with my foe;
> I told it not, my wrath did grow.
>
> And I watered it in fears,
> Night and morning with my tears;
> And I sunned it with smiles,
> And with soft deceitful wiles.
>
> And it grew both day and night
> Till it bore an apple bright—
> And my foe beheld it shine.
> And he knew that it was mine,
>
> And into my garden stole,
> When the night had veiled the pole.
> In the morning glad I see
> My foe outstretched beneath the tree.[39]

In Blake's notebook draft, this has the title "Christian Forbearance," and at one level it is a parable affirming openness against the repression induced by religious morality. Express your wrath, and all is well; suppress it, turn the other cheek, in the name of Christian forbearance, and it turns to poison. But this critique is also the vehicle for something else. All the poem's interest, all its energy as poetry, is invested in the repressed state, and in the perverse productivity and the pleasure in destruction which that repression makes possible. This is one of the Blake lyrics which, in *Doctor Faustus*, Leverkühn sets to music shortly after he has effectively entered into his pact with the Devil. Mann's narrator speaks of the poem's "evil simplicity,"[40] and this is exactly right: for something within the speaker—a something to which the poem gives voice—knows all the time what he is about. "Repression" is not, in fact, the best word for what the poem shows us: this is no Freudian unconscious, but an under-consciousness, beneath the fears and tears and smiles of the surface, that takes delight in its own duplicity and looks always toward that final moment of gladness and triumph. It is, after all, the speaker's *foe* who dies—so, a good outcome!—and the poem makes us much too intimate with this pleasure to condemn it. The speaker's triumph is also the poem's: "My foe outstretched beneath the tree" stretches out at the foot of the poem, giving us the satisfaction of the eight-syllable line which has been suppressed since the clear statements of the first stanza, but whose return we have been awaiting during the seven-syllable lines that intervene, with *growing* anticipation, until the moment when all is ripe and the trap is sprung. The poem's deepest pleasure is not so much in destructiveness as such as in collusion with the powers of darkness: the speaker's civilized or Christian forbearance (his fears and tears and smiles) is all the time colluding with his deadly intent, and there is the reader's collusion too, going along with Blake's apparent critique of repression, yet all the time relishing the nurtured enmity that repression generates. This dark and dangerous collusion is essentially diabolical, one might say, for the Devil with whom one enters into relationship, or makes a pact, is a figure in whom friendship and enmity are intimately intertwined. Moreover, the speaker's progress in the poem from ambiguous friend to declared enemy itself mirrors the history by which the Devil came into being, and plays on our abiding uncertainty about collusion or connection between the powers of darkness and light. Finally, this presence of the diabolical in the poem is strengthened by the imagery of apple, garden, and tree, which gives us, subliminally but certainly, a revisionary or parodic version of chapter 3 in Genesis. The Tree of Knowledge is revealed as the trap set for thieving humanity by a secretly malicious God who is indistinguishable from the Tempter.

Intimate Relations—Erotic and Parodic

"A Poison Tree" is one of three Blake lyrics that, in Mann's *Doctor Faustus*, Leverkühn sets to music after seeking out his prostitute and contracting the syphilitic infection which, the Devil promises him, will enable him to create great art. The others are "The Sick Rose" and "I saw a chapel all of gold." Later in his career Leverkühn also sets another short poem from Blake's notebooks, "Silent, silent night."[41] These poems all date from about the same period in Blake's writing. All of them engage us with a transgressiveness which we feel as dynamic, liberating, even revelatory, and yet recognize as destructive or as involved with corruption.

"I saw a chapel" is a difficult poem, perhaps imperfect—Blake did not include it in *Songs of Experience*—but of striking power.

> I saw a chapel all of gold
> That none did dare to enter in;
> And many weeping stood without,
> Weeping, mourning, worshipping.
>
> I saw a serpent rise between
> The white pillars of the door;
> And he forced and forced and forced—
> Down the golden hinges tore;
>
> And along the pavement sweet,
> Set with pearls and rubies bright,
> All his slimy length he drew,
> Till upon the altar bright
>
> Vomiting his poison out,
> On the bread and on the wine.
> So I turned into a sty
> And laid me down among the swine.[42]

The chapel is the site of weeping, worship, and fear; none dare to enter in; so the forcing of its doors by the powerful phallic serpent seems a profoundly desirable transgression. What is suggested here? The repressiveness of false religion, broken open by Blakean Energy?

The life-denying code of chastity and virginity, broken open by the power of desire? Both those thoughts are surely active. Yet any such scenario is complicated by the repulsiveness of the imagery that follows—the conjunction of sweet and slimy, the vomiting on the bread and wine, and the disturbing way the poem seems to figure sexual intercourse. The relishing of destruction that we found in "A Poison Tree" is more problematic here; the final lines are disconcerting, rather than gratified, and curiously indeterminate. Mann's narrator finds in them "the wild renunciation of a humanity dishonoured by the sight," but in such a morally definite reading he shows himself more sensitive to the "horror of pollution" than to its attraction—unlike the artist, the composer Leverkühn, who is said to reproduce the effect of the poem "with astonishing power."[43] "Power" there translates *Eindring-lichkeit*, from *eindringen*, to enter by force, break in, invade, penetrate: the unusual word suggests that the artwork does what the serpent does, or something very like it. This doubleness of response, of horror and empathy, corresponds to the indeterminacy of Blake's ending. The speaker's response to what he has seen is to lie down among the swine, but whether we should feel this as endorsing the befouling of the altar, essentially aligned with it, or rather as a dismayed turning away from the scene—retreating into an inert and defeated state of disillusionment, perhaps—is not clear. If in turning the speaker is turning *away*, is he failing to grasp the import of his own vision?

What is clear is that the poem's interest and vitality depend very largely on its ambivalence about the serpent. In gnostic thought, which seems to have been a powerful strain in early Christianity, the serpent is commonly a symbol of good, not evil. In bringing Adam and Eve into a state of knowledge, *gnosis*, and liberating them from obedience to the arbitrary rule of God, the serpent was possessed not by the Devil but by *sophia*, the principle of wisdom, or even by Christ himself. A. D. Nuttall's study has shown how Blake may have known about gnostic teaching, while arguing that no supposition of actual influence is necessary, since the gnostic emphasis on the rightness of the Fall is a perennial countercurrent in Christian thought, the undying heresy that gives orthodoxy its meaning. There is much that recalls the gnostics, Nuttall argues, in Blake's denigration of God the Father, authoritarian lawgiver and creator of a world fallen into materiality, in the name sometimes of the Devil, and sometimes of Jesus. It is then only to be expected that the serpent, as the great opponent of God's decree in Genesis, should be presented as a positive force. Nuttall therefore pauses on "I saw a chapel" as a crucial but problematic case in point—problematic because of the ambivalence with which the serpent is presented.[44] It is this ambivalence which fits the general case that I am making about the poet's relation with the Devil. Blake's poem draws appreciatively on the serpent's power to break open and break through, to violate what is closed off, to hold nothing sacred, while still holding to the dimension of ethical consciousness that reflects on, or perhaps simply recoils from, something intolerable in this. It returns to and remembers the truth-bearing energy of the original, gnostic serpent, without abandoning the received, traditional sense of the serpent as evil. Or to put this another way, if the serpent is the bringer of knowledge, the agent of reflective consciousness, Blake's representation of the serpent in this poem expresses precisely his shrewd poet's ambivalence about full consciousness, his wish to maintain that state of half-consciousness out of which his best poetry is written. The element of irreducible obscurity in the poem, its resistance to the full explication which it calls for, to the knowingness which it implies, is also part of this.

Blake's vision of the serpent in the chapel fascinates and disturbs through its sense of a close but normally forbidden connection— between the sweet and the slimy, the poison and the Eucharist. That sense of an intimate relation, powerful in proportion as it is improper, is reinforced by the poem's strong sexual subtext: the serpent rises, forces, enters, and ejaculates. All the Blake poems selected by Leverkühn would seem to touch on his sexual encounter: in "A Poison Tree" the poison incubating in the apple glances at the syphilis within him— the "Angel of Poison," as the Devil terms it[45]—and the other three poems all suggest sexual acts. This is most directly the case in "Silent, silent night," which invokes darkness and "deceit" as the proper accompaniments of sexual pleasure, given the strange but undeniable fact that "an honest joy | Does itself destroy | For a harlot coy." These lines can be read in two ways: an honest joy will be driven to self-destruction by the harlot's coy refusal to give herself freely; or alternatively, an honest joy will be polluted and destroyed in achieving the sexual relationship with the harlot which it desires. But the difference is not finally significant. The lines ask us to see sexual relation (or desire) as an experience of extreme otherness, a coming together of opposites normally so separate that their connection precipitates a crisis of pollution in which one element, at least, cannot survive in its original form. The otherness is not only between (we may assume) male and female, but between what lies "honestly" open to consciousness and what is the more desirable for being veiled, ambiguous, and "coy."

At the beginning of this book I argued that Leverkühn's encounter with the prostitute is connected with creativity, not only through the idea of syphilis as stimulant, but more fundamentally through the notion of a transformative relation with the other. In these Blake lyrics sexual relation touches on crisis; it is a pressure point throughout Blake's writing. Relations between his male mythological figures and their female partners are often badly strained; his female figures easily pick up connotations of the malignant harlot; and his erotic situations often involve pain, violation, and destruction, rather than pleasure. Sexual desire can seem almost synonymous with the torments of frustration and jealousy. There are several factors involved here. Blake is partly condemning his culture's prohibition of free sexual expression, the repressive code of chastity that "blights with plagues the marriage hearse."[46] He is partly expressing a visionary's anxiety about confinement to the realm of the senses, given that "nature is the work of the Devil," as he declared to Crabb Robinson.[47] But also deeply at stake is the relation to otherness. Desire, by definition, expresses want, expresses lack; insofar as all sexual desire is for the other, it is liable of itself to open that painful sense of separation and alienation which Blake calls *jealousy*, or projects as cruelty in the object of desire. The state of desire is the root of the problem, and where Blake celebrates consummation he often does so as the release from desire, and hence the erasure of otherness. He wrote in an early notebook,

> In a wife I would desire
> What in whores is always found—
> The lineaments of Gratified Desire.[48]

Setting aside Blake's naïvety about sex workers, the point is that her gratified desire would gratify his desire: a condition of identity, of difference obliterated, out of which new desire could hardly spring. Desire gratified is desire extinguished. And again in the notebook:

> What is it men in women do require?—
> The lineaments of Gratified Desire.
> What is it women do in men require?—
> The lineaments of Gratified Desire.[49]

In both entries the repetitions, especially the deadening rhyming of desire with itself, block any sense of otherness, and of any dynamic relationship with or through such otherness. Desire is answered by itself, and so annulled: an unfearful and wholly unerotic symmetry.

In the late prophetic books, "sexual" is often a term of reprobation, and Blake's ideal of a regenerated humanity in Eden is one without difference of sex;[50] or, where he wishes to preserve the notion of sexual delight, he does so through the idea of a fantastically self-effacing female partner. (Thus the "Divine Voice" in *Milton* looks forward to the happy day when Milton's female emanation shall cease her jealousy and, reconciled at last, "begin to give | Her maidens to her husband, delighting in his delight. | And then, & then alone, begins the happy female joy.")[51] Such passages hardly give us Blake at his soundest, but they suggest how much is being achieved in those finer poems which sustain the reach of desire to the other, with all the risk to integrity, the potential for corruption, which this entails. The last of these Blake poems to be picked out by Leverkühn is "The Sick Rose," from *Songs of Experience*:

> The SICK ROSE
>
> O Rose, thou art sick:
> The invisible worm
> That flies in the night,
> In the howling storm,
>
> Has found out thy bed
> Of crimson joy;
> And his dark secret love
> Does thy life destroy.[52]

Immediately striking is the relationship which this poem about the destructiveness of "dark secret love" claims with us, its readers. Although it refuses to give itself up to rational explication (no reader takes it to be about a gardening problem), it does not seem obscure or difficult in itself. Its power comes from the assurance with which it carries itself, the confidence with which it knows what it means, and with which it assumes that the reader—like the rose, its immediate addressee, with whom the reader is to some extent conflated—is sure to recognize its meaning. The dark secret thing in the poem is something with which we are, in fact, intimate: that is what the manner of the poem is telling us. The poem has found us out, as the worm has found out the bed of the rose. Its oblique knowingness holds a quality of threat, while its extreme economy makes it seem acquiescent if not in fact complicit in the life-destroying act of love.

This knowingness in the poem means that we cannot read it as lament, or certainly not only or mainly as lament. It is one of the greatest expressions in English of *Schadenfreude*—the indispensable German word for joy in damage suffered by others. This is the feeling that animates the poem, the energy that it shares with the worm flying in the storm. It is, of course, the emotion beyond any other that defines the Devil, as we must imagine him: which is also to say, it is the emotion beyond any other that we can least acknowledge in ourselves. Blake is acutely alert to its existence, as we have seen:

> In the morning glad I see
> My foe outstretched beneath the tree.

It features also in many passages of the prophetic books:

> They dance around the dying, & they drink the howl and groan;
> They catch the shrieks in cups of gold, they hand them to one another.
> These are the sports of love, & these the sweet delights of amorous play.[53]

But nowhere else in his work is it as intimately felt as here.

However, behind or alongside the poem's pleasure in destruction, there is a trace of something like wit, animating a certain parodic consciousness. Here is a trivial poem by Matthew Prior, who was widely read throughout the eighteenth century:

A True Maid

No, no; for my virginity,
When I lose that, says ROSE, I'll die:
Behind the elms, last night, cried DICK,
ROSE, were you not extremely sick?[54]

"O Rose, thou art sick." It can hardly be coincidence. Blake's first line exactly picks up the final line in the Prior. ("Rose" has a capital in Blake's manuscript draft and in the illuminated plate, although this is lost in Stevenson's edition.) More significantly, Blake's poem responds not only to the words, but also, very precisely, to the content of Prior's poem. The sexual morality of chastity which denies or regulates desire is revealed as affectation or hypocrisy, for it is undone by the activity that takes place in the night. Blake's poem roughly repeats the thought of Prior's and is written from broadly the same point of view.

Yet the poems are of course light-years apart. To become Blake's sick rose, Prior's sick Rose has been utterly transformed. Prior offers us a cheap, knowing anecdote: Rose is "a true maid," that is to say, all maidens are like that, *così fan tutte*. She is not really sick, just sexually active: the metaphor collapses instantly into the so-familiar actuality. What was repressed or concealed is brought fully into consciousness—Dick has seen everything, his all-too-knowing question makes everything clear—with the result that the whole matter of sexual desire becomes trivial. Full consciousness trivializes, perhaps because only what is trivial can be fully available to consciousness. But in Blake's rose there really is sickness: the poem speaks of some real corruption, a worm at the heart of beauty, in the cultural prohibition on desire which makes love something dark and secret and therefore destructive. Blake's poem is therefore immeasurably more interesting, because of the reality it accords to aspects of desire which cannot be rendered fully up to consciousness. It is this—the dark and secret aspect of desire—which the symbolic mode of the poem preserves and transmits.

Blake's poem is so much more powerful than Prior's, and transforms it so entirely, that it seems to obliterate its starting point, and to stand alone as a work of the symbolic imagination. Nevertheless, the difference between the two poems is part of the meaning of Blake's poem. By taking the worldly anecdote and the worldly poem, and seeing in them such symbolic significance, Blake opposes one order of understanding—the mundane order of Rose and Dick, of furtive gropings behind the elms, of the knowing smile that sums up Rose's self-division—with another that breaks in upon it, rather as the invisible worm breaks in upon the rose's bed, and transforms or destroys it. Here is again what I described earlier as the trace of wit. "O no no," says Blake to Prior: there is far more going on in this situation than your worldly eye is able to perceive. And so the worldly is redescribed, and transformed, in symbolic terms. But the half-consciousness of opposition is also part of the effect of the poem, shadowing the immediacy of the symbolism. Even if we do not know the Prior, Blake's poem still feels like a counterstatement that envisages some other statement of the case—such as would develop the poem's sexual symbolism into pornographic clarity, for example—only to oppose it.

The half-consciousness of that opposition is a way of *relating* those opposites: and this half-presence of relationship, held in the poem's fleeting consciousness of itself as parodic, is the more significant given its overt representation of sexual relations as blocked or destructive. The dark secret love of the worm destroys the life of the rose: sexual desire overcomes its tormenting consciousness of separation by destroying the otherness of the love object, which may be to destroy the other altogether. But the half-conscious, parodic mode of the poem relies on otherness; it holds both relation and opposition in play.

The concept of parody is being asked to do a lot of work here. Let me dwell on it a little, and in particular on the doubleness latent in the term. A parody, in Greek, is a song which is *para* another song; "*para* may be said to develop two trends of meaning, being used to express such ideas as nearness, consonance and derivation as well as transgression, opposition, or difference. . . . In compounds a synthesis of these two forces may sometimes be found."[55] Modern discussions often pause over the question of parody's relation to the text or practice which it has in view—is it sympathetic, playful and recuperative, or hostile and mocking?—and generally allow that it may be either; Margaret Rose's study would define it as encompassing both, and argues that an element of ambivalence is often crucial.[56] Although in modern usage "parody" often suggests polemical intent, it can also have a more open sense, as in Johnson's *Dictionary*: "a kind of writing, in which the words of an author or his thoughts are taken, and by a slight change adapted to some new purpose." The nature of that new purpose is not specified; what defines parody here is its formal quality of reworking, or borrowing combined with change. The *Songs of Innocence and Experience* could be said, therefore, to announce itself as a book of parodies without begging any question as to how we should interpret the relation of one poem to another.

In this capacious notion of parody, there is room for opposition to be true friendship. Dorothy Van Ghent has given a classic formulation of this way of thinking in connection with *Don Quixote*:

> It is possible for parody to be much more complex than debate. Instead of confronting two opposing views with each other, in order that a decision between them be arrived at, parody is able to intertwine many feelings and attitudes together in such a way that they do not merely grapple with one another antagonistically but act creatively on each other, establishing new syntheses of feeling and stimulating more comprehensive and more subtle perceptions. Parody—except that of the crudest kind—does not ask for preferential judgments. It is a technique of *presentation*: it offers a field for the joyful exercise of perception and not a platform of derision.[57]

"Without contraries is no progression," writes Blake in the *Marriage*. And when he later emphasizes that a "contrary" is not the same as a "negation,"[58] he is making space for a distinction like Van Ghent's. The more we think of parodic opposition as a dynamic relation, rather than a correction or displacement, the more this notion of a creative and joyful exercise of mind can come forward.

However, it is not an accident that parody often suggests a polemical or destructive attitude. In Bakhtin's concept of "double-voiced discourse," the parodist "speaks in someone else's discourse, but in contrast to stylization parody introduces into that discourse a semantic intention that is directly opposed to the original one. . . . Discourse becomes an area of battle between two voices."[59] Here the openness of dialogism is precariously held against the idea of victory for the parodist. Even if parody is more neutrally defined, as "repetition with critical distance, which marks difference rather than similarity,"[60] its direction is always toward an increase in consciousness and a multiplying of relations. It is therefore always liable to be unfriendly to certain kinds of literature: writing of great simplicity, writing which moves to rapture or to a single strong emotion, writing which crucially depends on the exclusion of certain considerations, or writing which draws its power from unconscious currents of feeling. In *Northanger Abbey* Jane Austen parodies the fashionable Gothic novel; but it is hard to imagine a Gothic novel incorporating a parody of Austen, for an Austen novel operates with a much higher level of self-awareness, whereas a Gothic novel's business is with what is stirring below the horizon of consciousness. Songs of innocence, also, or poetry of visionary inspiration, will be placed in a certain jeopardy (*jeu parti*, a divided game) within the field of parody. "The Lamb" is not *refuted* by "The Tiger"—which is a contrary, not a negation—but contraries make for progression, or for complication at least, and in the process "The Lamb" may be left behind, or appear to the divided consciousness in a different light.

Moreover, a developed consciousness tends to be alienated from its object, which is also to say, alienated from its own experience. This characteristically Romantic emphasis is exhaustively theorized by Hegel in the *Phenomenology of Mind*, but the relevant point here is not hard to grasp. To be conscious of relation and difference—to be reflectively conscious—is to be conscious of the other as other, and of the self as separate from, and in some sense opposed to, or set over against, its object. The parodic consciousness has thus fallen out of that state of grace in which it could be at one with its experience of the original work—and, by extension, with its experience more generally, toward which it finds itself to stand in an ironic relation. Such alienation is readily felt as fallen: either as separation imbued with the sense of loss (where parody suggests subcreation, something parasitic, decadent, inauthentic), or separation as opportunity for domination (so that parody becomes a malicious spoiling, or a cocksure taking over, which relegates the original to obsolescence). Both aspects lend themselves naturally to the association of parody with the diabolical.

Parody, therefore, can readily have a double aspect, expressing both affiliation and a destructive or alienated antagonism. Its potential to make connection between those apparent opposites aligns it with the figure of the Devil—the intimate enemy, the associate and adversary of God—and with the idea of liaison with the Devil that I invoke in this study. "Parody is fundamentally double and divided; its ambivalence stems from the dual drives of conservative and revolutionary forces that are inherent in its nature as authorized transgression."[61] Linda Hutcheon's phrase "authorized transgression" catches well enough God's permission of Satan's activities in *Paradise Lost*; it catches also the ambiguously devilish manner of the *Marriage*, where Blake's open parodies of Swedenborg dispose us to hear something scarcely less parodic when he speaks in the voice of the Devil.

Blake's general fondness for parody, especially in the form of counterstatement, is also to the point. For such a strikingly original writer, it is remarkable how much of his work reworks other texts or sets itself over against them—pervasively the Bible and Milton, but also Ossian, Young, Swedenborg, Gray . . . and also texts by Blake himself, as in the *Songs of Innocence and Experience*. His love of counterstatement is apparent in the splendidly trenchant marginalia that he wrote on the books that most exercised him. Several of his designs take an existing work or image as their point of departure.[62] Even the *Songs of Innocence* can be said to have a parodic relation to the strongly didactic songs for children written by eighteenth-century poets such as Watts, from which Blake's poems differ so sharply.

Yet is it right to call this kind of counterstatement parodic? If the description seems a precarious one, it is because Blake's oppositions continually threaten to become so strong as to abolish relationship. He is certainly not a consciously allusive, double-voiced writer in the manner of Pope or Fielding or Sterne. It would be hard to appreciate the beauty of innocence in the *Songs of Innocence* if one consistently heard their innocence as *pointed*. The power of symbolism in "The Sick Rose" depends on its obliterating the Prior poem to which it responds. "The Tiger" observes the chasm that separates it from the Lamb. In all these cases, the dimension of wit, the consciousness of relations, seems to be momentary or subliminal, a bridge which collapses after thought has passed across it. This is consonant with Blake's general mistrust of reflective self-consciousness as likely to cut us off from the true energies of our being, and to strengthen our wretched, deluded, and pernicious sense of self. Despite its tremendous analytic penetration, the general thrust of all Blake's writing is toward symbolic or mythopoeic modes that short-circuit rational paraphrase, and are immersive and immediate, rather than reflective. These modes typically give us images of Blakean Eternity, rather than narratives which unfold within space and time, in which the relation between events would give them their significance. This is clearly true of the handling of narrative in the longer prophetic books, where temporal sequence is everywhere disrupted or laid aside, and no one reads Blake for the story. It can be felt also in Blake's handling within those books of the individual line of verse, where he seems to have followed Young rather than Milton in writing strong stand-alone lines of emphatic self-sufficiency, where nothing whatsoever—aural or semantic—turns on the line-ending. Reflective consciousness is, fundamentally, consciousness of relations, indeed is constitutive of relation, but in Blake the recurrent threat is that relationship amounts only to antagonism and separation, opposition which involves no friendship—as in the nonrelations of clod and pebble, or the kind of situation depicted in the *Visions of the Daughters of Albion*, and crystallized in the design where Oothoon and her rapist lover, Bromion, are bound together naked, back to back, while the husband figure sits weeping a short distance away, too self-absorbed in his dismay and jealousy to make the connection with her that she implores. Consciousness is separation, and separation is fall.

Blake aspires to an unfallen writing, uncompromised by reflective consciousness. But to this, the parodic offers a valuable crosscurrent. In the parodic Blake there is a kind of half-consciousness. In "The Sick Rose" this makes possible the opening of relations with what remains other to the self: the poem can draw fully on the energy of the Adversary, the instinctual energy that rises up against the rose and relishes her sickness, without ceasing to register that energy as adversarial. What the poem gives us is the poetic exercise of a dark secret love for the other side, which knows itself well enough to find a wicked delight in its own action, but not so well as to lose the sense of transgression and the energies of otherness.

Blake's Milton: "I am that evil one"

When Blake wrote that Milton was "a true poet and of the Devil's party without knowing it," his phrasing left a degree of ambiguity as to the relation between true poetry and full consciousness. Could Milton have known himself to be of the Devil's party and remained a true poet, or does the alliance between creativity and the Devil depend upon a degree of unconsciousness? Why this indeterminacy around "knowing it" matters becomes clearer if we look at what happens when Blake attempts to resolve it. *Milton: A Poem* is a long work written in the early 1800s, some ten years after the *Marriage*. It expresses what is in some ways a more mature vision, less invested in the energies of opposition, more concerned to realize the possibility of integration. Yet as it approaches the point of integration, its interest lies not in its success but in its failure.

The poem returns to Milton's relationship with the Devil. It opens with Milton in Eternity, among the Immortals, listening to the song of an inspired Bard. The Bard sings of the fall of Satan (a different figure from the Devil in the *Marriage*) and the generation of the fallen world, so that what Milton hears is essentially Blake's revision or re-visioning of *Paradise Lost*. In this version, the Fall comes about after Satan usurps a function that is not proper to him, throwing Eden into terrible confusion. This act of usurpation is associated with repression, with the simulation of "love" and "pity" and "mildness" which Satan really feels, or believes that he feels. He pleads for the disastrous exchange of functions "with incomparable mildness . . . with most endearing love" (516–17; 7:5–6). But his brother knows him better than he knows himself and gives a true account of what this studied gentleness will lead to:

> You know Satan's mildness and his self-imposition,
> Seeming a brother, being a tyrant, even thinking himself a brother
> While he is murdering the just. Prophetic I behold
> His future course through darkness & despair to eternal death. (517; 7:22–25)

Satan's is a willed endeavour to be virtuous, an elevation of the conscious will over the realities of instinct. These feelings of love and pity have been improperly separated from their opposites, in particular from the passion of wrath, and so they become pernicious. It is this condition of separation that constitutes the Fall:

> And Satan, not having the Science of Wrath but only of Pity,
> Rent them asunder & wrath was left to wrath, & pity to pity.
> He sunk down, a dreadful death, unlike the slumbers of Beulah.
>
> The Separation was terrible. (522; 9:46–49)

In falling, Satan sets up as God—an authoritarian God of moral prohibition and condemnation who is to be identified with the jealous and judgmental aspect of God the Father in traditional doctrine.

> He created Seven deadly Sins, drawing out his infernal scroll
> Of Moral laws and cruel punishments upon the clouds of Jehovah
> ... saying, "I am God alone,
> There is no other! Let all obey my principles of moral individuality."
>
> (521; 9:21–26)

The Bard's Satan becomes, in his fallen condition, the authoritarian God-as-Urizen ("Satan is Urizen," 522; 10:1) worshipped in institutional Christianity, who enforces (as Blake saw it) a judgmental morality that generates all the miseries of the contemporary human condition. This is based on repression, that repression of the other entailed by an assertion of absolute selfhood that is both tyrannical and deeply insecure. "I am God alone, | There is no other!" It was this declaration by Jehovah that certain of the early gnostic writers seized on as error, invoking the idea of a divine family or community to which the creator-demiurge arrogantly denied his affiliation; the parallel with Blake's myth is striking.[63]

The song is thus an ethical inversion of *Paradise Lost*, and the Bard's Satan is a revisionary interpretation of that whole conception of God which informs Milton's great fable of sin and punishment. This is all broadly in line with the impudent counternarrative Blake had set out some years before in the *Marriage*, although Blake now uses some names differently, as I indicate in the notes added within square brackets:

> Those who restrain desire do so because theirs is weak enough to be restrained; and the restrainer or reason usurps its place and governs the unwilling [this becomes Satan's repressive usurpation of functions]. ...
>
> The history of this is written in *Paradise Lost*, and the governor (or reason) is called Messiah [i.e., God: the later Blake distinguishes sharply between God the Father and Jesus, but the *Marriage* ran them together, since it is the Son in Milton who drives Satan out of Heaven]. ...
>
> But in the *Book of Job* [and also, now, in Blake's *Milton*] Milton's Messiah is called Satan. For this history has been adopted by both parties.

> It indeed appeared to Reason as if Desire was cast out; but the Devil's
> account [now, the Bard's account] is that the Messiah [Satan, who will come
> to be thought of as God] fell, and formed a heaven of what he stole from the
> abyss.[64]

There is, however, one very significant difference. The Devil as the *Marriage* conceives of him, an energetic principle of opposition, has faded from view. In *Milton* there is no longer any positive role for the Devil, whatever name he is given.

The implications of this are immediately picked up in Milton's response to the Bard's song. We are told at the start of the poem that since his death Milton has been restless, uneasy, "unhappy though in heaven" (508; 2:18). Now, hearing the song and internalizing its meaning (the Bard takes refuge in Milton's bosom), he understands his great error. Dividing his own being, he has identified himself with a righteous selfhood that is set over against a principle of evil: but this repudiated, demonized principle is equally part of Milton. Understanding this moves him to embark on the heroic action with which the rest of Blake's poem is concerned: he will leave his place in heaven, descend to the world, and perform a great action of atonement and redemption, which Blake calls self-annihilation or eternal death (that is, annihilation of selfhood, or as we might say the ego), so that the Fall into division can be undone. Such an action would carry tremendous significance: as Blake sees it, it would amount to a version or instantiation of the incarnation, atonement, and resurrection of Jesus.

> And Milton said, "I go to Eternal Death! The nations still
> Follow after the detestable gods of Priam, in pomp
> Of warlike selfhood, contradicting and blaspheming.
> When will the Resurrection come to deliver the sleeping body
> From corruptibility? O when, Lord Jesus, wilt thou come?
> Tarry no longer: for my soul lies at the gates of death.
> I will arise & look forth for the morning of the grave.
> I will go down to the sepulchre to see if morning breaks.
> I will go down to self-annihilation & eternal death,
> Lest the Last Judgement come & find me unannihilate,
> And I be seized & given into the hands of my own Selfhood. . . .
> I in my Selfhood am that Satan; I am that Evil One,

He is my Spectre! In my obedience to loose him from my hells

To claim the Hells my Furnaces, I go to Eternal Death." (532; 14:14‑32)

Against the calamitous assertion "There is no other!" Milton will acknowledge and seek out his other, his shadow side. The key revelation which the song brings to consciousness in Milton is this: "I in my selfhood am that Satan; I am that evil one." Along with this change comes another, in the understanding of "Satan." The name primarily refers, as we have seen, to the righteous accuser‑God who is both source and manifestation of most of the real evils of life. Blake calls this figure "Satan" partly as a paradox—blackening God's name by identifying him with the evil he pretends to oppose—and partly because he is thinking of Satan's regular characterization as accuser in the Bible. That is what the Bard understands by Satan in his song. But something remarkable is involved when John Milton, author of *Paradise Lost*, recognizes *that* Satan as *his* Satan. God and the Devil merge into one. The double reference brilliantly brings together a double recognition: that the God whose ways Milton intended to justify is evil, and that the Devil whom Milton repudiated in *Paradise Lost* as evil is intimately part of him. It is this composite Satan, this compound of God and the Devil, which is his "spectre," a necessary shadow to that quality of ego consciousness which Blake calls "selfhood," and which is understood to be a blight and a curse.

What has happened here? The energetic Devil of the *Marriage*, who was both Blake's collaborator and very much kin to the Satan of *Paradise Lost*, has faded away, replaced by the Urizenic Satan of Blake's new myth. We can suppose that Blake has looked more soberly at the Satan of Milton's poem, has recognized his tyrannical traits, his egotism, his envy, and how closely his subjection to "the hateful siege of contraries" chimes with Blake's own understanding of what it means to be fallen. And, as we have seen, in the course of the 1790s the devil figure of Orc, principle of rebellious energy, came increasingly to be represented by Blake as entangled and compromised by what he opposes, until in the *Four Zoas* he dwindles into the instrument of Urizen's will.

There are consequences for the quality of the writing. *The Marriage of Heaven and Hell*, written back in the early 1790s, was a devilish piece of work. However seriously one takes it as a kind of manifesto of Blake's deepest beliefs, it is impossible not also to hear it as a wickedly transgressive piece, not least in its calculated indeterminacy as to the tone and implications of its satanism. Blake's claim to have written it in collaboration with the Devil generates an endless irony; the Devil is, of course, a slippery customer, but Blake's relations with him are slippery too. By contrast, in Milton's speech quoted above, where he recognizes that he *is* Satan, there is nothing that is devilish in that way. Everything in the poem lines up behind what he says here; there are no contrary voices that carry any weight; we hear him as simply right in what he proposes, in a way that creates a strong sense of a unitary, totalizing perspective. *There is no other* point of view. The lines have a certain rhetorical grandeur, and the ethical position they stand for is full of interest, but one wonders whether Blake will be able to support the tremendous, booming claim they make for the significance of what is to come.

At the climax of the poem, several thousand lines later, Milton comes at last to his great encounter with Satan, his creation or projection and his *alter ego*, and makes a long speech, which we understand as performative of the great act of self-annihilation which he had promised.

> Satan, my Spectre, I know my power thee to annihilate
> And be a greater in thy place, & be thy tabernacle,
> A covering for thee to do thy will—till one greater comes
> And smites me as I smote thee, & becomes my covering.
> Such are the Laws of thy false Heavens, but laws of Eternity
> Are not such. Know thou, I come to Self-Annihilation.
> Such are the laws of Eternity, that each shall mutually
> Annihilate himself for other's good, as I for thee. . . .
> I come to discover before Heaven & Hell the Self-righteousness
> In all its hypocritic turpitude, opening to every eye
> These wonders of Satan's holiness, showing to the earth
> The idol-virtues of the Natural heart, & Satan's Seat
> Explore, in all its Selfish Natural Virtue, & put off
> In Self-annihilation all that is not of God alone:
> To put off Self & all I have, ever & ever. Amen. (592–93; 38:29–49)

This would be morally shrewd were it not so poetically inert. Morally shrewd, because Milton not only understands that the position of righteous virtue which flows from the conception of God as moral authoritarian is really satanic, he also understands a subtler lesson: that directly to attack that authoritarianism, to "annihilate" it (as, for example, the French Revolutionaries annihilated the *ancien régime*), would only be to cover and preserve it, as part of an endless cycle of repression in the name of virtue. Hence he comes to dis-cover and expose the very principle of self-righteousness, annihilating not his opponent but his own self or ego, so that what remains may be of God alone. All very well. But as poetry, as a piece of imaginative creation, it fails to rise to the extraordinary and wonderful challenge Blake has set himself, of imagining how John Milton might speak to Satan if he were indeed to acknowledge him as part of himself. Milton's language here is thumpingly insistent yet also rhythmically flaccid, largely without shape or structure, and weakly declamatory or melodramatic insofar as it gestures toward dramatic speech. Most damagingly, Milton sounds in this speech like a prig, very full of Satan's wrongness and his own rightness: which is exactly how he must not sound if he has really taken the force of his own position.

As a piece of dramatic creation, Milton's speech will not bear comparison with those passages in the gospels that are broadly parallel: where Jesus finds ways of confronting accusation without being drawn into the power dynamics of counterassertion, which so readily becomes self-righteous or self-justifying.

> And the scribes and Pharisees brought unto him a woman taken in adultery; and when they had set her in the midst,
>
> They say unto him, Master, this woman was taken in adultery, in the very act.
>
> Now Moses in the law commanded us, that such should be stoned: but what sayest thou?
>
> This they said, tempting him, that they might have to accuse him. But Jesus stooped down, and with his finger wrote on the ground.
>
> So when they continued asking him, he lifted up himself, and said unto them, He that is without sin among you, let him first cast a stone at her.
>
> And again he stooped down, and wrote on the ground.
>
> And they which heard it, being convicted by their own conscience, went out one by one, beginning at the eldest, even unto the last. (John 8:3-9)

And Jesus stood before the governor: and the governor asked him, saying, Art thou the King of the Jews? And Jesus said unto him, Thou sayest.

And when he was accused of the chief priests and elders, he answered nothing.

Then said Pilate unto him, Hearest thou not how many things they witness against thee?

And he answered him to never a word; insomuch that the governor marvelled greatly. (Matt 27:11-14)

In both these passages something is withheld from us; more is conveyed than can be made explicit, or be spoken. The root of the problem in the passage by Blake has to do with the fullness of the claim to knowledge, to a totalizing consciousness. "I know . . ." Milton thunders, and again, to Satan, "Know thou . . ." This is the speech in which all is revealed, discovered, known.

There is no place here for otherness, for there is nothing "that is not of God alone"—that totalizing claim which Blake elsewhere identifies as deeply misguided and pernicious. Satan replies to this with a furious counterassertion: "But I alone am God, & I alone in heaven & earth | Of all that live dare utter this. Others tremble & bow | Till all things become one great Satan" (593; 38:56–39:1). There is a difference, of course, which Blake means to be crucial: Satan uses "I," whereas it is Milton's resolve to "put off self & all I have" that will reveal "God alone." But this is only the difference between pebble and clod. The effect of Milton's all-comprehending speech is to dissipate otherness: and therefore to dispel the possibility of relationship. This is reinforced when he immediately moves to a similarly climactic encounter with his female emanation, Ololon, hitherto alienated from him—but the gateway to union proves to be the repudiation and "burning away" of sexual difference. It is as though the tension involved in acknowledging *relation* with the other, undoing the absoluteness of opposition and alienation, is so great at these moments that it cannot be sustained, and otherness, once engaged with, must instantaneously combust or evaporate in the totality of the larger vision. This includes relations with that most significant of others, the Adversary. In Satan's brief reply to Milton his defiance rings hollow, and he is then immediately revealed as powerless to harm—a paper tiger. Howling vainly around the body of Albion, he "trembled with exceeding great trembling & astonishment" (594; 39:17). And that is the last we hear of him.

Milton is then free to make his final great declaration, a speech in which he "casts off," in a reiterated phrase, all aspects of selfhood. These include that reflective consciousness—"the idiot questioner who is always questioning | But never capable of answering, who sits with a sly grin | Silent plotting when to question"—which belongs to a separated self and is therefore naturally bound to "doubt" and "envy" (598; 41:12–16). Such consciousness may "pretend to Poetry," but only with the intent to "destroy Imagination" (598; 41:23). Among Milton's other castings off, he will, emphatically,

> cast aside from Poetry all that is not Inspiration,
> That it no longer shall dare to mock with the aspersion of madness
> Cast on the inspired. (598; 41:7–9)

At this moment of complete revelation, everything that is not of God alone is to be cast out. In particular, there shall be no element of mockery, no "sly grin," and no questions, only answers. In the terms of Blake's recently developed distinction, such skeptical consciousness is a "negation" to be destroyed, not a "contrary" with which to engage.

Blake had written that Milton was a true poet and of the Devil's party without knowing it: well now, in *Milton*, thanks to Blake, he does know it—and the consequence is the evaporation both of the Devil and of true poetry. The poetics announced at the end of *Milton* would cast off much of Blake's own finest writing. For a Devil's-party poet, the energies of poetry seem to be best served by the kind of half-consciousness that leaves space for a real, unresolved engagement with otherness, with a potentially mocking voice, and in particular with the entanglement of energy with evil.

William Hazlitt was much exercised by the close connection he perceived between the power of poetry and the will to power per se. He found himself driven to affirm "that poetry, that the imagination, generally speaking, delights in power, in strong excitement, as well as in truth, in good, in right, whereas pure reason and the moral sense approve only of the true and good." Hazlitt then poses a question which might have been prompted by the *Songs of Innocence and Experience*, had he known of its existence.

"Do we read with more pleasure of the ravages of a beast of prey, than of the shepherd's pipe upon the mountain?" No; but we do read with pleasure of the ravages of the beast of prey, and we do so on the principle I have stated, namely, from the sense of power abstracted from the sense of good; and it is this same principle that makes us read with admiration and reconciles us in fact to the triumphant progress of the conquerors and mighty hunters of mankind, who come to stop the shepherd's pipe upon the mountains, and sweep away his listening flock.[65]

If this is not quite to say that true poetry is of the Devil's party, it strongly suggests poetry's alliance with the darker impulses of our nature. The energy of poetry is not of God alone. In his study of Blake's thought, Morton Paley quotes that passage by Hazlitt and, citing "The Tiger" and the development of Orc, comments that "it may seem as if Blake was tending toward a similar view in the 1790s."[66] But if so, Paley hastens to show that he did not rest there: Blake's creation of a new, expanded mythology allowed him to move beyond Hazlitt's "disturbingly equivocal" view to a more positive, affirmative understanding which keeps faith with "divine humanity" and its potential for redemption or regeneration. That seems right; the end of *Milton* is nothing if not unequivocal. But however much of an achievement this may be in Blake's *thought*—which can be debated—my suggestion in this chapter has been that much of Blake's finest poetry arises out of that moment of extreme tension in the early to mid-1790s, when his openly ironic, provocative, parodic assumption of a devilish point of view became the means or pretext for engagement with energies genuinely dangerous, genuinely diabolical. In Blake's equivocal, double-voiced relation with those energies lies the vitality of his poetry, as well as the principle that keeps him from the grim conclusion which Hazlitt reluctantly envisages, the painful either/or that severs the ethical from the aesthetic.

I have presented *Milton* as marking the loss of Blake's poetic vitality and linked this to its loss of any energizing liaison with the diabolical. That is true, I think, of its general tendency, but it also contains passages that stand aside from the totalizing emphasis of the conclusion. In fairness to Blake, let me conclude with the wonderful moment when Urizen opposes Milton in his journey and like a malignant version of John the Baptist pours icy water from the Jordan onto Milton's brain. Milton's response is not to annihilate either Urizen or himself;

instead, he takes clay and sculpts the "Demon" into definite, human form. What subsists between them in this exchange is described as "enormous strife, one giving life, the other giving death | To his adversary" (541; 19:29–30).

> Silent Milton stood before
> The darkened Urizen, as the sculptor silent stands before
> His forming image, he walks round it patient labouring,
> Thus Milton stood forming bright Urizen. (544; 20:7–10)

It is a wonderful conception of the artist's dangerous task: the restoring of the darkened adversary to some of his original brightness.

4

Byron's Familiar Spirit

Satanic Byron

> . . . men of diseased hearts and depraved imaginations, who . . . labour to
> make others as miserable as themselves, by infecting them with a moral virus
> that eats into the soul! The school which they have set up may properly be
> called the Satanic school . . . characterized by a Satanic spirit of pride and
> audacious impiety, which still betrays the wretched feeling of helplessness
> wherewith it is allied. (Southey, Preface to *A Vision of Judgment*)[1]

When in 1821 the British Poet Laureate Robert Southey attacked the "Satanic school" in contemporary poetry, it was clear to his readers who, above all others, occupied that bad eminence. The immediate provocation was the opening cantos of *Don Juan*, a poem that gave huge offense for its perceived immorality and nihilism: but for years Byron had built his immense success around a series of darkly heroic figures who share many characteristics with Milton's great "archangel ruined." Byron's protagonists in the poems that made him famous—Childe Harold, the Giaour, Conrad the Corsair, Lara, Manfred—are charismatic yet profoundly isolated figures, exiles or outlaws from conventional society, alienated by a combination of their superior nobility of mind and some obscure act of crime or transgression in their past. Their consciousness is withdrawn, inflamed, and brooding; the pain they carry within is never fully communicated, but expressed in part by the attitude of disdain, severe and superb, which they show to human weakness in others as in themselves, and also to the littleness of life itself, its weakness to sustain their desires. They are *fallen* beings—or so at least they experience their existence—but tremendous in their fallenness: they can neither altogether regret what they have become, because of the dark knowledge which they now possess, nor reconcile themselves to their condition, but vibrate between the poles of grim acquiescence and unappeasable rebellion. It often seems to be the intensity of this consciousness itself that constitutes their alienated self: consciousness not only *of* but also *as* alienation.

This painful intensification of self, and the desire for relief from it, was, Byron believed, what made him a writer:

> To withdraw myself from myself (oh that cursed selfishness!) has ever been my sole, my entire, my sincere motive in scribbling at all; and publishing is also the continuance of the same object, by the action it affords to the mind, which else recoils upon itself.[2]

That image of the mind's self-recoil remembers Milton on Satan's

> dire attempt which, nigh the birth,
> Now rolling boils in his tumultuous breast
> And like a dev'lish engine back recoils
> Upon himself. Horror and doubt distract
> His troubled thoughts and from the bottom stir
> The Hell within him, for within him Hell
> He brings . . . (iv.15–21)

Satan cannot escape himself; and Byron's word "scribbling" shows how tenuous, how close to self-mocking, was his belief—in 1813, at least—in his poetry as a form of action that could release him from himself.

Indeed, most of the poems that made Byron famous are inescapably self-referential; the potency of his "Satanic" heroes was hugely enhanced by his own reputation. "Mad—bad—and dangerous to know,"[3] he was understood, like his creations, to walk on the wild side. He had travelled in the exotic East, lived the life of the libertine, taken the radical side in politics, driven his virtuous wife into separation, and was rumored to have slept with his half-sister; now he lived in exile in Italy, where he was said to indulge in all manner of sexual licence, and kept company with the atheist Shelley. His club foot suggested some more essential deformity, or brand of distinction, half-concealed like the Devil's cloven hoof. A plausible anecdote relates that "he used to declare that he was a fallen angel, not symbolically but literally, and told Annabella [his wife] that she was one of those women spoken of in the Bible who are loved by an exile from Heaven."[4] This impulse to court his own damnation in the eyes of the virtuous was to be powerfully expressed by the publication of *Don Juan*.

The proximity of the diabolical was felt by his readers almost from the start. Reviewing the first two cantos of *Childe Harold's Pilgrimage*, Francis Jeffrey was quick to see this connection between Satan and Harold, and to extend it to Byron himself.

> Like Milton's fiend . . . [Harold] "sees undelighted all delight," and passes on through the great wilderness of the world with a heart shut to all human sympathy. . . . The mind of the noble author has been so far tinged by his strong conception of the Satanic personage, that the sentiments and reflections which he delivers in his own name, have all received a shade of the same gloomy and misanthropic colouring.[5]

Jeffrey found a satanic quality not only in the author's sentiments and reflections, but also in his poem's ability to engage the reader with what should, or would otherwise, be repulsive or antipathetic. Harold is "a sated epicure" whose "disdainful" sentiments "run directly counter to very many of our national passions, and most favoured propensities." Yet Jeffrey could see that the poem would be a success. "The most surprising thing about the present work, indeed, is, that it should please and interest so much as it does."[6] This went to the heart of the Byron phenomenon, the extraordinary power of fascination exercised by certain of his poems. Like a solicitation from the Devil, they should not "please and interest," yet they do. They were felt to draw the reader in against his or her will: or rather, to excite in the will of the reader an inclination toward a mode of sensibility that was blighted or depraved. The more morally disconcerting this phenomenon, the greater must be the genius of the poet who can achieve such effects: but what was the status of such genius? Jeffrey developed this theme in subsequent reviews. Looking back on the poems leading up to *The Corsair*, he wrote of the "terrible energy" in Byron's writing, and of the "traits of divine inspiration, or demoniacal possession, thrown across the tamer features of humanity" as the "spell," the "natural magic," by which Byron "has fixed the admiration of the public."[7] Canto 3 of *Childe Harold*, with its "inextinguishable energy of sentiment," prompted Jeffrey to write, with admiration rather than approval, of "a sort of demoniacal sublimity, not without some traits of the ruined Archangel,"[8] and when *Manfred* came out the next year, this only sharpened Jeffrey's sense of Byron as an artist whose power came out of his association with the forces of darkness.

> The noble author, we find, still deals with that dark and overawing Spirit, by whose aid he has so often subdued the minds of his readers, and in whose might he has wrought so many wonders.[9]

Jeffrey presumably intends this as a figure of speech: but, one feels, only just.

A Turning Point

This satanic presence in Byron's work has always been much noticed and discussed. I deal only briefly with it here, for my interest is in its displacement or transformation in Byron's later work. At least until *Manfred*, Milton's Satan is the Devil evoked in Byron's poetry, but after that, it is a different dark spirit who influences his writing: the Mephistopheles of Goethe's *Faust*.

In canto 13 of *Don Juan* Byron writes of the turning point that comes with age. At the age of thirty, one passes "life's equinoctial line,"[10] and the passions and pleasures of love give way, to be replaced by other more constricted passions, such as the love of money, or the involvement in politics and the pleasures of hatred which that brings. Byron's own turning point, however, has been more profound; he has come to distance himself from *all* passionate involvement, whether love or hate:

> For my part, I am but a mere spectator,
> And gaze where'er the palace or the hovel is,
> Much in the mode of Goethe's Mephistopheles;
>
> But neither love nor hate in much excess;
> Though 'twas not once so. If I sneer sometimes,

It is because I cannot well do less,

And now and then it also suits my rhymes. (xiii.7–8)

Byron was here aligning himself with the trajectory of Goethe's own poetic career, as he would have known it from the account of Madame de Staël. In *De l'Allemagne* she wrote that Goethe had no longer that overwhelming ardor that inspired *Werther*, although the warmth of his thoughts was still sufficient to give life to everything. "It might be said that he is not affected by life and that he describes it only as a painter: he attaches more value now to the pictures which he offers us than to the emotions which he feels. Time has made him a spectator"—*le temps l'a rendu spectateur.*[11] "For my part, I am but a mere spectator." Byron's line links the detachment of the artist-narrator with the detachment of Mephistopheles. As Gretchen notices, Mephistopheles takes no *Anteil*, no sympathetic interest, in anything, and even his malice seems casual and occasional, subordinate to his intellect and a function of it. This makes him formidable: he regards all the goods of life with the cool, corrosive objectivity of the nonparticipant. Intellectual vocation, the pleasures of the senses, communion with the natural world, the rapture of passionate love—all shrink and wither under his intelligence. "I am the Spirit who always denies," he introduces himself to Faust, "and rightly so: for everything that comes into being is worthy only of destruction. Better, if it never came into being at all!" (1338–41).[12] His is not the only point of view, of course, but the play grants its reality as a point of view: yes, that is how human life appears when seen with a certain kind of detachment. Byron offers himself as a parallel case: circumstances may cause him to play the satirist, and "sneer sometimes," but he does so, nowadays, without passionate investment; his detachment extends even to his own role or "part," even to his own emotions, his residual spasms of love and hate.

"'Twas not once so." The notion of having passed some crucial turning point, in life as in poetry, gathers increasing force in the later cantos of *Don Juan*, but it was already there at the beginning of the poem. In the first canto Byron writes that he will not respond antagonistically to hostile reviews, although in his "hot youth" it would have been otherwise.

But now at thirty years my hair is gray—
(I wonder what it will be like at forty?
I thought of a peruke the other day)
My heart is not much greener; and, in short, I
Have squander'd my whole summer while 'twas May,
And feel no more the spirit to retort; I
Have spent my life, both interest and principal,
And deem not, what I deem'd, my soul invincible. . . .

No more—no more—Oh! never more, my heart,
Canst thou be my sole world, my universe!
Once all in all, but now a thing apart,
Thou canst not be my blessing or my curse:
The illusion's gone forever . . . (i.213–15)

Those last lines suggest the nature of the shift from the satanic toward
"the mode of Mephistopheles." The satanic principle is totalizing. It
seeks to be "all in all," a subjectivity that extends to the horizon. "The
mind is its own place and in itself | Can make a Heaven of Hell, a Hell
of Heaven."[13] Satan is alienated from God and from paradise, but insofar as he is Satan, the sense of the other only strengthens the opposing sense of self, in all its pain and pride. The earlier Byronic heroes
are satanic in that way, and so are the poems in which they appear,
insofar as everything in them reinforces the presence and the intensity
of that central consciousness. The reader is invited to an act of *total
identification*—not precisely with the protagonist, whose subjectivity
is finally inaccessible, but with a point of view filled and magnetized
by the contemplation of the protagonist. Hence Jeffrey's language of
"possession," of Byron's "spell" and "magic." Any trace of irony would
be fatal to this effect. But *now*—after the turning point, in *Don Juan*—
Byron's "heart," his passionate feeling, is no longer the universe. It is
"a thing apart," which he can address, reflectively, from a different,
discrepant, and potentially ironic point of consciousness. It was this
reflective quality in *Don Juan* which disappointed Kierkegaard's aesthete in *Either/Or*; he identified it as the reason that Byron's poem
failed to give the pleasure of *Don Giovanni*. All "opposition" is swept
away by the "demonic" immediacy of the *Don Giovanni* music, which
gives us passion's "infinite power that nothing can resist," whereas

Byron's reflective mode concedes that Juan's desires are in "conflict with the world about him."[14] "Reflection is fatal to the immediate,"[15] Kierkegaard's aesthete declares. Just so: and Mephistopheles, "the Spirit who always denies," is nothing if not reflective.

Enter Mephistopheles

Byron's admiration for Goethe is well attested. He dedicated *Sardanapalus* and *Werner* to Goethe as "the first of existing masters,"[16] and near the end of his life a visitor could report that although he knew nothing of the German language, "he was perfectly acquainted . . . with Goethe in particular, and with every passage of Faust."[17] There were a number of sources from which he could have gained a sense of the play. Goethe had published *Faust: A Tragedy* (i.e., *Faust: Part One*) in 1808. Madame de Staël's account in *De l'Allemagne*, which translates substantial passages into French, was published by John Murray in 1813, with some of Byron's close acquaintance—Francis Hodgson and William and Caroline Lamb—involved in the English translation. (De Staël declared roundly that "the Devil is the hero of the piece," and gave most of her admiration to the "infernal irony" of Mephistopheles.[18]) But Byron's first significant encounter with *Faust* came in the autumn of 1816, when Matthew Lewis, author of the sensational Gothic novel *The Monk*, was staying with him in the Villa Diodati. Lewis, who had met Goethe in Weimar, spent several days translating *Faust* to Byron, who recorded that he "was naturally much struck with it."[19] Within weeks he was, in *Manfred*, imitating specific passages as well as aspects of the whole Faust story.

When Lewis translated *Faust* for him, Byron must immediately have recognized the broad parallel between the figure of Faust and the "Byronic" protagonists of his own poems. Faust in Goethe is not the power-seeking magus of the sixteenth-century legend. He is a figure tormented by unfulfillment: the homeless one, as he grimly refers to himself, "der Unmensch ohne Zweck und Ruh" (3349), the antithesis of a human being, pointless, without aim or end or rest. All his academic, conceptual knowledge does not satisfy him: it is illusory, empty, amounting to nothing more than words; it gives him no access to the heart and source of life. He accordingly turns away from the life of knowledge, and the pain of consciousness, to seek immersion in the worldliness of the world, allowing Mephistopheles to lead him out of his study toward a life of dissipation and sensual pleasure. Hence his retranslation of John's Gospel: no longer "In the beginning was the word," but "In the beginning was the *deed*" (1237). Yet what kind of action would bring fulfillment? Its nature remains unimaginable. Faust's desires are essentially indeterminate, the expressions of a dynamic will without end or aim, since all ends and aims have been seen through. The darkness of his being is expressed in a great curse which he utters on all the illusions which hold us to life: the high ideas of the mind, the flatteries of fame and wealth, the soothing powers of wine, the bondage of family and material possession, and at the climax of this great bitter curse, love, hope, faith, and above all, patience. When he turns to the pleasures of the world and the flesh, therefore, it is with no expectation of fulfillment. He gives himself up to dissipation (and to love) with a certain bitterly indissoluble estrangement. Hence, in an extraordinary change to the old story, he does not contract his soul to the Devil absolutely, but stakes it on the wager that he can never be brought to experience, even for a single moment, a state of complete fulfillment. It is this painful restlessness of spirit, this consuming onward movement that characterizes Faust: a quality, perhaps, of genius, but one which also makes him a criminal figure—technically at first, in his association with the Devil, but then profoundly, in the destruction that he visits unwillingly, yet not altogether unknowingly or innocently, on Gretchen through his affair with her.

These characteristics—the restless anguish of spirit, the criminality, the estrangement, the tremendous contempt for life and the ideas and ideals that sweeten life for others—can readily be matched in the "Byronic" heroes of the *Childe Harold* period. Byron's favorite description of humanity as an unhappy compound of fire and clay is paralleled in Faust's self-description as painfully divided between the "two souls" that live within him, the one aspiring upward and elsewhere but the other forever earthbound (1112). Faust is a study in the same unappeasable, destructive restlessness of spirit that is Byron's signature theme.[20]

But we may speculate that what Byron was "much struck by" in *Faust* was, as that phrasing suggests, something more than the image of his own preoccupations. The difference in Goethe's treatment of those preoccupations is epitomized in his Devil. The Byronic heroes draw very substantially on Milton's fallen angel, as we have seen, and partake of that totalizing sublimity of mind which informs both Byron's charisma and his anguish. The mind is its own place, as Satan puts it—or as in *Don Juan* Byron remembered that period, the heart is all in all. But what Byron found in Goethe was that the Devil was someone else, someone other. In his classic essay "Byron and Goethe," Giuseppe Mazzini argued that Byron's heroes embody the absolutely free, but desperately solitary, individual; each is "Faust, but without the compact that submits him to the enemy; for the heroes of Byron make no such compact."[21] Exactly so: a Byronic hero is Faust without Mephistopheles, Faust as all in all. The new thing which Byron encountered in *Faust* was Mephistopheles: an entirely different way of imagining the Devil from that offered by Milton, and one which insisted on placing the Faustian subjectivity in relation to something other than itself.

As the spirit of denial, Mephistopheles explains to Faust, he is necessarily only ever "a part," an essentially relational figure, and can never give access to the whole (1345–78, 1780–84). His is a consciousness of unrelieved negativity, which sees life as worthless and aspiration as vain. Faust sometimes expresses a similar view, so that there is a sense in which Mephistopheles is part of Faust, or is expressing one aspect of Faust's consciousness. But whereas Faust feels the emptiness of life always as passionate disappointment and frustration, Mephistopheles expresses that vision quite differently: in a voice of irresistible, dry, ironic mockery, of unamused amusement. His measureless knowingness is reinforced by the many passages which invoke a certain theatrical self-consciousness; his presence continually threatens to expose the whole action of the play, with all Faust's sound and fury, as thin melodrama or poor comedy—perhaps akin to one of the puppet plays of Faust that Goethe remembered seeing as a child. Standing over against Faust in this way, Mephistopheles presented Byron with a perspective on the intensities of selfhood that offered new creative possibilities—even if the Devil's gifts come always at a price.

Manfred and the Encounter with the Earth-Spirit

Byron's immediate response to hearing Lewis translate *Faust* was to write *Manfred*, a turn to drama which shows both how strongly *Faust* had gripped his imagination and how little he had yet begun to assimilate the challenge of Mephistopheles. The opening closely recalls Goethe: Manfred is sitting, like Faust, in a "Gothic" room at night, passionately unsatisfied by all his knowledge. He rehearses the Faustian starting point in terms that show how completely this had meshed in Byron's mind with his own fascination with the Fall, and with the consciousness that heroically endures and resents its fallen condition:

> The Tree of Knowledge is not that of Life.
> Philosophy and science, and the springs
> Of wonder, and the wisdom of the world,
> I have essayed, and in my mind there is
> A power to make these subject to itself—
> But they avail not. (I.i.12–17)

Like Faust, Manfred calls up spirits that might satisfy his desire. As in *Faust*, they do not give him what he seeks, and as Faust "collapses" at this refusal, so Manfred "falls senseless" (I.i.191). Like Faust, he then contemplates suicide, and like Faust is barely deflected from taking the fatal step. What torments him is not only the emptiness of "Knowledge," but also a more specific remorse; Byronic heroes are regularly haunted by some act of crime committed in their past, but nowhere else is this so clearly identified as the destruction of the beloved. "I loved her, and destroy'd her!" (II.ii.117), Manfred declares, in a line which—whatever its roots in Byron's own experience—is precisely applicable to the Gretchen tragedy. It was Goethe's innovation to develop the Faust story as a tragedy of seduction, and some readers have found it hard to see the connection; it is striking that Byron so readily followed Goethe in linking the alienated or hell-devoted consciousness with a destructive sexual relationship, albeit one set in Manfred's past.

Yet there is no equivalent to Mephistopheles in Byron's drama, no counterweight to the Faustian Manfred. Arimanes, enthroned power of evil, whom Manfred visits but to whom he calmly refuses to kneel, is a being of a quite different kind. And when the Devil arrives in the final scene, as in the Faust legend, to claim his soul at the point of death, Manfred sends him and his fellow demons most tremendously packing. "Back to thy hell!"

> What I have done is done; I bear within
> A torture which could nothing gain from thine:

The mind which is immortal makes itself
Requital for its good or evil thoughts—
Is its own origin of ill and end—
And its own place and time . . .
I have not been thy dupe, nor am thy prey—
But was my own destroyer, and will be
My own hereafter.—Back, ye baffled fiends!
The hand of death is on me—but not yours! (III.iv.124–41)

Paraphrasing Milton's heroic Satan—"the mind is its own place" (i.254)—Manfred makes the Devil redundant. Encounter with the Adversary is therefore inconceivable. Manfred is a Faustian figure, but one who has never met Mephistopheles; his posture of anguished, rebellious egotism is "all in all," without any genuinely dramatic interaction with a site of consciousness that is other to itself, and is, in that individualistic sense, unequivocally (if melodramatically) heroic.

This satanic affiliation—the titanic assertion of individual mind, the heroic gesture as compensation for all—was not to be all at once undone by Mephistopheles, whose presence can be felt in *Manfred* only in the resistance he provokes. Reviewing Byron's play, Goethe wrote that he "has used motifs [from *Faust*] which suited his purpose in his own way, with the result that none is the same anymore."[22] The most revealing example is the passage early in the play which recalls Faust's encounter with the Earth-Spirit. Manfred conjures the "spirits of the unbounded Universe" (I.i.29), but when they appear they cannot give him the "oblivion, self-oblivion" (I.i.144) which he demands of them. He collapses, and a dark incantation is spoken over his body, dedicating him to further suffering. His stature is, however, simply enhanced by this encounter. He passes out not because the spirits disappoint him but at the intensity of his own suffering, seeing in the vision they present to him the woman whom he loved and destroyed. The spirits conclude that there is nothing they can do to add to his torment, and curse him simply with himself, since, like Milton's Satan, he is himself already his own "proper Hell" (I.i.251). This concedes the truth of what he had already told them:

The mind, the spirit, the Promethean spark,
The lightning of my being, is as bright,

Pervading, and far-darting as your own,
And shall not yield to yours, though coop'd in clay! (I.i.154–57)

Faust's encounter with the Earth-Spirit ends very differently. He summons this spirit out of his desire to rise above the disappointments of conceptual knowledge, to enter instead into the immediate principle that holds the world together at its core. In the Earth-Spirit it seems that he has found what he seeks; it announces itself as the dynamic, glowing, ever-changing principle of the totality of life, embracing "birth and grave—an eternal sea—weaving the living fabric of divinity at the loom of time" (501–9). Faust greets its appearance with rapture, and with an impulse of identification: "Spirit of activity, how near I feel myself to you!" (511), but this meets with an immediate rebuff, as the jingle of words in the German mocks his presumption:

Du gleichst den Geist, den du begreifst,
Nicht mir! (512–13)

You resemble the Spirit that you comprehend—not me!

The spirit disappears; Faust collapses in an agony of chagrin; and the bathos of the actual is consolidated by the arrival of Wagner, who has heard Faust "declaiming," as he puts it—"reading a Greek tragedy, perhaps?" (522–23). The moment of soaring lyrical aspiration is flattened into the kaleidoscope of diverse modes and fragments which is *Faust*. It is a moment of rejection that burns itself into Faust's consciousness, haunting him later in the drama. The spirit that he truly comprehends—and, worse, which he resembles—is not the Earth-Spirit, the sublime totality of things, which by its very nature defies intellectual comprehension, but Mephistopheles, the spirit of denial, necessarily only ever "a part," not the whole. Faust is thrown back on what he can comprehend or conceptualize, on the mode of reflective consciousness, which carries with it the separation or alienation of the "mere spectator."

The Earth-Spirit encounter is the moment when Faust is first brought up against his own littleness, the moment that releases irony into the play. That Byron should have chosen that encounter to reconfigure as a tribute to Manfred's indomitable, Promethean mind, can be understood as an act of resistance to Goethe's deglamourising irony which confesses the pressure of that point of view. (Faust frequently wishes to resist or deny what he hears from Mephistopheles, but is never quite able to.) The heroic note in *Manfred* is both thinner and more extreme than in Byron's nondramatic writing, with a ringing declamatory hollowness that, if not quite at the edge of self-parody, still seems almost to invite an ironic reply, an answering bathos, as if it were a provocation, a conjuration, of Mephistopheles.

For it is the approach to the Earth-Spirit that *generates* Mephistopheles, by a kind of necessary reaction. This is implied in the line just quoted, and confirmed in the later soliloquy which Faust addresses to the "sublime Spirit" who holds out the possibility of communion with the life of nature:

> Oh, but now I feel how nothing comes to perfection for human beings. Along with this joy, which brings me ever closer to the gods, you gave me that companion, whom already I can no longer do without—even though his cold mockery belittles me in my own eyes, and with a word turns all your gifts to nothing. (3240–46)

Eat this fruit, and you shall be as gods, knowing good and evil, said the serpent. Faust's aspiration to divinity, to embracing the totality of life, is likewise thrown back into a fallen mode of consciousness, which degrades the gifts of life precisely through its knowingness about them. Whereupon Mephistopheles enters, right on cue, and changes Faust's elevated blank verse into a set of rhyming exchanges in which the ardent romantic's protestations are exposed to the critical commentary of his shadow. Breaking in upon Faust's retirement, Mephistopheles brings into consciousness considerations that Faust would rather suppress. He raises an ironic eyebrow at Faust's curious preference for passing his time in the countryside while his lover sits weeping, apparently abandoned, at home. Surely it would be better if Faust acknowledged the carnal desires that underlie all his fine feeling, and returned to the poor girl? "Go in and comfort her, you fool!" (3367). This counsel is the more disconcerting for being not *evidently* malicious; the possibility of diabolical intent merges equivocally with the note of down-to-earth good sense. Yet even while he accedes to it, Faust understands it, not wrongly, as destructive.

This movement of bathos following afflatus is the ground rhythm of *Faust*. Bathos is supplied sometimes by the sententiousness of Faust's scholar assistant Wagner, by the ingenuous directness of Gretchen, or by a countermovement in Faust's own consciousness. But it is supremely the mode of Mephistopheles. Again and again, Mephistopheles pinpoints with deadly precision what is inflated or self-deceiving in Faust's intuitions of transcendence. Whether this is Faust's contemplation of a heroic suicide, his feeling of something divine in his love for Gretchen, or his withdrawal into a state of Wordsworthian communion with nature, Mephistopheles unfailingly reminds him of the baser element which his affirmation leaves out. Or, to make the point in a less character-based way, Mephistopheles' idiom, as much as his critique, forces a switch into a less exalted imaginative mode or register. His familiar manner, antidote to sublimity, pulls Faust's expansive subjective lyricism back down into a *dramatic* relation, where it is met and abruptly challenged by other voices, perspectives, or generic modes.

From Romantic to Burlesque

Although Byron could not admit Mephistopheles into *Manfred*, in *Don Juan*—begun two years later—the Mephistophelean bathos is everywhere. It is built into the manner of the writing, which—like Faust before the Earth-Spirit, though without Faust's dismay—continually collapses, or stages its own collapse, in the approach to finality or transcendence: a poetic reenactment of the Fall.

Let us look at the account of how Juan falls in love for the first time. Although the effects Byron creates here are broad, they already suggest the subtleties that will recur, in increasingly charged and complex forms, throughout the poem. The adolescent Juan has spent much time together with the lovely Donna Julia, and finds himself afflicted by a discontent whose nature he hardly understands:

> Silent and pensive, idle, restless, slow,
> His home deserted for the lonely wood,
> Tormented with a wound he could not know,
> His, like all deep grief, plunged in solitude:
> I'm fond myself of solitude or so,
> But then, I beg it may be understood,

> By solitude I mean a sultan's, not
> A hermit's, with a haram for a grot. (i.87)

A characteristically Romantic idea of solitude—meditative, melan-
choly, *deep*—is allowed a certain real weight and presence in the first
four lines before turning into burlesque, as in an aside to the reader
Byron invokes his own reputation as libertine, laced for good measure
with an image of Orientalist excess. In Blakean terms, a kind of innocence is sharply juxtaposed, or rather exposed, to the voice of experience. As the passage develops, the knowingness of that voice not
only contrasts itself with innocence, but encroaches upon it. Juan pur-
sues "his self-communion with his own high soul," lost in his thoughts
about the wonders of man, and nature, and the heavens—and also about
Donna Julia's eyes:

> In thoughts like these true wisdom may discern
> Longings sublime, and aspirations high,
> Which some are born with, but the most part learn
> To plague themselves withal, they know not why:
> 'Twas strange that one so young should thus concern
> His brain about the action of the sky;
> If *you* think 'twas philosophy that this did,
> I can't help thinking puberty assisted. (i.93)

Mephistopheles—the spirit of negation—mocks Faust's impulse
to find something divine or elevated in his passion for Gretchen. In
Byron's stanza the register of seriousness descends line by line, until
arriving with perfect comic timing at the terminal bathos of the final
couplet, with its facetious four-syllable rhyme. The mockery here is
not so much of Juan as of any reader who might be inclined to take
these sublime longings seriously. "If *you* think" these expressed some
transcendental spark within the mind, then Byron "can't help" replying
that puberty assisted. This voice of knowing denial is locally irresistible; the sense of privileged insight is guaranteed by Byron's worldly
experience.

Yet this is more than simply the comedy of unmasking, or the correction of the mind's affectation by the reality of the body. The opening lines about "true wisdom" come by the end of the stanza to seem

as if they must have been sarcasms, but this is a retrospective revision; they did not read as sarcasm at the time. And the phrase "some are born with" marks an important exclusion: these "longings sublime" are not *always* affectation, or the mere mimicking of sentimental literature. This exclusion is then, apparently, abandoned and forgotten as we descend into knowingness. The stanza tells a debunking truth about adolescent feeling, yes, but it also itself enacts a fall. There is a comparable moment in Goethe's *Faust* in the witch's kitchen, where Faust gazes with rapture at the image of female beauty he sees in the magic mirror. Mephistopheles' quietly sardonic remark at the end of the scene reduces this to the aphrodisiac effects of the rejuvenating potion. "Du siehst mit diesem Trank im Leibe | Bald Helenen in jedem Weibe": "with that potion in your body, you'll soon be seeing Helen of Troy in every woman" (2603–4). The heavy rhyme on *Leibe/Weibe* (body/woman) subjects Faust's erotic rapture to a derisive bathos, as knowingly as the clinching couplet in Byron's stanza. Yet it is a crucial detail that Faust first sees the lovely vision in the mirror independently, and *before* he drinks the witch's potion. There is at least a possibility that Mephistopheles' final lines do not comprehend Faust's rapture as entirely as he may suppose.

If it seems overstated to associate these falls into bathos in *Don Juan* with the Devil, Robert Southey did not think so—and neither did Byron himself. This is how he opens the fourth canto:

> Nothing so difficult as a beginning
> In poesy, unless perhaps the end;
> For oftentimes when Pegasus seems winning
> The race, he sprains a wing, and down we tend,
> Like Lucifer when hurl'd from heaven for sinning;
> Our sin the same, and hard as his to mend,
> Being pride, which leads the mind to soar too far,
> Till our own weakness shows us what we are. (iv.1)

"We" in this stanza refers particularly to Byron, but has also a general application. The continual falling into bathos which marks *Don Juan* writes large the sense in which all poetry is liable to be the record of failure. The mind which soars will soar too far, until like Lucifer it is forced to reflect upon its own fall. This movement is written into

Byron's handling of the *ottava rima* stanza throughout *Don Juan*: six lines of aspiration, rhyming once too often for safety, then falling or flattening into the final couplet. (Many variations are played on that basic model, of course.) Where will this movement, "oftentimes" repeated, eventually take us? The next stanza continues:

> But Time, which brings all beings to their level,
> And sharp Adversity, will teach at last
> Man,—and, as we would hope,—perhaps the devil,
> That neither of their intellects are vast:
> While youth's hot wishes in our red veins revel,
> We know not this—the blood flows on too fast;
> But as the torrent widens towards the ocean,
> We ponder deeply on each past emotion. (iv.2)

Every idealistic, affirmative, or lyrical movement in the poem calls out its negative, ironic countermovement ("sharp Adversity"), an adversarial voice taught by time and experience. "The torrent widens towards the ocean." Will this mean wisdom—or entropy, the levelling out which is the end of living? The prideful, aspiring Lucifer will perhaps lose his illusions, and for a moment Byron seems to glance at the ancient heresy that at the end of time even the Devil will reform and be redeemed. The alternative possibility, however, is that he will become the disillusioning devil of absolute negation which is Mephistopheles. The same question is then mapped onto Byron's personal history as a poet. In the next stanza he invokes the idea which is recurrent in *Don Juan*, of a turning point which has precipitated the mode of Mephistopheles.

> As boy, I thought myself a clever fellow,
> And wish'd that others held the same opinion;
> They took it up when my days grew more mellow,
> And other minds acknowledged my dominion:
> Now my sere fancy "falls into the yellow
> Leaf," and imagination droops her pinion,
> And the sad truth which hovers o'er my desk
> Turns what was once romantic to burlesque. (iv.3)

There is a poised ambivalence here, felt in the way that the imagery of falling leads paradoxically to an image of something *hovering*. This decline brings knowledge and a cure for vanity, it "shows us what we are," it recognizes truth, albeit a "sad truth." It is in that sense a desirable fall. Yet this knowledge is also an expression of decline, a drying up or burning out of the high romantic, impassioned Byron who had so captivated his readers. It is Macbeth whose way of life "is fall'n into the sere, the yellow leaf," and whose fall into a withered autumnal life is also, of course, a fall into damnation, or into the nihilism of "tomorrow and tomorrow and tomorrow."

Byron liked to quote the saying of a Methodist preacher, "no *hopes* for *them* as *laughs*."[23] He quoted it satirically, as one of the laughers—but without altogether cancelling the suggestion that such mockery is on the road to hell, or to a place where all hope has been abandoned. The mocking comic bathos in *Don Juan*, its continual turning to burlesque, is ambiguous in its tendency: both salutary and dismayed.

The Ambiguous Devil

During the period of *Don Juan*, Byron composed three works in which the Devil himself appears. They are *Cain*, *The Vision of Judgment*, and *The Deformed Transformed*. Each represents the Devil in ways which recall Goethe's Mephistopheles; they all came after a period when we know that Byron was refreshing and sharpening his sense of *Faust*. In 1820 he sent for Retzsch's Analysis of the play, which arrived in Ravenna early in 1821; this included large extracts translated by Daniel Boileau, supplementing the 1,600 lines of translated selections published in the *Blackwood's Magazine* of June 1820. This was also the period of Byron's closer contact with Shelley, who was translating passages from the play for publication in the *Liberal*, the periodical founded by Byron with Shelley and Leigh Hunt.

In *Cain*, Byron's Lucifer does not sound much like Mephistopheles, although Byron did link them when defending his play. Where he is, however, comparable is in the negativity he expresses, and in the ambiguous status given to that negativity. When the drama opens, Cain is already in a state of sullen resentment at the injustice of the Fall and at the pain of being human which it so unfairly bequeaths. "Content thee with what *is*," Eve pleads (I.i.45), but such an attitude is precisely what Cain's intellectual restlessness rebels against. He is in this state of mind when Lucifer comes to him and shows him further grounds for discontent. In the central act of the drama, Lucifer takes Cain out into the immensities of the universe, in a great tour through time and space. Lucifer reveals to him the existence of millions of other worlds, the mutations of our own world over eons of distant time, and the shadowy underworld of the dead, which includes the exalted race of pre-Adamite beings, destroyed in geological catastrophe, in line with the recent scientific theories of Cuvier. Cain thereby discovers the utter insignificance of human life when seen in the long perspectives of astronomy and geological time. If the universe looks beautiful, that, Lucifer explains, is merely the effect of distance, promoting delusion—and when Cain objects the loveliness of Adah, his wife and sister, Lucifer replies that her beauty too will pass away, with so much the greater loss for those who cherish it. It is a bleak education, which Cain is inclined to resent:

> CAIN. And to what end have I beheld these things
>> Which thou hast shown me?
> LUCIFER.   Didst thou not require
>> Knowledge? And have I not, in what I show'd,
>> Taught thee to know thyself?
> CAIN.   Alas! I seem
>> Nothing.
> LUCIFER.   And this should be the human sum
>> Of knowledge, to know mortal nature's nothingness. (II.ii.417-22)

What knowledge brings is radical disenchantment.

Is this the voice of the Devil? Lucifer could pass for a certain kind of Enlightenment moralist, for whom disenchantment is the price of rational maturity. *Sapere aude*, dare to think, was according to Kant the motto of the Enlightenment, and like a true son of the Enlightenment Lucifer urges Cain to test the motives to piety against the realities of his own experience. He should cultivate intellectual independence:

> One good gift has the fatal apple given—
> Your reason:—let it not be over-sway'd
> By tyrannous threats to force you into faith
> 'Gainst all external sense and inward feeling:
> Think and endure,—and form an inner world
> In your own bosom—where the outward fails;

So shall you nearer be the spiritual

Nature, and war triumphant with your own. (II.ii.459–66)

These are Lucifer's last words in the play, his valediction to Cain. They do not sound like an instigation to evil, but rather an attempt to deliver his audience from the delusions of religion as superstition, or religion as tyranny. This thoroughly modern critical consciousness extends also to his own role as Devil. As we have seen in an earlier chapter, Lucifer detaches himself firmly from his traditional role as tempter to sin. "I tempt none, | Save with the truth," he declares (I.i.196–97). When Adam and Eve ate from the tree, he points out, it was God who was really the Tempter, planting "things prohibited within | The reach of beings innocent, and curious | By their own innocence" (I.i.200–202). He himself had nothing to do with the serpent—as Genesis can confirm.

Shelley, too, observed that the Devil makes no appearance in the early books of the Old Testament, and that it is the Christians who "have turned this Serpent into their Devil"[24] in an attempt to get God off the hook. But Byron does something more interesting than Shelley when he gives this deconstruction of the Devil to the Devil himself. This ability to reflect at a distance upon his own cultural role and identity is something which Byron's Devil shares with Goethe's. In the "Witch's Kitchen" scene in Faust, Mephistopheles declines the name of Satan, as a figure "long since consigned to the book of fables— although humans are no better off: the evil one is gone, the evil ones remain" (2507–9). Mephistopheles knows perfectly well how humans use the Devil as scapegoat for their own weaknesses and crimes. When Faust is gripped, belatedly enough, by horror at the consequences for Gretchen of their relationship, he turns on Mephistopheles in passionate reproach, addressing him for the first time as the monstrous figure of evil familiar from tradition and from nightmare ("Roll your devilish eyes furiously in your head"), as if trying to force the register of the play into that of Gothic horror. But he has no reply to Mephistopheles' calmly lethal response: "Who was it, who ruined her? I or you?"[25] Like Byron's Lucifer, Mephistopheles refuses to take the blame. He may be the Devil; but he is not *that* Devil. The more overtly supernatural or Gothic the situation in which he appears—his conjuration by Faust, the witch's kitchen, the Walpurgisnacht—the more coolly and ironically he distinguishes himself from what might be expected of him.

It is an effect that Byron drew on once more in *The Deformed Trans-formed*, when the Stranger—a "tall black man" who materializes out of a cloud to interrupt Arnold's suicide—begins by differentiating himself from the Devil that Arnold supposes he may be.

> STRANGER.   If I be the devil
>   You deem, a single moment would have made you
>   Mine, and for ever, by your suicide;
>   And yet my coming saves you.
> ARNOLD.   I said not
>   You *were* the demon, but that your approach
>   Was like one.
> STRANGER.   Unless you keep company
>   With him (and you seem scarce used to such high
>   Society) you can't tell how he approaches. (I.i.90–97)

The ironic manner strongly recalls Mephistopheles. As Mephistoph-eles arranges for Faust's magical rejuvenation, so the Stranger offers Arnold—a deformed hunchback—physical transformation into the body of an Achilles, and does so in a version of the traditional contract with the Devil which self-consciously departs from it: "You shall have no bond | But your own will, no contract save your deeds" (I.i.150–51). Mephistopheles, Lucifer, and the Stranger are Devils who stand con-sciously apart from both the theological supernaturalism of the old story and the literary supernaturalism of contemporary Gothic fic-tion. Such fiction can be interpreted as the rising up of fears and pow-ers repressed or neglected by Enlightenment rationality. But Lucifer and Mephistopheles incorporate such rationality; there is about them nothing of the uncanny or the repressed; they give us, so to speak, the Devil seen by daylight.

But the Devil by daylight is the Devil still, and perhaps all the more formidable for it.[26] The scandalized readers of *Cain* saw that Lucifer is given many persuasive things to say that go unchallenged in the play. But they were too hasty in assuming that Lucifer was therefore noth-ing more than Byron's mouthpiece, the mere vehicle for an attack on established religion. When Shelley was asked about his alleged influ-ence on *Cain*, he replied regretting his inability "to eradicate from his [Byron's] great mind the delusions of Christianity which, in spite of his reason, seem perpetually to recur."²⁷ *Cain* offers no simple vindication of Lucifer. Although he dismisses the traditional story that implicates the Devil in the Fall, his bleak enlightenment of Cain can be understood as itself another version of the knowledge that brings death into the world, and all our woe. Cain's initial discontent is exacerbated by his long conversation with Lucifer and the knowledge which Lucifer opens to him. In the final act Cain offers his sacrifice to God in terms so grudging, so defiant, and so full of virtual accusation that it is hardly surprising (and certainly not clear evidence of tyranny) that God should reject it. Angered, Cain moves to throw down his brother's favored altar, in repudiation of such a God; Abel piously defends it; and Cain strikes him down, in an impulsive act at which he is himself immediately appalled. This is finely done, as Goethe remarked,²⁸ and the finesse lies most of all in the equivocal relationship between the act of murder and the long colloquy with Lucifer which preceded it. The act is felt as partly a consequence of the conversation, *but to an indeterminate degree*. Was it foreseen or intended by Lucifer? And how far does the education he gives Cain contribute to the murder? It is impossible to say. Lucifer does not suggest the murder (though he does at one point put Abel's irritatingly acceptable piety into Cain's mind). Much of the time he sounds convincingly disinterested, and he appears sincere in suggesting that a short course in nihilism will have a certain anesthetic value for suffering mankind—understanding the "nothingness" of human life will spare Cain's children "many tortures" (II.ii.422–24)—although if so he misses the way that nihilism is itself painful for human beings, who cannot detach themselves from the conditions of creation with the Devil's sublime contempt.

> LUCIFER. I pity thee who lovest what must perish.
> CAIN. And I thee who lov'st nothing. (II.ii.337–38)

But when he speaks to Cain of "the joy | And power of knowledge" (I.i.209–10), it is not only as a child of the Enlightenment, but also with an obliquely sinister exhilaration:

> Nothing can
> Quench the mind, if the mind will be itself
> And centre of surrounding things—'tis made
> To sway. (I.i.213–16)

That dark investment in the sense of power is not the same as the calm confidence with which Kant proposes the autonomy of intellect. It identifies enlightenment—more precisely, the realization of the freedom of the individual mind and will—as a Faustian compact, as the Devil's bargain. Is Lucifer acting, after all, as the Tempter? What he told Cain at the start—"I tempt none, | Save with the truth"—is a more equivocal, more dangerous statement than it at first appeared. It is equivocal in the same way that the Stranger is equivocal in *The Deformed Transformed*, when he assures Arnold that what is involved between them is something quite other than the traditional contract of damnation between the Devil and his client.

> ARNOLD.   But name your compact:
>   Must it be signed in blood?
> STRANGER.   Not in your own.
> ARNOLD. Whose blood then?
> STRANGER.   We will talk of that hereafter.
>   But I'll be moderate with you, for I see
>   Great things within you. You shall have no bond
>   But your own will, no contract save your deeds. (I.i.146–51)

The gesture—perfectly modern, secular, and self-conscious—by which the Stranger waives the traditional contract, may be less generous than it seems. It may, in fact, be an act of diabolical malice. The play was unfinished at Byron's death, but his memorandum suggests that it was to finish with Arnold destroying the woman he loves. But we cannot tell how far the Devil is to blame. The Stranger does seem to be offering Arnold a real expansion of his life, just as Lucifer offers Cain a real expansion of his understanding. This ambiguity—the sense of the Devil as an equivocal companion, or as only equivocally the Evil One— is functional. Such ambiguity dissolves the presumption of *dichotomy* that supports the traditional notion of the Devil; in so doing, it opens the possibility of engaging in more complicated, dynamic relations with the Adversary.

There is here a significant parallel with, and surely also an actual debt to, Goethe's Mephistopheles. The not-quite contract offered by the Stranger clearly recalls the wager in *Faust*. As Byron does with Lucifer, so Goethe keeps ambiguous Mephistopheles' intention with regard to Faust and his contribution to the final catastrophe. He rejuvenates Faust in preparation for a life of sexual license, but he does not seem actively to tempt Faust to the seduction of Gretchen, whom Faust appears to meet by chance. His supernatural contribution to the process amounts to nothing very essential: a supply of Viagra and a credit card would do as much. True, he tells us in a rare soliloquy that he plans to destroy Faust by exposing him to a life of worldly dissipation, whose hollow pleasures will only reinforce his torment of unfulfillment. But this straightforwardly malevolent plan makes no sense in relation to Faust's wager that Mephistopheles can never bring him to a moment of contentment, a moment of such complete fulfillment that Faust could wish it might last forever. Only then, it is agreed, may Mephistopheles claim him. By plan A, Mephistopheles should be scheming to frustrate Faust's desires; by plan B, to fulfill them; and this ambiguity only compounds our doubt as to whether, much of the time, Mephistopheles is scheming against Faust at all. He seems rather to be offering his sharp, ironic, belittling commentaries without any malicious or manipulative intent, but simply because that is how he is, and how things are. Much of the time, he seems to be primarily a reactive figure, responding to Faust's circumstances and demands as these present themselves, though always with that chilling ultimate indifference—chilling, yet also engagingly cool—which is his trademark.

There *is*, of course, a great and terrible evil in the play. It is what happens to Gretchen, implicated in the deaths of her mother and brother, abandoned by her lover, rejected by her community, driven to infanticide and madness, and condemned to execution. But Goethe does not tell us how much of this, if any, Mephistopheles engineers or even foresees. In its original, unpublished form, *Faust: Part One* consisted of two clusters of passages: the early Faust/Mephistopheles scenes, and the Gretchen tragedy. Between these came what Goethe called "the great gap,"[29] which he sought for years to find the right way to fill. In the final version there is material connecting the two sections, but there is also a strong residual sense of discontinuity—between motives and events, between the Devil and the evil—and this is very much part of the play's power. We are left uncertain as to whether Mephistopheles' detachment is in fact the mask for his evil, or whether his flashes of malice are merely the remnants of a superseded conception. This uncertainty is not resolved. The palimpsest or double-exposure effect may well have originated in the layering processes of composition over thirty years, but its preservation in the published version is a stroke of art.

This ambiguity is not just a matter of Mephistopheles' intentions, as we may try to imagine them; it involves what might be called his ultimate ethical orientation. He famously introduces himself to Faust as "a part of that power that always wills what is evil, and always creates what is good" (1335–36). Faust is puzzled by this "riddle," and any reader of *Faust* as published in 1808 is likely to share in his puzzlement. *Faust: Part One* does not lead to good in any obvious sense. It ends with Faust's failed attempt to rescue Gretchen from her prison cell the night before her execution. In her terribly lucid madness, she at first clings to the returning lover who abandoned her, but then refuses to escape with him on the Devil's magic horses, passionately repudiating her freedom to escape the horror and remorse which afflict her with hallucinatory vividness, and horrified most of all at the end by Faust himself. Unable to persuade her to come, Faust flees without her. It is the most emotionally devastating passage Goethe ever wrote, of unsurpassable tragic intensity.

To say that, however, is also to say that it is beyond the reach of Mephistopheles' belittling critique. Mephistopheles declares at the end of the scene, "She is condemned" (*gerichtet*); just before publication, Goethe wrote in a "voice from above" which supplies a corrective echo: "She is saved" (*gerettet*) (4611). That voice offers a minimal, precarious glimpse of the idea behind what I have called the secret history of the Devil: the idea that the Adversary is working for God in working against him, his opposition being functional within the larger whole.

This idea gets a fuller expression in the "Prologue in Heaven," another relatively late addition in the 1808 *Faust*. When defending his representation of Lucifer against the storm of protest it created, Byron's mind went not simply to *Faust*, but to the prologue in particular.

> What would the Methodists at home say to Goethe's "Faust"? His devil not only talks very familiarly *of* Heaven, but very familiarly *in* Heaven. What would they think of the colloquies of Mephistopheles and his pupil, or the more daring language of the prologue, which no one will ever venture to translate?[30]

The prologue bases itself on the opening of the book of Job, where Satan—who comes among "the sons of God"—discusses with God the case of Job, and is licensed to throw Job into affliction as a test of his piety. Goethe's prologue opens with the archangels singing to the Lord in splendid verse of the splendors of the creation. Also present is Mephistopheles, who regrets that he cannot make "great speeches" about the cosmos, but reports that on earth human life goes on as badly as ever. Human beings are a torment to themselves, made miserable by their imperfect glimpse of the divine: like grasshoppers, they spring upward, only to fall back into the dung. He himself hardly cares to hurt the poor things. At which God mentions Faust, whom he declares his servant: but Mephistopheles raises an eyebrow at this description. In his absurd and restless discontent, Faust is indeed a case in point, and Mephistopheles bets that God will "lose" him if he is allowed a free hand. God accepts the wager without concern; error, he declares, is an inevitable part of that "striving" that marks a good man's dim consciousness of the right path.

It is true that Mephistopheles has brought a critical, discordant voice into the heavenly rejoicing, and God is somewhat exasperated with him: "Do you have nothing else to say to me? Can you only ever come with accusations? Does nothing on earth ever seem good to you?" (293–95). But beneath God's exasperation there is a largely cordial note: "I have never hated your kind. Of all the spirits of denial, a rogue like you is the smallest burden to me. Human beings all too easily slacken in their activity, and grow fond of peace and quiet: that's why I like to give them a companion who draws them on and works upon them and must be devilish busy" (337–43). That last phrase, *muss als Teufel schaffen*, also carries the implication "must, as a devil, be productive," or in Shelley's particularly affirmative rendering, "must create forever."[31] The Faustian discontent which Mephistopheles will further stimulate and exacerbate (for that seems to be the idea) will end not in damnation but in something else—salvation, perhaps, as indeed it does at the end of *Faust: Part Two*, published many years later. Or perhaps it will not *end* in anything at all but find a kind of redemption in the endlessness of striving. God concludes by commending to the other archangels the beauty of dynamic process in the cosmos, "das Werdende, das ewig wirkt und lebt" (346), "that which is in process of becoming, which is eternally active and living"; *wirkt* picks up the same word used three lines earlier to describe how the Devil works upon human beings. What is suggested here is an extraordinary reassimilation of the Devil into the larger, productive functioning of the whole, in which the roguish kind of negativity is ultimately salutary. The prologue thus offers the ethical imagination something precious: the glimpse of a rapport between the Adversary and God which reveals the Adversary as not unequivocally the enemy, and so models an intuition of the good and evil of the world as woven together, Earth-Spirit–like, to ultimately affirmative effect.

How taken Byron was by this quality in the Prologue can be seen from the marvellous passage in *The Vision of Judgment* which it inspired.[32] The Archangel Michael encounters Satan, prior to their debating the destiny of the soul of George III:

> He and the sombre, silent Spirit met—
> They knew each other both for good and ill;
> Such was their power, that neither could forget
> His former friend and future foe; but still
> There was a high, immortal, proud regret
> In either's eye, as if 'twere less their will
> Than destiny to make the eternal years
> Their date of war, and their "Champ Clos" the spheres.
>
> But here they were in neutral space: we know
> From Job, that Sathan hath the power to pay
> A heavenly visit thrice a year or so;
> And that "the Sons of God," like those of clay,
> Must keep him company; and we might show,
> From the same book, in how polite a way
> The dialogue is held between the Powers
> Of Good and Evil—but 'twould take up hours. . . .
>
> The spirits were in neutral space, before
> The gate of heaven; like eastern thresholds is
> The place where Death's grand cause is argued o'er,
> And souls despatched to that world or to this;
> And therefore Michael and the other wore

A civil aspect: though they did not kiss,
Yet still between his Darkness and his Brightness
There passed a mutual glance of great politeness. (249–80)

The manner of recalling Job, and the idea of "polite" relations between the Devil and his opposite, are unmistakably after Goethe. The *Vision* was published in the first number of the *Liberal*, where it was to have been accompanied by Shelley's translation of the prologue, making the connection immediately apparent. Michael and Satan are eternal enemies, but in the special imaginative conditions of "neutral space," the poetry modulates into a realization of the reciprocity that underlies, or complicates, the great opposition of "Good and Evil," the ultimate dichotomy of "that world" or "this." It is "both for good and ill" that Michael and Satan know each other, a knowledge of good and evil that weaves that dichotomy into a different pattern, and an entire poetic is implicit in the "civil aspect," the "mutual glance," that temporarily connects Michael and "the other."[33] Though unresolved, there can be a dialogue with the Devil. This intuition is wonderfully supported by the life and energy of the writing: manifest in the supple parodic intelligence (simultaneously parodying Job, Goethe, and Southey), parody being itself a staging of "civil" or mock-civil engagement with the other, and above all manifest in Byron's shameless *familiarity* throughout the poem, which holds nothing sacred: familiarity with the death of his king, with the teaching of Scripture, with the idea of a divine judgment, and with the Devil himself. (To say nothing of the poet laureate. At the poem's comic climax Satan and Michael will be united once more, in their common anguish induced by Southey's recitation of his poem.) The tightrope walked by the insolent comedy of the *Vision*, an insolence always simultaneously genial, is the tightrope of good manners that keeps relations open between Satan and Michael.

The moment of rapport is, however, both brief and limited. Satan may not be the Enemy absolutely, but he will soon return to that role (without enthusiasm) and demand George's soul, just as Byron himself will within a few stanzas return to his oppositional role as antiestablishment satirist. Only a timeserver like Robert Southey—who, having written Wesley's biography, is equally keen to write Satan's (785–86)—can actually change sides, or be all things to all men. The genial comedy of the *Vision* barely counterbalances its polemical offensiveness. The sense of a living, mutual connection "between his Darkness and his Brightness" is no more than glimpsed. And in this too Byron is true to Goethe's prologue. The positive scenario at which the prologue hints does not reappear in *Faust: Part One*, rather as in the book of Job the sense of *liaison* between God and Satan appears only in the opening frame. And even in the prologue, it is held in tension against the independent dramatic life given to Mephistopheles. After God has expressed his confidence in Faust, he withdraws, the archangels disperse, and Mephistopheles is left in possession of the stage to speak the closing lines.

> Von Zeit zu Zeit seh' ich den Alten gern,
> Und hüte mich, mit ihm zu brechen,
> Es ist gar hübsch von einem grossen Herrn,
> So menschlich mit dem Teufel selbst zu sprechen. (350–53)

> I like to see the old fellow from time to time, and take care not to break with him. It's really quite charming for a great lord to speak so humanly even to the devil.

If God has felt able to regard Mephistopheles with a tolerant condescension, Mephistopheles meets that condescension with a certain irresistible condescension of his own. The rapport between them is audaciously figured as a matter of social politeness, which keeps on speaking terms two individuals who differ strongly in their attitudes, their interests, and their position in the world. Such behavior is (in Shelley's translation) "civil enough,"[34] says Mephistopheles, and he commends this great lord for speaking so humanly or humanely— *menschlich*—to his poor relation: but the word carries a certain sardonic irony, for it is curious indeed if relations between the Deity and the Devil can be described as *menschlich*. This feline tribute to the Lord's good manners is itself civil enough, but also suggests something that may be weak or vulnerable in God's sublime tolerance of what would otherwise be called evil. Just for a moment we see the Lord as something of an old buffer, an amiable colonial administrator who may be rather out of touch with conditions on the ground. When Mephistopheles tells us that he takes care not to break with him, this simultaneously reminds us that he could, and that other stories tell us that he has, and that there is in that cool ironic self-possession something formidable that is still to be fully reckoned with.

All this is perfectly conveyed in the quality that Byron referred to when he thought of this scene: Mephistopheles' *familiarity*. "His devil not only talks very familiarly *of* Heaven, but very familiarly *in* Heaven." Familiarity is a good word here in the way it holds two meanings together. On the one hand, Mephistopheles is family; his way of talking speaks of the secret history which tells that God and the Devil are intimately related. But also, to talk familiarly is indecorous, disrespectful, conceivably insolent; it presumes (improperly) upon acquaintance; it is to behave as family when one has no right to do so. "Talking familiarly" might remind us that the root of *diabolical* has to do with slander, talking improperly about people. Familiarity (which breeds contempt) is diabolical also because it is insidious: the deliciously casual way in which Mephistopheles speaks of God—which Byron thought unpublishable in England,[35] and which must startle almost any religious sensibility—draws us irresistibly in. This is because Mephistopheles is so familiar with us; left alone on stage, given the last word, he shares this with us in a manner that presumes upon our complicity.

The Devilish Narrator

If Mephistopheles' ultimate ethical orientation is ambiguous, and if much of his vitality and interest lies in this ambiguity, can we say the same about Byron's adoption of the mode of Mephistopheles?

From the very start, *Don Juan* flaunted its own wickedness. The choice of subject was, coming from Byron, an immediate provocation. The Don Juan of legend is an insatiable, amoral seducer, bound for hell. And although the young Juan we meet in the first two cantos is not (yet) that figure, a good deal of sexual activity takes place, while the narrator mimics moral dismay to openly comic effect. The poem forces upon its readers the reality of sexual desire and the hypocrisy of disapproval of sexual desire, and it was to that extent a libertine work, which no woman of good character could discuss in polite society. Still more provocative was its implication that the titanic, heroic, tormented restlessness of Byron's earlier protagonists—to whose dark glamour his readers had thrilled—could be reinterpreted as the mere mobility of a Don Juan. Childe Harold's pilgrimage across Europe had been impelled by a profound spiritual weariness and despair, likened to that of the wandering Jew who was cursed by Christ; but Juan is sent packing on his travels after being caught in bed with a married woman. "Dear *Adorable* Lord Byron, *don't* make a mere *coarse* old libertine of yourself," wrote Harriette Wilson in response to those first two cantos; it was not the sex that offended her, a Regency courtesan at the top of her profession, but she was dismayed to find that Byron, in becoming "*vulgar*," was "wilfully destroy[ing] the respect and admiration of those who deserve to love you and all the fine illusions with which my mind was filled."[36] Such devotees found their enthusiasm for Byronic intensity vandalized by the new poem's casualness with its own procedures and purposes, its apparent refusal to take itself or anything else seriously.

Don Juan was outrageously improper in other ways too. It took every opportunity to refer flippantly or skeptically to matters of religion. There were openly personal attacks on contemporaries. Most offensive of these was the satirical portrait of Juan's mother, Donna Inez, as a repressed, hypocritical, hyperzealous paragon of virtue; intertwined with a situation of marital breakdown and scandal, this transparently invited application to Byron's wife. Then in the second canto came the shipwreck and the episode of cannibalism among the famished survivors. Byron dwells on the full horror and pathos of the situation, but also speaks of it with a sardonic levity that Keats thought "one of the most diabolical attempts ever made upon our sympathies."[37] William Gifford, a great admirer of Byron's work, wrote to Murray about the second canto that he had "lost all patience at seeing so much beauty so wantonly and perversely disfigured. . . . As it is, it is better than any other could have done; but this is poor praise for Lord Byron. What a store of shame and sorrow is he laying up for himself!"[38]

It would be easy to assemble contemporary notices denouncing the depravity of *Don Juan*, in sometimes hysterical terms, and to feel that these illustrate simply that peculiarly nineteenth-century blend of reactionary politics and canting morality which Byron was born magnificently to affront:

> The truth is that in these days the grand "primum mobile" of England is *Cant*—Cant political—Cant poetical—Cant religious—Cant moral—but always *Cant*—multiplied through all the varieties of life.—It is the fashion—

& while it lasts—will be too powerful for those who can only exist by taking
the tone of the time.[39]

It is true that Byron's "immoral" flourishes are directed, in part, against
his prudish, sentimentalizing, or hypocritically censorious English
readership. But the dismay of such readers as Keats and Gifford must
give us pause. At what point does deriding the cant of morality become
the insinuation that all morality is cant? The line is not clearly drawn
in *Don Juan*, as it had been, for example, by Byron's admired Fielding.
Evangelical readers like Hannah More, who wanted the poem burned,
believed that no such line existed, and Mephistopheles would be
inclined to agree with her—for Mephistopheles, too, is an astringent
critic of cant, of Faust's claim, for instance, that his love for Gretchen
is a high and exalted passion.

With this question in mind, let us return to Juan and Julia in the
first canto, where the comedy would seem to be at its lightest and most
unclouded. Julia is a young wife with a much older husband—which
means that, for the knowing narrator, there can be only one outcome.

> Wedded she was some years, and to a man
> Of fifty, and such husbands are in plenty;
> And yet, I think, instead of such a ONE
> 'Twere better to have TWO of five and twenty,
> Especially in countries near the sun:
> And now I think on't, "mi vien in mente,"
> Ladies even of the most uneasy virtue
> Prefer a spouse whose age is short of thirty.
>
> 'Tis a sad thing, I cannot choose but say,
> And all the fault of that indecent sun,
> Who cannot leave alone our helpless clay,
> But will keep baking, broiling, burning on,
> That howsoever people fast and pray
> The flesh is frail, and so the soul undone:
> What men call gallantry, and gods adultery,
> Is much more common when the climate's sultry. (i.62–63)

Given a physically unfulfilling spouse and a quantity of sunshine, adultery follows as a matter of course. Respectable women, as the antithesis

of ladies of easy virtue, must therefore be ladies of most uneasy virtue: the deft verbal joke smiles at the wish to be chaste or faithful in marriage. Such virtuous resolution is bound to be most uneasy when set against the strength of other desires, against the strength of that indecent Mediterranean sun, and against the strength of that self-possessed, easy, so-knowledgeable narrative voice.

The comedy here is irresistible. But there is also something authentically dangerous in this voice, with its casual countenancing of "the soul undone." The idea of the soul being undone in the act of adultery is partly mock-religious ("howsoever people fast and pray"), a worldly burlesque of how a pious reader would regard the act, set up to precipitate the comic bathos of the final, trivializing couplet. But it also stands independently of that trivializing movement, and in dialogue with it. The safety of Julia's soul really is involved in her attraction to Juan. For this is how Byron describes the moment of her yielding, when she finds herself together with Juan in the moonlight. "The devil's in the moon for mischief," and Byron explains why:

> There is a dangerous silence in that hour,
> A stillness, which leaves room for the full soul
> To open all itself, without the power
> Of calling wholly back its self-control;
> The silver light which, hallowing tree and tower,
> Sheds beauty and deep softness o'er the whole,
> Breathes also to the heart, and o'er it throws
> A loving languor, which is not repose. . . .
>
> And Julia's voice was lost, except in sighs,
> Until too late for useful conversation;
> The tears were gushing from her gentle eyes,
> I wish, indeed, they had not had occasion,
> But who, alas! can love, and then be wise?
> Not that remorse did not oppose temptation,
> A little still she strove, and much repented,
> And whispering "I will ne'er consent"—consented. (i.114, 117)

Vorrei e non vorrei—I would like to, and I would not like to—sings Zerlina in the duet with Don Giovanni, in the moment before she yields to him. The situation shows us an unprincipled seducer and a spectacularly faithless bride: but the music solemnizes an erotic power that overwhelms resistance or denial. Byron presents us with a comparable doubleness: the knowing voice remains present—"too late for useful conversation"—but it still cannot reduce to its own terms that "opening" of the full soul beyond or away from words (so apt to be either canting or knowing) to which the poem also opens itself at this moment. What happens between Julia and Juan is unknowable by the knowing voice; the silence really is "dangerous," in a sense that is more than just evangelical-baiting.

It is true that Byron goes on to reflect on the power of pleasure over his own good resolutions with his familiar mocking nonchalance, and that the next scene is one of perfectly delicious sexual comedy in the bedroom. But what follows is in a quite different key. Divorced, disgraced, and sent into a nunnery, Julia writes her farewell letter to Juan as he is sent away on his travels. The letter fills six stanzas, of which this is one:

> You will proceed in beauty, and in pride,
> Beloved and loving many; all is o'er
> For me on earth, except some years to hide
> My shame and sorrow deep in my heart's core;
> These I could bear, but cannot cast aside
> The passion which still rends it as before,
> And so farewell—forgive me, love me—No,
> That word is idle now—but let it go. (i.196)

The stanza following the letter pays Julia the tribute of setting aside the knowing narrative voice; its quiet objectivity is oddly moving:

> This note was written upon gilt-edged paper
> With a neat crow quill, rather hard, but new;
> Her small white fingers scarce could reach the taper,
> But trembled as magnetic needles do,
> And yet she did not let one tear escape her;
> The seal a sunflower; "*Elle vous suit partout*,"
> The motto, cut upon a white cornelian;
> The wax was superfine, its hue vermilion. (i.198)

Only then does Byron's worldly voice return and abruptly enforce our detachment from the pathos of her situation:

This was Don Juan's earliest scrape . . . (i.199)

The poem does not present Julia's adultery with Juan as a sin or crime or immoral act; its worldliness mocks any such moralizing inter- pretation. But the loss of "self-control" in sexual passion which it equa- bly countenances and facilitates—for rather like Don Alfonso in *Così fan tutte*, the mere presence of Byron's knowingness makes the inno- cence of others unsustainable—is nonetheless acknowledged as truly dangerous. Such loss of self-control is life-changingly consequential for Julia; her desolation puts her beyond the reach of knowing com- edy. And it is dangerous for Juan also, insofar as it may be taking him the first step along the road which leads to the knowingness of his narrator, the infinitely disillusioned Lord Byron. This is a man who is known to have all the worldly experience of a Don Giovanni under his belt, and who reports that experience has brought him merely to the detachment of a Mephistopheles, neither loving nor hating but sneering sometimes, and capable (for example) of referring to the love affair between Juan and Julia, with a perfectly calculated shallowness and flippancy, as "Juan's earliest scrape."

We are made aware that this figure commends the life of immedi- ate pleasure and sensation only because there is nothing else: those who would regulate or disapprove of it in the name of some higher value are merely talking cant. *Viva la libertà*, sing the voices in *Don Giovanni*, as the climax of act one approaches: but they do so with an ominous, hectic insistence. Long live the spirit of liberality and open- ness (mean the guests)—of total freedom in human relations (means Leporello)—of the libertine way of life which laughs at all moral prohi- bition (means Giovanni): but the meanings threaten to collapse indis- tinguishably into one another, and while each singing line strives to assert itself against the others, the music holds them all together in a sardonically emphatic unison that is both thrilling and terrifying.

There is something of that sardonic quality in the way that Byron's narrator can countenance or commend an engagement in worldly plea- sures, which he knows, just as well as any canting moralist, never lead

to fulfillment. When Juan arrives in London, he is confronted with the
glittering high-society merry-go-round which Byron knows so well:

> Then dress, then dinner, then awakes the world!
> Then glare the lamps, then whirl the wheels, then roar
> Through street and square fast flashing chariots, hurled
> Like harnessed meteors; then along the floor
> Chalk mimics painting; then festoons are twirled;
> Then roll the brazen thunders of the door,
> Which opens to the thousand happy few
> An earthly Paradise of "Or Molu."
>
> There stands the noble Hostess, nor shall sink
> With the three-thousandth curtsey; there the Waltz,
> The only dance which teaches girls to think,
> Makes one in love even with its very faults.
> Saloon, room, hall o'erflow beyond their brink,
> And long the latest of arrivals halts,
> 'Midst royal dukes and dames condemned to climb,
> And gain an inch of staircase at a time.
>
> Thrice happy he, who after a survey
> Of the good company, can win a corner,
> A door that's *in*, or boudoir *out* of the way,
> Where he may fix himself, like small "Jack Horner,"
> And let the Babel round run as it may,
> And look on as a mourner, or a scorner,
> Or an approver, or a mere spectator,
> Yawning a little as the night grows later.
>
> But this won't do, save by and by. . . . (xi.67–70)

The sense of energy and excitement, the taste of lived experience, are
palpable. So is the satirical note, the sense of *vanitas* which invests
this earthly paradise of ormolu. The three stanzas are a little exercise
in entropy; the initial excitement runs down, slightly weakened with
each repetition (of "then" and "there") until we arrive at the slow queue
slowly ascending the endless staircase, "condemned to climb" like a
troop of sinners in Dante. Serial repetition—an inch at a time, the

same ball every evening—confesses itself in this image as life-draining tedium. The happy man is therefore he who withdraws from participation. Yet the happiness of retirement, too, runs down toward ennui, toward the quietly resonant line that seals the downward movement: "Yawning a little as the night grows later."

The sense of entropic decline is felt in the sequence of options: from mourner to scorner to approver to "mere spectator." We have met this phrase before. A "mere spectator . . . in the mode of Goethe's Mephistopheles" is what Byron says he has himself become: Mephistopheles, who has seen everything, and seen through everything. The phrase also appears earlier in the poem, applied to the figure who stands next to Juan, his fellow prisoner, in the Turkish slave auction. He has

> An open brow a little mark'd with care:
> One arm had on a bandage rather bloody;
> And there he stood with such *sang-froid* that greater
> Could scarce be shown even by a mere spectator. (v.11)

Later in the poem Byron will name this figure as John Johnson, but meanwhile he remains anonymous. English, thirty years old, with curling dark hair and resolution in his eye, he is a kind of double for Byron himself, in his post-turning-point mode of detached, dispassionate commentator. Being sold into slavery is something Johnson endures calmly as one of fortune's little whims, and although he wept when his first wife died, and also when his second ran away, by the time of the third, he explains, he knew to run away himself.

> "You take things coolly, sir," said Juan. "Why,"
> Replied the other, "what can a man do?
> There still are many rainbows in your sky,
> But mine have vanished. All, when life is new,
> Commence with feelings warm and prospects high;
> But time strips our illusions of their hue,
> And one by one in turn, some grand mistake
> Casts off its bright skin yearly like the snake." . . .
>
> "All this is very fine and may be true,"
> Said Juan, "but I really don't see how

> It betters present times with me or you."
> "No?" quoth the other, "yet you will allow
> By setting things in their right point of view,
> Knowledge at least is gained." (v.21, 23)

This exchange between Juan and "the other" is essentially the dialogue between Cain and Lucifer, which Byron was to write shortly after finishing this canto. It also epitomizes the tension between Byron's disillusioned narrative voice and the young, passionate lovers of the early cantos, Juan, Julia, and Haidée, here played out as actual dialogue. Consequently, there is some tension in the presentation of Johnson himself. His *sang-froid* (the quality de Staël found in Mephistopheles and in Goethe)[40] does not make him inhuman; he speaks supportively to the young Juan, is resourceful under fire, and regrets the way that society destroys the little kindness that might naturally subsist between human beings. But he makes his living as a mercenary—the perfect career choice for a man who has seen through everything—and amid the carnage and the atrocities at the taking of Ismael, there is something chilling, in fact coldblooded, in the professional shrewdness with which he kills, survives, and plunders.[41]

The blood of the "mere spectator" in London society grows cold in a different way—"Yawning a little as the night grows later"—but here too the reflective consciousness conferred by experience is bleak in its implications. And so Byron, having first led us to it, waves it away. "But this won't do, save by and by." Such weariness *will* come, with time and experience and detachment; but it does not belong to youth; and since it is of no value in itself, why anticipate it? Therefore Byron, as Juan's expert guide to London life, advises him to fling himself into the social whirl and all the opportunities for flirtation and seduction which it brings.

> But "Carpe diem," Juan, "Carpe, carpe!"
> To-morrow sees another race as gay
> And transient, and devoured by the same harpy.
> "Life's a poor player,"—then "play out the play,
> Ye villains!" and above all keep a sharp eye
> Much less on what you do than what you say:
> Be hypocritical, be cautious, be
> Not what you seem, but always what you see. (xi.86)

This is ambivalent, dangerous, double-edged advice. "Carpe diem . . . Carpe, carpe!": the repetitions empty the idea of substance, yet draw their urgency from that emptiness. The life recommended for Juan's embrace is known to be transient and worthless; still, as the alternative—middle-aged ennui, withdrawal, and disillusionment—is hollow also, so hollow indeed that it has nothing better to advise than this, then, after all, why not? *Viva la libertà!* And so the despair of Macbeth ("Life's a poor player"), which we have seen Byron appropriate to himself in his burned-out middle age, generates a countermovement, a burst of Falstaffian bravado; the quotation from the tavern scene in *1 Henry IV* affirms hedonism and life lived as role-playing against the threat of a final judgment. But the bravado here, in Byron, knows itself as a gesture, and throws itself away in the moment of utterance. The final piece of advice on how to play the social game successfully— "be | Not what you *seem*, but always what you *see*"—is peculiarly tense, at once temptation and accusation, and in that way peculiarly diabolical. It comes as the climax of a great sequence of exclamation at how rapid, frantic, and incessant the changes in England have been in recent years. "I have seen . . . I have seen . . ." reiterates the narrator, sixteen times in the preceding twenty-four lines; the phrase insists on his position as the "mere spectator," the detached observer for whom there is only *vanitas* everywhere. For him then to urge Juan to be "always what you *see*," to be participant and knowing spectator both, is a kind of double bind.

Such advice, given in that all-too-knowing spirit, would poison the ability to embrace it if its grounds were truly understood. It has the ring of Mephistopheles about it:

> Grau, teurer Freund, ist alle Theorie,
> Und grün des Lebens goldner Baum. (2038–39)

> All theorizing, my dear friend, is grey: the golden tree of life is green.

Mephistopheles is there speaking to the novice student who seeks his advice as to what course of study to pursue. Academic disciplines are hollow, Mephistopheles explains, mere bubbles of language—except only medicine, because of the opportunities which it brings for handling women's bodies. There stands the golden tree of life. The student is duly grateful for such practical advice. But the Devil's irony is never keener—and never more diabolical—than when, from the vantage point which has seen through everything, he urges his protégé to *choose life.* It is in just that same spirit that Mephistopheles urges Faust to leave his miserable study and embrace the world of sensuous experience; he is confident that "das wilde Leben" (1860)—a wild way of living, or the wildness of really living—will, in the long run, only exacerbate his restlessness, his painful insatiability, his dependency on the Devil.

The consequences in *Faust* are catastrophic, although in ways that escape Mephistopheles' intention. There is much of the self-deceiving sentimentalist in Faust's love of Gretchen—she is at every point his superior—but there are also elements in his attraction that are beyond the Devil's reckoning. In Gretchen, for the first time, Faustian desire does not remain within the vortex of the subjective but attaches itself to something in the world, and the tragedy of their relationship takes it outside the Devil's knowingness: for Mephistopheles knows nothing of tragedy.[42] *Don Juan* breaks off before we can tell what was to become of Juan in high society, although the description of Aurora Raby also suggests possibilities that fall beyond the scope of the narrator's sardonic "Carpe, carpe!" But in any case *Don Juan* is, throughout, a poem not summed up and comprehended by the intermittent negativity of its narrative voice, but written *between* the disillusioned narrator and the living world. Its life lies in its continual dynamic movement between those poles, and its Mephistophelean negativity is valuable because, continually undermining any ideal sentiment, it enforces that mobility.

But it is, of course, classically dangerous to call up the Devil in the belief that you can retain control of the situation; the spirit of denial is a genuinely dangerous presence. Francis Jeffrey—the most intelligent of *Don Juan*'s hostile critics—saw clearly the dialectic at the heart of the poem, acknowledged Byron's inwardness with the values which he sees through as illusions, but believed that only made the poem all the more pernicious:

> Love, patriotism, valour, devotion, constancy, ambition—all are to be laughed at . . . but the author . . . has the unlucky gift of personating all those sweet and lofty illusions, and that with such grace and force and truth to nature, that it is impossible not to suppose, for the time, that he is among the most devoted of their votaries—till he casts off the character with a jerk—and, the

moment after he has moved and exalted us to the very height of our conception, resumes his mockery at all things serious or sublime—and lets us down
at once on some coarse joke, hard-hearted sarcasm, or fierce and relentless
personality—as if on purpose . . . to demonstrate practically as it were, and
by example, how possible it is to have all fine and noble feelings, or their
appearance, for a moment, and yet retain no particle of respect for them—or
of belief in their intrinsic worth or permanent reality.[43]

Among the examples Jeffrey offers is Julia's letter, which gives us "the
holiest language of the heart"—but is contaminated by the bedroom
farce which precedes it and by the seasickness which overcomes Juan
as he reads it. Jeffrey is splendidly alert to the extraordinary mobility
of *Don Juan*, but he resolves that mobility into a position. Whereas
Byron himself offers his inconsistency as a principle of vitality, even
a kind of truthfulness—"But if a writer should be quite consistent |
How could he possibly show things existent" (xv.87)—Jeffrey assumes,
half against the grain of his own perception, a real, fundamental Byron
in the poem, whose nihilistic voice is the terminus to which all roads
lead. But if it is true that Byron "personates" positive moral ideals—
and to Jeffrey's list might be added the passion for liberty and the
passion for truth—it can be argued that he equally "personates" the
negative, mocking consciousness which burlesques them. In writing
about the narrative voice in *Don Juan* it is difficult, and sometimes
impossible, to know whether to speak of Byron or of the narrative
persona, for Byron is continually personating himself as "Byron,"
whether this be Byron the entertaining raconteur or Byron the cynical
immoralist. Crucial here is Byron's celebrity, which by writing more
or less autobiographically he inescapably invokes: *however* he presents
himself, this appears as a role adopted to play up to, or to contradict,
his readers' preconceptions, and so is immediately inflected with a
note of self-personation or self-parody. To seek to pin down the real
Byron here, as Jeffrey does, is to miss the *indeterminacy* of parody as
Byron employs it, and perhaps of all good parody.

Consider for example this stanza from canto 4, reflecting on the
moral outrage aroused by the first two cantos:

Some have accused me of a strange design
Against the creed and morals of the land,

And trace it in this poem every line:
I don't pretend that I quite understand
My own meaning when I would be *very* fine,
But the fact is that I have nothing plann'd,
Unless it were to be a moment merry,
A novel word in my vocabulary. (iv.5)

The poise of candor and irony—the involvement of candor and irony in one another—is beautifully done. Byron protests his innocence. Those hyperanxious moralists (like Robert Southey) who find a satanic intention in the opening cantos are absurdly paranoid; they need to lighten up, and to recognize a joke, a piece of light entertainment, when they see one. The poem has no design on the reader; Byron has "nothing plann'd." And that all seems right: it has the whole weight of the poem behind it. But at the same time as protesting his innocence, Byron also plays the innocent—as we hear in the trace of mock-naïvety in the word "strange," or the touch of Simple Simon in lines 3 to 5. We become aware that the innocence may be a kind of mask, something performed, comical, obliquely mocking. Can it really be that Byron has *nothing planned*, no design in telling us this? And indeed there is an "unless" that takes us to the final line, the grim reflection that to be a moment merry is "a novel word in my vocabulary." This calls up the famously brooding and bitter Byron of *Childe Harold*, and his emergence in the stanza, at what is so often the punch line final couplet, would seem to expose the candor as disingenuous by comparison. And yet not quite so: for the final line is itself a little too much, an instant self-parody, and ends by relishing its own overstatement, a relish felt in the comedy of the double rhyme.

The fine comedy of this stanza turns on an ambiguity: we cannot finally either acquit or convict Byron of having something *planned*. Those terms of acquittal or conviction are appropriate because what is in question is his malice, his wickedness of intent. But—as with Mephistopheles—we cannot finally settle the ethical orientation of that wickedness, for reasons that have to do with the play of parody and the special kind of doubleness or indeterminacy which the parodic spirit creates.

Closure, Parody, and Comedy

In Mann's *Doctor Faustus*, the Devil refers to hell as the place where "everything ends."[44] The mobility of *Don Juan* resists the definitive. Byron disclaims "design," despite raising that idea so strongly: he disclaims that he has an end in view. This can also be understood structurally or temporally: the poem resists finality, evades or defers the *last judgment*. Although bathos lies continually in wait, it is not terminal, as I have tried to show; the nihilistic voice cannot be sustained for more than a line or two without beginning to become its own ironic self-parody. The poem then responds to it as further stimulus, not as closure.

In this resistance to finality there is, once more, a parallel in *Faust*. The Don Juan story has often been recognized as a kind of comic analogue to that of Faust. (When Goethe asked himself what kind of music could be appropriate for the setting of *Faust*, he thought of *Don Giovanni*; Kierkegaard's aesthete sees Faust as a "reproduction of Don Juan" at a more developed stage.)[45] Each story deals with an insatiable protagonist whose desires break established moral codes in ways which elicit a complex mixture of admiration and disapproval, and which lead in the end to his death and damnation. But Goethe, crucially, calls the traditional outcome into question: and so does Byron. Juan, whom we meet at the very start of his sexual career, is too naïve, too young, too warmhearted, and altogether too much seduced rather than seducing, to be a credible candidate for hell.

The comedy Byron draws from this is complicated, however; the prospect of damnation is never an entirely facetious idea in the poem. This is true even, or especially, in Juan's most idyllic relationship, that with Haidée. This is the moment at which they first make love:

> Alas! they were so young, so beautiful,
> So lonely, loving, helpless, and the hour
> Was that in which the heart is always full,
> And, having o'er itself no further power,
> Prompts deeds eternity can not annul,
> But pays off moments in an endless shower
> Of hell-fire—all prepared for people giving
> Pleasure or pain to one another living. (ii.192)

Beneath the comic mimicry of religious disapproval, there is a note of lament that survives the irony. For the future is ominous: not just because Haidée's pirate father will return, but because the freshness of young love could not in any case (Byron insists) survive the passing of time. What waits for the young Juan at the end of his story may be the disillusioned and perhaps damnable Don Juan who is already present in the reflective, all-too-experienced voice of the narrator. Negativity comes with reflection and with time; it is age and experience that turn what was once romantic to burlesque.

This is an idea that cuts more and more sharply as the poem goes forward and "the night grows later." In the early cantos the narrative voice does not establish itself as dominant, but is continually in dialogue with a counterbalancing sense of youthful idealism and passion whose loss the narrator mourns even as he mocks it. As the poem goes on, this counterbalancing idealism drains gradually away. In the "English cantos," which comprise roughly the final third of the poem as it stands, the narrator's voice is dominant, and the proportion of reflection and commentary to action is much greater. Juan himself does little; little happens to him; and we get little access to his consciousness. He no longer functions as a straightforward foil or counterbalance to his worldly narrator. His recent service, in war in the carnage at Ismael and then as hard-worked stud to Catherine of Russia, makes him a more experienced, but somewhat jaded, perhaps shop-soiled hero, however dashing and desirable a figure he cuts in London high society. By setting these cantos in that empty, glittering world he knew so well, Byron is satirizing a very specific way of life, and in one sense this puts him on firm moral ground. Yet the note of a bottomless negativity is also sounded, since it is not clear by what viable positive values the ennui of high society life can be condemned or even, more simply, set aside. It is an utterly superficial world: but can a return to sexual comedy, in this setting and at this stage in the poem, have the vitality that speaks of depth? There is little sign of such vitality in the Duchess Fitz-Fulke, who seduces Juan just before the poem breaks off. The threat hangs in the air that the poem might be drawing toward a point from which no vital development is conceivable. We'll go no more a-roving: there will be no more Greek island banquets or adventures in harems, just the definitive bathos of reality, as revealed to the detached spectator, "yawning a little as the night grows later."[46]

To feel this threat is to see why it matters that *Don Juan* is such a radically antiteleological poem. Episodic, digressive, ad hoc, and apparently unplanned, it presents itself as conceivably endless. Its comic energies are mobilized in its resistance to finality. The lines quoted earlier from canto 4 ("Nothing so difficult . . .," iv:1) allege that beginning and ending are the most difficult things in poetry: to end well is virtually impossible because of the Lucifer-like fall into bathos and burlesque that lies in wait for soaring aspiration. This fall is seen as a continual falling that holds off conclusion. Reflecting on these matters is in fact Byron's way of *beginning* canto 4. Finality would necessarily discover some things to be of consequence (since they lead somewhere), but in *Don Juan* nothing is allowed to be of consequence for very long, neither love nor war nor politics nor Byron's own personal history, so that the negative critique enacted in the narrative voice works to some degree against itself. Without ever wiping the slate clean, it makes it impossible to do the sum and finalize the account.

The parallel with *Faust* lies in the special arrangement which Faust negotiates with the Devil. The possibility that Faust will evade damnation for his dealings with the Devil arises when he substitutes a wager, a conditional bargain with Mephistopheles, for the unconditional contract of the legend. Faust wagers that Mephistopheles will never be able to bring him to a moment of experience which is such that Faust will wish the moment to last. *If* he ever does wish such a thing, *then* Mephistopheles can take him: at that moment, Faust declares, let the bell toll and the clock stop, let time, for him, be over (1692–1706). At one level this is about bringing Faust to a sense of fulfillment or at least contentment. That seems to be what Faust intends by it, for he offers it only rhetorically, as a sure impossibility, in bitter confidence that happiness is not for him, and that none of the Devil's worldly gifts can satisfy the spirit. But at another level, which Mephistopheles appreciates more keenly (for he moves swiftly to accept the wager and claim it as a binding contract), the wager is about finality, about bringing Faust to a point where he has nothing to hope or desire or strive for, where Mephistophelean disillusionment is total and stretches unbroken to the horizon. That would truly be the end of Faust: the end of the rest-lessness of spirit which *is* Faust's identity. Time, as the principle of ongoing change and mobility and striving, would indeed be over for him. But at the end of the 1808 *Faust* his story is not over, his destiny still unfixed. The play ends shatteringly but indeterminately, with Gretchen "condemned" but also "saved," according to the voice from above, and Faust abruptly carried away by Mephistopheles to some kind of safety and some kind of future.[47]

Faust's wager essentially repeats the wager—the same word, *Wette*, is used—between Mephistopheles and the Lord in the "Prologue in Heaven." The Lord is confident that despite all Faust's anguish and confusion, in his "dark or obscure impulse" (*in seinem dunklen Drange*) he will retain a sense of the right path. Not so, says Mephistopheles, if you give me free rein. The Lord accepts the bet and raises the stakes: not only, he predicts, will Mephistopheles be ultimately powerless against a fundamentally good man like Faust, but his roguish kind of negativity is a positively beneficial stimulus in keeping human beings active, blocking their fondness for peace and quiet (324–43). Faust's wager thus turns not simply on his own behavior but on the ultimate function of the Devil, the ultimate tendency of negativity if fully released.

In writing *Don Juan*, Byron remakes that Faustian wager in his own name, and tries the outcome. He gives himself over to the mode of Mephistopheles, the cynically mocking spectator, in a gamble that such negativity will not prove terminal or total. He is betting, we might say, that he can conjure the Devil without being overwhelmed by him. His ability to keep the poem going for the time being, despite or indeed in response to the prospect of an end—"But this won't do, save by and by"—is the evidence that the wager has not, at least, been lost. Keeping the poem going does not just mean writing more and more, of course, although that is part of it. It is really about the open-endedness of Byron's irony at every moment. It means voicing mockery or bur-lesquing earnestness without reservation or inhibition, in a manner that holds nothing sacred and yet never arrives at what I am calling the last judgment. It is often not possible in *Don Juan* to fix the boundary where responsible critique ends and devilish negativity begins, but it is in that ambiguity that the writing has its life.

Important to this ambiguity is the poem's parodic quality, because of the way parody can erode the opposition between self and other, and can mesh critical detachment with participation. *Don Juan* offers itself as a parody explicitly of epic, and implicitly of the picaresque novel as well as of other versions of the Don Juan legend. Specific passages parody (closely or broadly) a host of particular writers and texts: Homer (the Nausicaa episode), *Paradise Lost*, Shakespeare (especially *Hamlet*, *Macbeth*, *Henry IV*, *The Merchant of Venice*, and *The Tempest*), Virgil (the death of Priam), the "Ancient Mariner," the Psalms, Horace, Pope, the *Ubi sunt?* topos, the opening of the *Inferno*, Wordsworth . . . and others. Byron also likes to parody the voice of moral propriety, mockingly; more subtly, as Jeffrey asks us to recognize, he "personates" more ideal or sympathetic feelings with a consciousness that stands to one side of them, and sees them simultaneously in a distancing perspective. This pervasive parodying of other texts or discourses sensitizes us to how Byron also continually parodies himself in one guise or another: the fallen "Napoleon of the realms of rhyme" (xi.55), for example, or the notorious immoralist, or the spontaneous extemporizer with "nothing plann'd" who speaks as the fancy takes him. Each of these is patently both a real aspect of the historical/legendary Byron and a role that Byron is playing at that moment in the poem, a role in the sense that it does not fill or determine the play of consciousness which accompanies it. Even the Mephistophelean "mere spectator" is such a role, although this is a more hazardous assertion, since it is from the detached viewpoint of Mephistopheles that all other roles appear as such, and become vulnerable to the Devil's critique. But a narrator who reflects that he looks on "much in the mode of Goethe's Mephistopheles" (xiii.7) cannot be *identical* with Mephistopheles; "mode" carries a certain self-reflexive irony. The extravagance of the sentiment is self-aware, and therefore becomes comic—as is felt in the facetious rhyming on "Mephistopheles," which, although ending the stanza, refuses the responsibilities of closure.

When Bernard Beatty quotes that line, he comments, "this sounds plausible enough until we recall that there is no Faust with whom this Mephistopheles can talk."[48] This is part of Beatty's concern that the later cantos are in danger of running down as the single narrative voice grows dominant. In my terms, Beatty is concerned that Byron may be losing his wager with the Devil. But to this it is possible to reply that the narrative voice is not single, but through its mobility implies an ongoing dialogue. The narrator's self-comparison with Mephistopheles, for example, comes next to moments where he associates himself with Johnson and with Cervantes—also figures of intelligent disillusionment, but disillusionment of different kinds, which Byron moves between rather than amalgamates:

> Rough Johnson, the great moralist, professed,
> Right honestly, "he liked an honest hater"—
> The only truth that yet has been confest
> Within these latest thousand years or later.
> Perhaps the fine old fellow spoke in jest:—
> For my part, I am but a mere spectator,
> And gaze where'er the palace or the hovel is,
> Much in the mode of Goethe's Mephistopheles;
>
> But neither love nor hate in much excess;
> Though 'twas not once so. If I sneer sometimes,
> It is because I cannot well do less,
> And now and then it also suits my rhymes.
> I should be very willing to redress
> Men's wrongs, and rather check than punish crimes,
> Had not Cervantes in that too true tale
> Of Quixote, shown how all such efforts fail. (xiii.7–8)

Perhaps Johnson "spoke in jest"; the possibility of irony that Byron hears even in Johnson's most "honest" professions invests even his own with the provisionality that comes with the comic energy of performance. After these stanzas come three on Cervantes that express both warm endorsement of his vision and dismay at its destructive implications, as the narrator moves—ever onward—to a new, differently critical standpoint. It is always hard to know where to stop a quotation from *Don Juan*; the accent, the point of view, is always changing. As Jerome McGann puts it, *Don Juan* is "a poem that is, in fact, always in transition."[49] And this is in a real sense Faustian, if one recalls the terms of Faust's wager: only if he stands still, filled by the current moment, can Mephistopheles claim him. Until that moment comes, the same incapacity for fulfillment that exposes him to Mephistopheles, and that Mephistopheles sustains and symbolizes, also preserves him from Mephistopheles. The mocking knowledge that informs "Carpe, carpe!" may not, after all, be wholly malevolent.

In his essay on laughter, Baudelaire describes the comedian or comic artist as someone who possesses "the capacity of being both himself and someone else at one and the same time."⁵⁰ This doubleness matters because Baudelaire sees laughter as fundamentally "Satanic," coming as it does "from a man's idea of his own superiority"—which, in a fallen, wretched creature such as man, is an "essentially contradictory" phenomenon.⁵¹ The comic artist, unlike the person who simply laughs at others, grasps this contradiction; they can adopt and express the satanic view of things without being confined to it. Such an artist shares in the power of the "philosopher" who knows how to laugh at his own fall, because he possesses "the power of getting outside himself [*se dédoubler*] quickly and watching, as a disinterested spectator, the phenomenon of his ego [*phenomènes de son* moi]. But cases of that sort are rare."⁵² Baudelaire's disinterested spectator has much in common with the "mere spectator" whose Mephistophelean perspective Byron invokes in *Don Juan*. Mephistopheles himself might be said to appear as Baudelaire's comedian when he addresses God in the "Prologue in Heaven": "the pathos of my situation would surely make you laugh—if you hadn't got yourself out of the habit of laughing" (277–78). His self-description to Faust as one who, willing evil, performs good, describes a quintessentially comical state of affairs. What he offered Byron, we may say, was a way of apprehending the negativity of the Devil not within his own core self, as the earlier Byronic heroes do, but as a kind of double, an *alter ego*: part of a double act. In *The Deformed Transformed*, Byron responded to *Faust* literally along those lines; the Stranger adopts the deformed body which Arnold discards, so that "you shall see | Yourself for ever by you, as your shadow" (I.i.447–48).⁵³ In *Don Juan* a comic version of that doubling effect is played out between the reflective narrator and the action narrated, between the parodic Byron and the texts he parodies, but most of all in the mobility of the poetic voice.

"No hopes for them as laughs." Byron thought at one point of using the Methodist's declaration as the epigraph for *Don Juan*.⁵⁴ But the doubleness to be found in a certain kind of laughter allows Baudelaire to suggest the possibility that "the phenomena produced by the Fall will become the means of redemption."⁵⁵ Readers have always been divided over whether the mobility of *Don Juan* speaks, finally, more of hollowness or of vitality. It is perhaps less helpful to settle its *final* tendency than to recognize the significance of the question. Can the spirit of negation be acknowledged, and even embraced, in a way that is ultimately fruitful, or, once admitted as a companion, a familiar spirit, will it insist on the last word? *Faust* explores that question in one way; Byron's whole poetic career, and the writing of *Don Juan* in particular, explores it in another, which was surely influenced by his own encounter with the mocking Mephistopheles.

5

TELLING THE DEVIL'S STORY
Doctor Faustus and *The Master and Margarita*

In my opening chapter I drew certain ideas from Thomas Mann's *Doctor Faustus* with which to frame the discussion that followed: ideas in particular about an opposition between aesthetic immediacy, such as may be associated in particular with music, and a reflective consciousness that inevitably carries with it a sense of alienation. This dichotomy, in Mann's novel, is advanced by the Devil; yet a liaison between the artist and the Devil may also be the condition of negotiating it. In this chapter I want to return to *Doctor Faustus* to consider not only its *ideas* about opposition, but the way in which, as a work of art, it both expresses and seeks to overcome such opposition. In particular, I want to consider the figure of the storyteller, the natural site of a reflective, mediating consciousness, which Mann directly opposes to the figure of the inspired artist.

Doctor Faustus is presented by Mann not as a novel but as a biographical memoir, with the subtitle *The Life of the German Composer Adrian Leverkühn as Told by a Friend*, and in my first chapter I said nothing about that friend. The biographer is a strong presence in the work, commenting extensively and at every turn on the content of his narrative; his foregrounded consciousness both mediates Leverkühn to us and separates him from us. What this does is to interpose between Leverkühn and ourselves precisely that dimension of reflective consciousness which Leverkühn's aesthetic rejects. Although *Doctor Faustus* is clearly a work energized by the idea of Leverkühn's genius, by the hypothesis of his late music, and by the Devil's hugely persuasive aesthetics, through the narrator Mann's art insists on its difference from the art of Leverkühn in composing *The Lamentation of Dr. Faustus.* That difference, the space between them and the possibility of bridging it, might be said to be its true subject.

The narrator carries the faintly comic name of Serenus Zeitblom. He was Leverkühn's closest friend in childhood and has followed his development all his life, with the greatest sympathy and concern; he is Leverkühn's passionate admirer. For most of Leverkühn's life, Zeitblom was the only person outside his immediate family whom Leverkühn addressed with the familiar *du.* Yet he was never truly the confidant of Leverkühn, who "admitted [no one] into his life," and Zeitblom is temperamentally very different from his friend, as he himself well knows. In the opening pages of the book, he describes himself as "by nature wholly moderate, of a temper, I may say, both healthy and humane, addressed to reason and harmony." He fears, therefore, that his reader may reasonably doubt whether "my whole existence does not disqualify me" for the task of writing Leverkühn's life.[1] This is a doubt which he shares. "For a man like me it is very hard, it affects him almost like wanton folly, to assume the attitude of a creative artist to a subject which is dear to him as life and burns him to express; I know not how to treat it with the artist's playful self-possession."[2]

This is more than a merely conventional *apologia.* Zeitblom is a writer who would have profited from some sharp literary editing. He is rather long-winded, sometimes clumsily circumstantial, anxious to get things right in a way that draws our attention to his own writerly self-consciousness; often he pauses to reflect on what he has just said, or to interject some detail about his own life and circumstances, or to express the turmoil of his emotions, and always with a certain formal deliberateness, a slightly pedestrian or methodical quality, as if careful to leave no word unsaid. A former classics teacher (he resigned his post under the Nazi regime) and a comfortably married man, the single most striking thing about him, which has no obvious connection with the rest of his life, is his lifelong fascination with Leverkühn. Our impression is of a mind disposed toward familiar human decencies, struggling to do justice to a subject—the nature of daemonic genius—which both touches him to the quick and is altogether alien to him.

"The daemonic, little as I presume to deny its influence upon human life, I have at all times found utterly foreign to my nature."[3] His relation to his subject is something like that of Dr. Watson to Sherlock Holmes—except that this is a much more thoughtful, deeply exercised, and dramatically present Dr. Watson.

This narrative heaviness, this imperfect artistry, is of course a stroke of art by Thomas Mann. Nevertheless, many readers of the novel—especially the first 200 pages—must have fretted with a sense of authorial long-windedness, as well as admiring Mann's powers of characterization. The reader does not find that they can see all the way round Zeitblom, or over his head, as they might expect to do with a different kind of foregrounded narrator. For Zeitblom is an intelligent, articulate representative of the great tradition of humanist culture which derives from the classical world, and is sensitive too to the modern pressures to which it stands exposed. That tradition has seemed to some to collapse and die in the first half of the twentieth century—destroyed by the revelations of two world wars; undermined by the theories of unconscious processes put forward by Marx, Darwin, Nietzsche, and Freud; supplanted by modernist art forms more adequate to a new understanding. The daemonic source of Leverkühn's music makes just such a challenge to Zeitblom's humanist values. He has always believed that his feeling for culture is strong in being inclusive of the forces that might seem to challenge it, from outside or from below. When in his youth he visited the sacred places of Greece, he tells us,

> I experienced by divination the rich feeling of life which expressed itself in the initiate veneration of Olympic Greece for the deities of the depths; often, later on, I explained to my pupils that culture is in very truth the pious and regulating, I might say propitiatory, entrance of the dark and uncanny into the service of the gods.[4]

Mann allows Zeitblom to be thoughtful and intelligent about these matters. At the same time, there is in his manner of expression (and not only in the English translation) a certain careful formality, a faint note of the stereotypical German professor, such as is not to be heard in the prose of Nietzsche or of Freud. This allows us to feel a limit to the inclusiveness of Zeitblom's stance, a limit that lies precisely in the lucidity of its conceptualization—as in a lesson that can in principle be "explained" to one's pupils. And Zeitblom, reflecting on his reflections, knows this too, and is troubled by it. He knows that in reflecting on genius he is drawn to make a distinction—which he also knows that he cannot justify or even clearly articulate—between "pure" and "impure," good and evil. The word "genius" has "a noble, harmonious, and humane ring,"

> and yet it cannot be denied (and has never been) that the daemonic and irrational have a disquieting share in this radiant sphere. We shudder as we realize that a connexion subsists between it and the nether world, and that the reassuring *epitheta* which I sought to apply: "sane, noble, harmonious, humane," do not for that reason quite fit, even when—I force myself, however painfully, to make this distinction—even when they are applied to a pure and genuine, God-given, or shall I say God-inflicted genius, and not to an acquired kind, the sinful and morbid corruption of natural gifts, the issue of a horrible bargain. . . .
>
> Here I break off, chagrined by a sense of my artistic short-comings and lack of self-control.[5]

This is from the first chapter; the whole novel explores that "breaking off." Zeitblom begins with the presumption that "the daemonic and irrational" have their proper place in the "radiant sphere" of genius, but when—with Leverkühn burning in his mind—he dwells upon that mysterious connection, he reacts against it with a dichotomizing reflex that reflects his "artistic short-comings," his deficiency in the kind of artistry that could hold these opposites in synthesis (as Leverkühn's late music, we are told, succeeds in doing). His chagrin expresses the gap, the difference, between Leverkühn and himself, which is also the inability of the reflective consciousness to transmit the reality of Leverkühn's genius, and perhaps even to find terms in which to approve of it.

The intractable otherness of that genius is underlined by Mann's decision to make his Faustian artist a composer. There is a strong nineteenth-century tradition of thought that sees music as having, of all the arts, the deepest affinities with the realm of instinct, and the most equivocal relations with the realm of culture. Not in any obvious sense mimetic, music can claim to bypass or transcend our normal, experience-based faculty of understanding; more readily than the other arts, it admits the notion of direct, unmediated intuition or inspiration. (Paganini was rumored to have sold his soul to the Devil in exchange for his virtuosity, as, later, was the blues guitarist Robert Johnson; would such stories about *writers* have equal appeal?) Music was associated with elemental forces that are prior to, and reach deeper than, the forms of consciousness, selfhood, and civilization. Kierkegaard, as we have seen, had found Mozart's *Don Giovanni* to epitomize that "daemonic" power which obliterates moral considerations; Schopenhauer had seen music as giving unique access to the reality of the world will that underlies all representation; Nietzsche, with Wagner's *Tristan and Isolde* in mind, had written of the power of music to release the Dionysiac. To this way of thinking, it is a question whether music is a force for culture at all. Zeitblom tells us at the start that he is inclined to exclude music from "the pedagogic-humanistic sphere," the humanities properly so called, which he pointedly refers to as the *bonae literae*. They are *bonae*, good, because they are built on language, and appeal to that "old philological interest" which inspires "a lively and loving sense of the beauty and dignity of reason in the human being." Music, however—"that other, perhaps more intense, but strangely inarticulate language"—stands to these humanist values as a dangerous, morally equivocal force; it seems to Zeitblom "to belong to a world of spirits for whose absolute reliability in the things of reason and human dignity I would not just care to put my hand in the fire."[6]

The fact that he is nevertheless a passionate admirer of Leverkühn's music is, he reflects, "one of those contradictions which, whether one deplores or takes joy in them, are inseparable from human nature."[7] This appears as a contradiction from the viewpoint of humanist culture—which also seeks to make ethical judgments: "whether one deplores or takes joy in them." Zeitblom as narrator stands for that order of thought, both by virtue of his humanist values and, more fundamentally, by virtue of embodying the activity of reflective consciousness: yet, through his feeling for music and his relationship with Leverkühn, he is also aware of a space that is altogether outside the order of thought and its oppositions. When he comes to Leverkühn's late music, he is intensely exercised by its ambiguity, its manner of dissolving, through musical means, the absoluteness of the opposition between heaven and hell, salvation and damnation—just as he is intensely exercised by the dual aspect of salvation and damnation that the *Lamentation* presents as an event in Leverkühn's artistic life. But there is no doubt that—precisely despite and because of this ambiguity—he is passionately convinced by the music itself as "breakthrough," epiphany, something beyond "speculation," work of genius, unquestionable manifestation of spiritual reality in the realm of experience.

What is crucial is that *we cannot hear this music*. Mann emphasizes the otherness of Leverkühn's artistic achievement by embedding it in a narrative that is, by the Devil's criterion of "rapture," profoundly inartistic, a densely deliberative medium. When, early in the novel, we get an account of a late Beethoven sonata, we can marry the words to the music, for we know this independently; but when Zeitblom gives us pages of verbal description of Leverkühn's music, without at any point transcribing a musical phrase, the effect is curious: we can say a good deal about the structure of the music, its emotional and imaginative effect, and its symbolic significance, but we have no access to it as an immediate reality of our experience, and the longer Zeitblom goes on describing it, the more we feel this to be the case. The effort to evoke music through language exhausts itself, and describes finally its own limitations. We remain within the order of thought, which is the order of language, and the inevitability of this is enforced by the all-too-solid presence of Zeitblom, the medium of reflective consciousness which comes between us and the immediacy of music. Zeitblom's chagrin at his artistic shortcomings has a certain comical aspect, and he does not escape Leverkühn's ironical, mocking smile, but it is at bottom the chagrin of the novel as a whole at its separation from the subject on which it reflects: a chagrin at the necessity of substituting words for music, the necessity of reflecting on rapture.

It is a necessary chagrin. There may be moments when we are tempted to wish Zeitblom to the devil—to wish that Mann were a more direct, less cerebral, more Dionysiac writer, who would grant us some measure of direct access to Leverkühn and the power of his art. But that temptation is stopped in its tracks by one further aspect of Zeitblom's role. Zeitblom's narrative self-consciousness places Leverkühn's genius in historical reality: the reality of Germany in the first half of the twentieth century. Leverkühn himself is not much engaged with the contemporary world: his creative years are spent withdrawn from society, and his masterpieces draw on works of the sixteenth century (Dürer's woodcuts of the Apocalypse, the original Faustbook) in treating what appear to be timeless religious subjects. Zeitblom, however, writes his memoir in Germany between 1943 and 1945, and his references to contemporary events—the bloodbath of Germany's military defeat and the horror of her moral corruption—effectively map Leverkühn's life onto the larger tragedy. The twenty-four years during which Leverkühn is incubating syphilis are those between 1906 and 1930, the period during which Germany could be said to have been incubating fascism. His weariness with existing musical forms and the outdated culture from which they sprang, as well as his inclination to mockery, reflects a general cultural malaise, a political and intellectual rootlessness which Zeitblom documents through various secondary characters and conversations. And his desire for a "breakthrough" into some more vital, dynamic, rejuvenated mode has strong echoes both in the self-image of fascism and in the terrible instinctual energies which it, in truth, generated or released. Zeitblom uses the term "daemonic" both for the power of genius and for the energies of fascism, and speaks of the "pact" signed in her blood by which Germany intended to conquer the world.[8] It is as we come to the final terrible scene of Leverkühn's collapse, when Leverkühn reveals his great transgression to those around him, that Zeitblom hears of the first opening of the concentration camps, the revelations which force Germany to confront her knowledge of what she is and what she has done. The *Lamentation*, therefore, is irresistibly felt to belong to Germany as well as to Leverkühn; the two stories are intertwined.

What is the effect of this? Most obviously, it means that Zeitblom's reflective consciousness, with its capacity for moral anguish, strikes us as indispensable. His existence as narrator expresses the conviction that questions of aesthetics cannot stand alone, outside history; they cannot be isolated from the political sphere, least of all by any German artist writing at that time. In particular, all idea of a realm "beyond good and evil," or of celebrating the Devil's party, is sharply confronted by reference to the real, wholly unambiguous evils of Nazi Germany. We are immediately forced to recognize that such an idea has its validity, if anywhere, only in a symbolic sense, with reference to levels of deep psychic organization or to the imaginative world of the artist. Translated into the world of action and event, it drastically changes its character.

What is important here is the *differentiation* between historical reality and the realm of art. It is sometimes carelessly said that Leverkühn's pact with the Devil is offered as an allegory of the rise and fall of Nazi Germany, but that cannot be right. For one thing, it would be clumsy and needless, in that case, to include the condition of Germany within the narrative. In allegory, *x* stands for *y*, not alongside *y*. For another, Leverkühn—in whatever sense he damns himself—commits no act that is remotely comparable with the evils of war or the acts of the Nazi state. The sense in which he joins with the Devil, horrifying though it is from one point of view, is simply incommensurable with the sense in which Germany goes to the devil in the same period. The idea of a longed-for "breakthrough" occurs insistently in the novel, in both artistic and militaristic contexts, but the two do not merge. When Zeitblom interprets Germany's participation in the First World War in terms which look beyond the immediate evil toward an ultimate justification, Leverkühn is quietly dismissive:

> "What the break-through to world power, to which fate summons us, means at bottom, is the break-through to the world—out of an isolation of which we are painfully conscious. . . . The bitter thing is that the practical manifestation is an outbreak of war, though its true interpretation is longing, a thirst for unification."
>
> "God bless your studies," I heard Adrian say here in a low voice, with a half-laugh.[9]

This difference between them continues into the postwar climate of decadence and "loose speculation":

> He found my efforts to see in the evil the good which it might conceal, to be in the same vein as the comment which I had made at the war's beginning— and that makes me think of the cold, incredulous "God bless your studies!" with which he then answered me.[10]

Zeitblom is here himself thirsty for unification, for the involvement of evil with good, but for Leverkühn such radical ambiguity is not to be sought in political reality, only in art. When he agrees that "a real breakthrough is worth what the tame world calls a crime," he instances the Kleist essay on puppet theatre—"here too it treats of the break-through

. . . but it is talking only about the aesthetic"—and when Zeitblom protests, "do not say *only*! One does wrong to see in aesthetics a separate and narrow field," he smiles his cold, mocking smile and turns away.[11] Mann is conducting a real dialogue here, but if both speakers are right, Leverkühn is surely right in the more important sense. German militarism achieves no "breakthrough," only extremity, as Zeitblom himself will acknowledge by the end. The horrifying analogy between political abomination and artistic achievement is horrifying precisely because it refuses to resolve itself, but remains an obstinate dissonance, a fissure running through the work that is expressed in the space between Leverkühn and Zeitblom.

In important respects, then, the dichotomy between the aesthetic and the reflective, the Kierkegaardian either/or, is simply reinforced by Zeitblom's narrative presence. His lack of artistry, his anxious contrasting of the *bonae literae* with music, his ethical consciousness, and his groundedness in historical reality all contribute to this. At the end of the book, he doubts that he can ever return, after the events of the Nazi period, to the teaching of humanist culture, with its faith that "reason and clarity" can be integrated with "the deities of the depths."[12]

But in other ways he also *connects* these opposite spheres: at the level of human content, through love, and at the level of art, as parody.[13]

To begin with love. In a novel where immediacy is so much desired, the book we read is the immediate expression and embodiment of Zeitblom's great love for Leverkühn. His love for "Adrian" is written into almost every page. This is not to force the word; Zeitblom uses it himself, at the start, with a directness that is rare in his prose. Love is, he declares, his chief qualification to be Leverkühn's biographer, and specifically makes up for his lack of affinity with the daemonic sphere of genius:

> First and last—and this justification was always the most valid, if not before men, then before God—I loved him, with tenderness and terror, with compassion and devoted admiration, and but little questioned whether he in the least returned my feeling.[14]

Indeed, Zeitblom knows that such a return was out of the question. "With Adrian that did not happen. Human devotion he accepted, I would swear, often without even noticing it. . . . I might compare his isolation to an abyss, into which one's feelings towards him dropped soundless and without a trace."[15] This asymmetric love is the response of consciousness to an ideal form of unconsciousness, or of that which lies beyond consciousness, here figured as the defining mark of genius. Without thought of reciprocity or union, it aligns itself with Leverkühn's account of love, quoted in my opening chapter, which emphasizes otherness or strangeness as its foundation. Leverkühn spoke of "a conquest of previously existing resistances, based on the strangeness of I and You, that which is of the self and that which belongs to the other."[16] Zeitblom subscribes to this theory of love, as well he might, and recalls it later, rephrased in his own more cautious terms:

> Probably it is my fate to be able to speak only stiffly, dryly, and analytically about the phenomenon of love: of that which Adrian had one day character-ized to me as an amazing and always somewhat unnatural alteration in the relation between the I and the not-I. Reverence for the mystery in general, and personal reverence as well, combine to close my lips or make me chary of words when I come to speak of the transformation, always in the sign of the daemonic, the phenomenon in and for itself half miraculous which negatives the singleness of the individual soul.[17]

This is very much in Zeitblom's idiom, with its careful formality, its consciousness of its own shortcomings, its deliberated chagrin. He is meticulously conscious that the "transformation" lies beyond his words, just as Leverkühn lies beyond him. But for all that, his final phrase has no less of the ring of felt experience than Leverkühn's words about "strange flesh." They are the words of a lover, and if Zeitblom, in the separated position of the reflective narrator, emphasizes the breakthrough from singleness, while Leverkühn, thinking of the sex-ual act, emphasizes the element of strangeness in the desired other, their accounts nevertheless match one another well enough. To speak of love as an "alteration in the relation between the I and the not-I" is a desperately abstract way of putting it, and partakes of that atmosphere of strained intellectualism which in this novel is both medium and sub-ject, but perhaps only such an abstract formula could lend itself to that richness of implication which the novel demands.

In particular, it allows the connection with parody. Zeitblom is a kind of double for Mann, a figure in whom Mann parodies aspects of himself: which is to say that he is a figure through whom "the rela-tion between the I and the not-I" becomes fluid. We can feel this sim-ply from Zeitblom's self-positioning as author, and from the blend of inwardness and irony with which that self-positioning is given. The novel's first readers were able to perceive how Zeitblom and Mann were both writing at the same moment, in the light of contemporary events; when the fall of Germany and the reports of the opening of the concentration camps intrude upon Zeitblom's writing of his biog-raphy, they were intruding equally upon Mann's writing of his novel. The reader who knows Mann's other writing may well hear Zeitblom's extended elaborations of phrase, his anxious meticulousness in lan-guage, as "mocking and mourning Thomas Mann's own style," in the words of Erich Heller.[18] In Mann's memoir of the writing of *Doctor Faustus*, he wrote how Zeitblom's "nervousness was mine; I was paro-dying my own overbrimming eagerness. And it was a boon to play this part; to let the book be written for me, as it were." And again: "I had never loved a creature of my imagination . . . as I did Adrian. . . . Quite literally I shared good Serenus' feelings for him, was painfully in love with him from his days as an arrogant schoolboy, was infatuated with his 'coldness,' his remoteness from life . . . with his conviction that he was damned."[19] The day in 1943 on which Zeitblom records that he began the biography is the day on which Mann tells us he began to write Zeitblom's book.

How much such doubling meant to Mann is suggested by other aspects of the memoir. Its subtitle, in German, is *Roman eines Romans*— the novel of a novel—as if to suggest the convergence of Zeitblom's memoir and Mann's. Mann ponders his own diary notes—dating from only, at the furthest, five years earlier—as though they were written by a stranger. He finds, for example, a letter in which he asked for the loan of the old Faust chapbook and the letters of Wolf, and remarks, "The combination suggests that I had long been pursuing a rather defi-nite outline of an idea." After reproducing a diary entry, he comments, "Music, then, and Nietzsche. I would not be able to explain why my thoughts and interests were turning in this particular direction at that time."[20] Where we might have expected a direct remembering, instead we get Mann the biographer on the elusive trail of Mann the artist, a Zeitblom struggling to piece together understanding of a Leverkühn.

For if Zeitblom is Mann's double, so is Leverkühn. The memoir encourages us to see in Mann's writing of *Doctor Faustus* a partial parallel to Leverkühn's artistic career. What is presented as a factual, documentary record repeatedly recalls and echoes the fiction. There are several references to the novel as a *musical* work.[21] Events and writings peculiarly relevant to Mann's task "seemed to come my way of their own accord,"[22] as though some larger narrative agency were involved. Theodor Adorno enters Mann's life as the necessary "helper, adviser, and sympathetic instructor . . . precisely the right person"[23] to help him get forward with the book: just so, one might say, Leverkühn is visited by the Devil, who assumes Adorno's appearance, paraphrases his views, and speaks to him about Kierkegaard, as Adorno did to Mann. Leverkühn's infection, too, is echoed in Mann's chronic illness during the composition of *Doctor Faustus*; he notes that "the infection, as it often is with me, was hard to expel. It continued to smoulder in the organism and produced unpleasant after-effects."[24] As the writing of *Faustus* approaches its conclusion, and Leverkühn approaches his final syphilitic crisis, Mann is discovered to have a shadow on the lung and undergoes major surgery. Lying in hospital after the operation, he reflects upon the guilt of the artist in terms that connect him with the damnably cerebral composer:

> Surrounded in a critical situation by so much love, sympathy, solicitude, one asks oneself what one has done to deserve it—and pretty well asks in vain. Has any man who ever bore the incubus of creation upon his back, always concerned, obsessed, preoccupied with the work of days and years—has any such man ever been an enjoyable companion? *Dubito*. And I doubt it particularly for myself. How is it, then? Can the consciousness of one's arrears in this respect, the knowledge that one's work is claiming what one should be able to give freely to one's intimates—can the colouring of existence by this sense of guilt make up for the great lack and reconcile others to it, even win their affection? Here is a speculation impious enough to be ascribed to Adrian Leverkühn.[25]

Mann also records a diary entry made at the point when he came to Leverkühn's composition of the *Apocalypse* music. "How much *Faustus* contains of the atmosphere of my life! A radical confession, at bottom. From the very beginning that has been the shattering thing about the book."[26] This confession of a confession expressed through an artwork parallels Leverkühn's own climactic confession that his *Lamentation of Dr. Faustus* and his reasons for working on the Faust story were acutely, agonizingly personal.

Part of the interest of this doubling is biographical—though it should be remembered that Mann called his memoir a "novel," and that these parallels are at least partly constructed by Mann himself. But my concern here is with the play of this double consciousness in *Doctor Faustus*, the parodic mode through which the relation of self to other, I to not-I, consciousness to immediacy, can be something other than one of sheer opposition, and a safe connection can be opened with the daemonic. "How necessary the mask and the playfulness were, in view of the earnestness of my task."[27]

The topic of parody comes up at a crucial turn in the conversation between Leverkühn and his visitor. The Devil argues that the strength of modern critical consciousness undermines all the traditional forms of art; their harmonious formal play, as it once was, would now be exposed as hopelessly sanguine. Leverkühn accepts this, but, like a wrestler seeking for a hold that exploits the strength of his opponent, tries to hold back the radical conclusion for which the Devil is pressing:

> I: "A man could know that and recognize freedom above and beyond all critique. He could heighten the play, by playing with forms out of which, as he well knew, life has disappeared."
>
> He: "I know, I know. Parody. It might be fun, were it not so melancholy in its aristocratic nihilism."[28]

Does the Devil win this exchange? By dismissing parody as nihilistic, the Devil drives Leverkühn on to the extremity of his late, apocalyptic music, and in particular to the *Lamentation*, whose pure expressiveness is composed, Zeitblom tells us, "without parody."[29] This is described as a work of overwhelming anguish and desolation, unqualified and total, except only that Zeitblom invites us to hear, in the "dying away of the sound of mourning" in the cello's final note, "a hope beyond hopelessness," something that remains "as a light in the night."[30] Much critical discussion of *Doctor Faustus* seeks to assess the novel's attitude toward a diabolically inspired art through the descriptions we are given of Leverkühn's late music—its appalling negativity, or its tragic grandeur, or its hints of redemption—since here, it would seem, the Devil's gift is fulfilled, and his aesthetic can be evaluated. But this, I think, is a fruitless enterprise. To repeat the point made earlier: as readers, we cannot hear this music. Its pure expressiveness, its immediacy, however inspiring as an idea, remains hypothetical; the medium of reflective consciousness, thickened by the voice of the narrator, is not to be put aside. When Zeitblom urges us, "listen to the end, listen with me,"[31] the effect is to remind us of what we cannot do.

There is, however, one work by Leverkühn which *is* immediately present to us, and it is a work diabolically inspired. The Devil appears in *Doctor Faustus* only in chapter 25; this chapter gives us a *verbatim* transcription of the document in which Leverkühn recorded the Devil's visit and their conversation together. The document came to Zeitblom after Leverkühn's death. In introducing it, Zeitblom says that he is torn between two horrifying alternatives: that it represents a real dialogue with another being, or that those diabolical cynicisms "came out of the afflicted one's own soul."[32] Either way, he presents it to the reader as an object of Gothic terror; his hand trembles as he transcribes it.

What fails to occur to Zeitblom is that this document might be a work of art. This is despite the fact that it bears many marks of deliberated literary composition. It is written in dialogue form. It is brilliantly structured. The Devil changes shape to match what he has to say at that moment, from ugly bullyboy to Adorno-like intellectual and back again. And most significantly, the document is pervasively and openly parodic. There are passages of sustained parody within it, as when the Devil closely paraphrases Adorno in one place, and Nietzsche in another. Leverkühn's challenge to the Devil to prove his objective existence reprises Ivan Karamazov's challenge to his own sinister visitor in Dostoevsky. In these marks of art, the authorship of Leverkühn overlaps, of course, with that of Thomas Mann, ambiguously or rather indistinguishably: for in this document the two artists come together, in a heightened version of that doubling effect which is already the effect of parody. In one stylistic feature in particular we can see that Leverkühn certainly has a hand. The whole document is written in an intermittently archaic style that recalls the sixteenth-century German of Luther and the original Faustbook; this takes us back to a late medieval world where the Devil was palpable and real, while also, as parody, preserving a distance from it, in an intensified, miniaturized version of what Mann is doing in the novel as a whole. Leverkühn uses this archaic idiom on two other occasions in the novel: in an earlier letter to Zeitblom, recounting his accidental visit to the brothel, and at the very end, as his mind collapses. On the first occasion he adopts it whimsically, consciously, deliberately; on the final occasion, parodic no longer, it possesses him. This document falls between those two modes, with a powerful indeterminacy: neither affected nor transparent, it is the style of art.

To say that the document may be a work of art is not to say that it is a mere fiction, that it does not record a real encounter. If we are gripped by chapter 25—and it may well strike us as the core of the novel, the chapter for which the novel was written—we may even say that it could not have been written *without* a real encounter. Derek Attridge's argument, cited in an earlier chapter, is relevant here: the true artist invents only what is really out there, engages with an otherness generated by the contours of the known. Artistic invention is also discovery; yet what is discovered cannot be wholly assimilated. That is why the true work of art strikes us as both recognizable and unprecedented. One might also put Attridge's insight like this: the work of creation never belongs wholly to the author, is never the work of the author only. On a theological plane, this would suggest that "God only" is a condition always deferred; meanwhile the Devil claims his share. On the plane of narrative, this means that the story never belongs wholly to the storyteller, or to one storyteller alone, which is precisely the crisis which Leverkühn's document forces upon Zeitblom:

> I myself must cease to speak. . . . In this twenty-fifth chapter the reader hears Adrian's voice direct.
>
> But is it only his? This is a dialogue which lies before us. Another, quite other, quite frightfully other, is the principal speaker, and the writer sets down only what he heard from that other.[33]

This is wonderfully suggestive as to the nature of artistic creation. But in swinging between alternatives—*either* Adrian *or* the Devil—Zeitblom misses the point of his own insight. In this dialogue the artist and the Devil engage with one another—antagonistically, but also collusively—and out of that engagement, that *agon*, comes the literary creation. The dramatic tension between them—for despite the Devil's dominance in the argument, some part of Leverkühn remains importantly resistant—is thrillingly repeated at the formal level: our perception that this is what happened to Leverkühn (the dialogue as documentary record) plays off against the perception that this is what Leverkühn has made of it (the dialogue as work of art). Whether the Devil exists as an independent entity is finally irrelevant, a meaningless question, as he himself observes. If we think of him as part of Leverkühn's mind, then the artist has succeeded in projecting and finding a voice for those thoughts to the point where the *agon* becomes possible; if we think of him as the being who is "frightfully other," then the artist has succeeded in engaging with the stranger to the point where dialogue becomes possible. In any case, the challenge presented by the Devil is such that it has produced the writing that gives him a voice: but for that very reason it is not the only voice that we hear. Reflective consciousness and artistic genius are opposed in *Doctor Faustus*: but they come together in the moment of dialogue, unresolved and dangerous but self-evidently productive, between the Devil and the artist.

———

By way of coda, let me conclude by telling or, rather, retelling another story of the Devil's involvement in creative process, in which the fluidity or plurality of authorship again is crucial.

Mikhail Bulgakov's *The Master and Margarita* was written during the late 1920s and 1930s and is set mostly in contemporary Moscow. We meet the "Master" of the title only halfway through. He is, or was, a writer, who has written a book about Pontius Pilate which describes his desolation at the execution of Jesus. This was so savagely treated by the literati of the Soviet establishment that he burned all copies of the manuscript in fear and despair, and sits now in an asylum for the mentally ill. Bulgakov himself found it impossible to publish almost any of his work during this period, under Stalin, and at one point took the bound draft of his novel, cut the pages diagonally from top to bottom, and burned them, keeping the spine and mutilated remnant to show that the work had once existed. The Master is clearly a kind of double for Bulgakov himself, or a representation of what he might have become or might still become.

Nevertheless, the book about Pontius Pilate, or a significant part of it, exists. Four freestanding chapters within Bulgakov's novel—chapters 2, 16, 25, and 26—are written in a quite different style from the rest. They are set in Jerusalem in the time of Pilate and recount Pilate's interrogation of Yeshua Ha-Notsri, a vagrant teacher; Yeshua's crucifixion; and Pilate's response to that event. That these chapters exist is the work of the Devil, who appears in Moscow at the beginning of the book and leaves the city at the end. For his epigraph, Bulgakov took Mephistopheles' self-description in *Faust*: "I am a part of that power that always wills what is evil, and always creates what is good."[34] What the Devil "creates" in the course of the book is to make it possible for a certain work of literature, unacceptable and virtually unthinkable under the Soviet regime, to come into existence.

This, however, is not apparent for some time; nor does it seem to be the Devil's purpose in coming to Moscow. He arrives one evening and introduces himself as a foreign traveller named Woland, "a specialist in black magic."[35] Accompanied by his bizarre retinue—a couple of shape-changing henchmen, a naked witch who serves as his maid, and a huge talking black cat called Behemoth—he takes over an apartment, puts on a performance of magic at the Variety Theatre, and causes mayhem throughout the city. The activities of this group mostly take the form of a dark practical joking, a sinister buffoonery. At the theatre the women in the audience may exchange their outfits, free of charge, for the latest, most expensive fashions from Paris—which disappear when they are outside in the street. Money is showered upon the citizens—which later turns to worthless paper. The master of ceremonies has his head torn off (and replaced) by the cat; the theatre manager is spirited instantaneously to Yalta; the chairman of the residents' association finds the bribe he accepted has turned inexplicably into illegal foreign currency, about which the authorities have been informed. And so on.

These goings-on chime so well with the extravagant but deadpan surrealism with which these chapters are written that we are bound to feel ourselves largely complicit with the Devil's operations. This sense of affinity with the forces of darkness is set up at the very beginning. The book opens when Woland joins the conversation of two literary figures. The chairman of Moscow's foremost literary association is explaining to a young poet that no story about Jesus should be written, since it is certain that Jesus never existed. A fluent, confident intellectual, he makes this point with some self-importance and much ostentatious scholarship, and explains to the strange foreigner who has joined them that in the enlightened state of the Soviet Union all the old proofs of God's existence have been discredited, and atheism is the only rational position. The superstitious belief in man's dependency on higher powers has been replaced by the assertion of autonomy: man himself is in control. There is a delicious absurdity in dogmatizing thus to the Devil himself. Woland certainly relishes it: he professes himself fascinated to hear of these remarkable views, with a dangerous mock-politeness that is precisely paralleled by the wicked mock-realism of Bulgakov's writing. The chairman's complacent rationalism makes him vulnerable as well as absurd; he is mistakenly skeptical when Woland accurately predicts the manner of his imminent death. "Never Talk to Strangers" is the chapter's mischievously disingenuous title.

This gives the cue for what follows. In the face of the Devil, the secular rationality and materialism of modern Moscow prove absurdly limited, overwhelmed by a force of ferocious comic energy that is both deeply disorienting and obscurely revelatory. In the carnival of violence and trickery that now break out, we feel an element of fantastic poetic justice, a corrective acknowledgment of realities neglected or suppressed. If some of these diabolical assaults seem arbitrary, most of the Devil's victims are recognizably on the make, in small, banal, all-too-human ways: hustling for a free lunch or a better apartment, maneuvering for advantage, cheating on their wives, exploiting their privileges or toadying to their superiors. The Devil's carnival sweeps across this world of petty self-concern, of the familiar here and now, almost like a refining fire: and indeed near the end of the novel the official, state-sanctioned writers' club goes up in flames.

The half-complicit reader, then, can find much to relish in these energies. But they convey a damning judgment on contemporary life; and the citizens of Moscow experience them, not surprisingly, as threatening and destructive: as evil. Caught within their expectations of realism and rationality, they protest; they flee; they call in the police; they beg to be locked inside the safety of armor-plated chambers. Bamboozled, humiliated, astounded, and terrorized, ever-increasing numbers find themselves as patients in the hospital for the insane, an asylum indeed, a place of gentle words, unbreakable windows, and tranquilizing injections.

The exception is Margarita. When she receives an invitation from the Devil, she accepts it, metamorphoses (euphorically) into a witch, and acts in the exhausting role of queen and hostess throughout the long night of the Devil's ball. She makes herself over to the Devil without reserve: and yet is not corrupted. For her motive for consorting with the Devil is the hope of recovering her lost lover, the "Master" of the book's title, whom she loves with an absoluteness as distant as the wildest supernatural event from the reasonableness of normality. She loves him for himself, but also as the author of the story about Pontius Pilate, which she cares for as devotedly as she cares for him. At the end of the ball her service is rewarded: the Devil grants her heart's desire. He restores to her not only the Master himself, teleported from the asylum, but also the manuscript of his book. The Master had destroyed the last surviving copy, but, Woland drily remarks, "manuscripts don't burn."[36] Intimacy with the Devil has opened an unexpected door to restoration.

We can now trace the Devil's connection with the four Jerusalem chapters. At the start of Bulgakov's novel, when Woland breaks in upon the discussion of the historical nonreality of Jesus, he politely points out that Jesus certainly existed; he knows, because he was there, and can tell the story. And he begins to recount what then becomes the next chapter in Bulgakov's text and the first of the Jerusalem chapters, which gives us Pilate's interrogation of Yeshua and his part in the events immediately leading up to the crucifixion.

The second Jerusalem chapter comes into being as a direct consequence of this. Listening to the Devil's story was the young poet Ivan Bezdomny, or Ivan the Homeless. The encounter with Woland turns Ivan's mind (the Devil had hinted that schizophrenia lay in store for him), or more precisely induces such deranged behavior that he is committed to the mental hospital. He is obsessed by the need to take action against the dangerous foreigner—and obsessed also by the story of Pontius Pilate. He tries to write this down, for he is, or was, a writer, but his account becomes confused and he gives it up. Then, just as he is falling into a heavily medicated sleep, he is visited by the Master, an inmate in the same hospital. This nighttime visitant comes to Ivan like a figure in a dream, or like Ivan's overwrought hallucination; they share, of course, a burning interest in the story of Pontius Pilate, and when the Master tells Ivan that he has written a book about him, Ivan can reply by telling him of the Devil's firsthand account. "The guest then folded his hands as if in prayer and whispered, 'Oh, I guessed right! I guessed everything right!'"[37] When his guest leaves, Ivan then dreams what happened next in Jerusalem, and this dream then becomes "The Execution," the second of the four Jerusalem chapters.

The third and fourth chapters can be more briefly accounted for. They come straight from the manuscript which the Devil caused to be magically restored, as reward for Margarita's service. As Margarita returns to the precious manuscript, the two chapters which she rereads appear as chapters in Bulgakov's own book. In these chapters, Pilate arranges for the covert murder of Judas of Kerioth, the man who informed against Yeshua: for Pilate is gripped by a strange anguish over the death of Yeshua. A rumor will be circulated that Judas killed himself.

Let us now review this story of Yeshua and Pilate and its provenance. The first of the chapters is the Devil's narrative; it begins as if spoken by Woland, as an immediate witness of the events: on the face of it, an unimpeachable historical source (if delivered by the figure whom some regard as the father of lies). The second is Ivan's dream, induced in him by the triple influence of the Devil's story, the Master's visit, and his medication for mental illness: on the face of it, a highly subjective fantasy. The third and fourth chapters are presented as the text written by the Master and restored to existence by the Devil: on the face of it, a literary fiction. But when we read these freestanding chapters, our consciousness of narrative frame drops away. The text gives us Jerusalem just as securely and immediately as it gives us Moscow, indeed more so, for there is nothing surreal or supernatural or carnivalesque about the Jerusalem narrative, which is naturalistic throughout. If the chapter "Pontius Pilate" is the Devil's story, it is also Bulgakov's.

The effect of this is to suggest an indeterminately shared or shifting authorship, as the story begun by the Devil migrates to or is taken up by other narrators, including Bulgakov himself. Even as the story seems at last to come into focus as a literary fiction within the novel, a text written by the Master, so it overflows its bounds, penetrating the Moscow narrative within which it seemed to be enclosed. Near the end of the novel, as the Devil prepares to leave Moscow, a messenger comes to him from the Jerusalem world. The messenger is Levi Matvei, Yeshua's disciple, who figured importantly in the Jerusalem chapters. He now emerges from them with the extraordinary message that Yeshua has read the Master's book, and requests that the Master be granted eternal peace—which Woland duly arranges.[38] Two characters within the Master's narrative thus act to influence the Master's fate. The story within the story becomes the story of the story.

This formal slippage is crystallized in another telling detail. When the Master visits Ivan in the hospital, he tells Ivan that when he was writing the story of Pilate, he already knew the exact phrase with which it would end: "the fifth procurator of Judea, the knight Pontius Pilate." In fact, the last chapter of the Master's narrative as we have it, "The Burial," chapter 26, ends with a slightly different phrase: "the fifth procurator of Judea, Pontius Pilate." It is the final chapter of *Bulgakov*'s novel, chapter 32, in which the Master is sent into eternal peace—a kind of idyllic retirement cottage in the afterlife, accompanied by the loving Margarita—that ends with the identical phrase the Master had foretold. The Master's book has become, or been reimagined as, Bulgakov's, the book we hold in our hands. "Someone was releasing the Master into freedom,"[39] we are told, an indeterminate "someone" in whom Woland, Bulgakov, and a more impalpable authorial agency all come together. The absolute power exercised (we may suppose) by a single, stable author—mirroring an all-powerful Creator who is God alone—is here abdicated and dispersed, in a flamboyant expression of writing as collaborative or multiple, dependent upon another or a muse.

This dynamic indeterminacy of authorship picks up the way that nothing about the story of Yeshua and Pilate can be definitive. There are small but significant discrepancies between the second and the third of the Jerusalem chapters, notably with regard to the words reported as spoken by the dying Yeshua. More obviously, there is the relation of these chapters to the gospel narratives. Matthew was thought in Bulgakov's time to be the earliest of the gospels; Yeshua complains that his crazy follower Levi Matvei is always recording his words—but inaccurately. "Once I happened to see the parchment and was aghast. Absolutely nothing that was written there did I ever say."[40] At one level, this is the Devil's joke against the authority of Scripture. The Jerusalem chapters are the Devil's version of the gospel in this particular sense, that although Yeshua is a remarkable human being who makes an extraordinary impression on Pilate, there is no suggestion of his divinity or his resurrection, of transcendence or ultimate triumph. The crucifixion is described with unrelieved naturalism, and Yeshua's body, although carried off by Matvei, is retrieved by the Roman guard and buried, along with the bodies of those crucified beside him. Yet naturalism too is only one way of seeing, and this version of the Passion narrative is no more definitive than the evangelists' stories (which it partly corroborates, and partly calls into question), being itself so elaborately foregrounded as a piece of storytelling, a particular representation of a reality felt as anterior to representation. The darkness which engulfs Jerusalem at Yeshua's death is the result of bad weather, apparently nothing more, yet is uncannily echoed in the darkening storm that engulfs Moscow as Woland and his entourage take their leave, and the Master is set free. The Devil's/Master's narrative ends on the Sabbath, before the Sunday which may or may not have brought resurrection. With so much left open, it is worth noting that, at the end of the final Jerusalem chapter, space is made for a further narrative: Levi Matvei asks Pilate to give him a piece of clean parchment to write on.

In both Faust's and Byron's dealings with Mephistopheles, everything depends on not coming to an end. If nothing about the story of Yeshua and Pilate is definitive, that is perhaps because it is itself a story of unfinished business. Pilate—the master of *realpolitik*, who understands the abyss of human depravity, and whose one warm relationship is with his dog—finds himself strangely fascinated by the openness of the naïve Yeshua, who sees all men as good (even the brutal guard who strikes him) and holds that "every kind of power is a form of violence against people."[41] Pilate, the man of power, is also a man in great pain—he suffers from terrible migraines, which seem to express some deeper anguish—and Yeshua's presence speaks to him, obscurely, of the possibility of some great relief or release. Short of risking his own position, he does everything he can to prevent Yeshua's crucifixion taking place, with some hope of keeping Yeshua indefinitely by him. When the crucifixion has become inevitable, Pilate is overwhelmed by a terrible desolation:

> That same incomprehensible anguish, which had come over him on the balcony, pierced his entire being once again. He immediately tried to explain

this anguish, and the explanation was strange: the procurator had the dim sense that there was something he had not finished saying to the condemned man, or perhaps something he had not finished listening to.[42]

Pilate is haunted by the desire to continue that unfinished conversation. He cannot pursue it because, at one level, he submitted to the pressure of political reality and had Yeshua executed. But at another level, he cannot pursue it because the Master's narrative is itself unfinished, interrupted by the pressure of political realities under the Soviet regime. Meanwhile, Pilate waits eternally for his story to continue. Woland explains this to the Master as they journey into the afterlife, and it is Woland who helps to move the story of Pilate toward a kind of conclusion.

> "They have read your novel," began Woland, turning to the Master, "and they said only one thing, that, unfortunately, it is not finished. So I wanted to show you your hero. He has been sitting here for about two thousand years, sleeping, but, when the moon is full, he is tormented, as you see, by insomnia. . . . He says," Woland's voice rang out, "the same thing over and over. That the moon gives him no peace and that he has a bad job. That is what he always says when he cannot sleep, and when he does sleep, he always sees the same thing—a path of moonlight, and he wants to walk on that path, and talk with the prisoner Ha-Notsri, because, as he keeps maintaining, he did not finish what he wanted to say long ago. . . ." Woland again turned to the Master and said, "Well, then, now you can finish your novel with a single sentence!"
>
> The Master seemed to have been waiting for this as he stood motionless, looking at the seated procurator. He cupped his hands over his mouth like a megaphone and shouted so that the echo rebounded over the desolate and treeless mountains. "Free! Free! He is waiting for you!"[43]

Whereupon Pilate is released from his chair to run, "laughing or crying," down the path of moonlight to where Yeshua, we can assume, is waiting to resume their conversation.

The single sentence with which the Master "finishes his novel" is nothing like the final words he had predicted; they dwelt on Pilate the official, "the fifth procurator of Judea," a figure in history, determined by history, whereas this sentence speaks of freedom. This seems right, for these words set Pilate free from determination by the past, to enter into an ongoing dialogue. "Let's not disturb them," Woland says to the Master. "'Maybe they will come to some agreement.' Woland then waved his hand toward Yershalaim [Jerusalem], and it was extinguished."[44] Any ultimate *agreement* between Jesus and Pontius Pilate, with their opposite understandings of human nature, is hypothetical, and lies altogether beyond the story. As we saw in Blake, a marriage between heaven and hell is not easily achieved; and if Leverkühn's late music reflects each of those opposites in the other, we cannot hear it. That such reconciliation is *conceivable*, even as a remote possibility, is enough: what matters, for the moment, is the continuation of the dialogue between these opposites, the open-endedness which the Devil generates, and which he leaves behind him when he departs.

The inheritor of that open-endedness is Ivan Bezdomny, the poet who met the Devil at the start of the book, and to whom we return in the novel's brief epilogue. Years have passed, and life in Moscow has returned to normal, with the interventions of the Devil first rationalized and then forgotten—except by Ivan. Although partially recovered from his "schizophrenia," a great restlessness and trouble comes upon him every year in the spring when the moon is full. On those nights he is driven first to revisit those places in Moscow which have featured in the story, and then to dream of Golgotha, in an agony which gives way, after a tranquilizing injection, to further, happier dreams—of Pilate and Yeshua walking on a path of moonlight, "engaged in heated conversation, arguing about something, and trying to reach some kind of agreement."[45] In Ivan's dream, Pilate begs Yeshua to tell him that the execution never really happened, and Yeshua, "his eyes smiling for some reason," assents: "You only imagined it." "So that was how it ended?" Ivan asks the Master, who also appears in his dream, and the Master likewise assents. Ivan is then at peace, set free from these troubling memories—until the next full moon.[46]

That was *not* how it ended, we know. The sedated Ivan only imagines that Pilate only imagined it. The ending is not definitive, but one more variation on the story. As if to make this point, the phrase that the Master predicted would be the final words in his book, and which concluded the final numbered chapter of Bulgakov's novel, chapter 32, is repeated once more at the end of the epilogue, but this time with a tiny verbal variation,[47] as if to express both the endless, recurrent claim of Pilate's anguish upon the imagination, and the fragile possibility of dynamic change which that tiny variation suggests. And the full moon will come round again, with its troubling, deranging intimation that the material world of the here and now is likewise not definitive. What Bulgakov leaves us with is no conclusion, but rather Ivan's recurrent need to return to the story and to continue it, to pursue a conclusion, in a mirror image of Pilate's need to return to his conversation with Yeshua.

There are two things about Ivan which illuminate the importance Bulgakov gives him at the end, and entitle him to conclude this study also. One is that he is the figure most permanently affected by his encounter with the Devil. At the start he is eager to be instructed in the Soviet party line; he feels a strong, instinctive aversion to Woland, and insists to him that "man himself is in control."[48] But his obsessive, deranged pursuit of Woland through the Moscow streets already hints at interesting possibilities: his adventures leave him dressed in a Tolstoyan-style torn peasant shirt, holding a candle, with a paper icon pinned to his chest—a travesty version of a holy fool. And in the asylum we hear how, in his schizophrenia, the "old Ivan" who was obsessed with opposing and overcoming the Devil, is addressed by "the new Ivan," who accepts rather than opposes these strange events. The new Ivan retorts to the old that Woland

> is, no doubt about it, a mysterious and exceptional personality. But that's what makes it so interesting! The fellow was personally acquainted with Pontius Pilate, what could be more interesting than that? And instead of making that ridiculous scene at Patriarch's Ponds, wouldn't it have been better to have asked him politely about what happened next to Pilate and the prisoner Ha-Notsri?[49]

Like Pilate himself, Ivan finds himself wishing that he had continued his conversation with his antagonist. This desire is, in both of them, a wish met by literary creation, a wish for another chapter in the Jerusalem story. When he meets the Master, he urges him: "Tell me what happened next to Yeshua and Pilate. Please, I want to know." And when the Master refuses—his novel now makes him shudder, "your friend from Patriarch's Ponds [i.e., the Devil] could have done it better than I"[50]—Ivan then dreams that next chapter, as we have seen, and so brings or returns it into existence.

For the second thing that matters about Ivan is that he is a writer. He begins as a poet publishing under the regime, but in the asylum the new Ivan feels a "sudden and inexplicable aversion to poetry." "I won't be writing any more poems."[51] Literature of that kind seems hatefully dishonest to him; he gives up his writing. Yet not entirely, or unambiguously. He is given pencil and paper in the asylum (somewhat as Matvei is given a piece of clean parchment by Pilate) and writes a "confused and incomprehensible" narrative of the encounter with Woland and Woland's narrative of Pilate.[52] He makes a better job of retelling all this to the Master, and is "excited by the success of his storytelling."[53] And near the end, when the Master takes leave of him forever, "Ivanushka smiled and stared with crazed eyes into the distance" and tells the Master, "I want to write something else," to which the Master replies, "That's good, that's good. You'll write the sequel about him."[54] Ivan thus joins the Master as another virtual double of Bulgakov, one of the book's several circles of overlapping narrative consciousness. The Master first enters the book as if he were Ivan's hallucination in the clinic, and even in the second half of the novel, where we see events largely from Margarita's point of view, we are reminded at key moments of the existence of the central characters in Ivan's consciousness. When Margarita meets the Devil, he is first described as "the one whom poor Ivan, at Patriarch's Ponds, had recently tried to convince of the Devil's non-existence," and when the Master is restored to her, he is first described as "Ivan's night visitor, who called himself the Master."[55] How does the Master know that he is in the presence of the Devil? Because "that boy Ivan Bezdomny told me about you."[56]

All this subtly prepares us for the book's return to Ivan at the very end, and for how the sense of a great unfinished business has passed to him. Unbearably restless in the spring full moon, marked forever by his encounter with the Devil, he lives between two worlds, and in his dreams reanimates an old story and strives to bring it forward to a new conclusion. There could be no better fable—or perhaps, demonstration—of the Devil's efficacy as Muse.

NOTES

Chapter 1

1   Keats to Shelley, 16 August 1820, in *The Letters of John Keats, 1814–1821*, ed. H. E. Rollins, 2 vols. (Cambridge, Mass.: Harvard University Press, 1958), 2:322–23.

2   See Spenser, *The Faerie Queene*, book 2, canto 7, sts. 24–28.

3   Keats to Woodhouse, 27 October 1818, *Letters*, 1:386–87 (spelling modernized).

4   *The Complete Poetry and Prose of William Blake*, ed. David V. Erdman, rev. ed. (Berkeley: University of California Press, 1982), 634.

5   *Blake: The Complete Poems*, ed. W. H. Stevenson, 3rd ed. (Harlow: Pearson/Longman, 2007), 124; *Byron: The Complete Poetical Works*, ed. Jerome McGann, 7 vols. (Oxford: Oxford University Press, 1980–1993), vol. 5: *Don Juan*, xv.22.

6   See in particular A's essay "Rotation of Crops": Søren Kierkegaard, *Either/Or*, ed. and trans. H. V. Hong and E. H. Hong, 2 vols. (Princeton: Princeton University Press, 1987), part I, 281–300.

7   Kierkegaard, *Either/Or*, part I, 70.

8   Kierkegaard, *Either/Or*, part I, 100–101. I do not consider here the adequacy of A's account of *Don Giovanni*, though this is both tenable and powerful. Bernard Williams' thoughtful reflections on it ("Don Giovanni as an Idea," in W. A. Mozart, *Don Giovanni*, ed. Julian Rushton [Cambridge: Cambridge University Press, 1981]) effectively endorse its view of Giovanni as "the life principle . . . energy in action, unselfconsciousness" and acknowledge as problematic the question of whether there is

"anything left to the idea of an order against which he is to be judged"
(85). In *The Roots of Romanticism* (London: Pimlico, 2000), Isaiah Berlin
took the nineteenth-century excision of the opera's final sextet to epitomize Romanticism's rejection of fixed or given truth structures in favor
of allegiance to the ever-onward, insatiable will and the larger-than-life
mythmaking which the Romantic attitude fosters. According to the
Romantic view, "here is this vast, dominating, sinister symbolic figure,
Don Giovanni, who stands for we know not what, but certainly for something inexpressible. He stands, perhaps, for art against life, for some principle of inexhaustible evil against some kind of philistine good; he stands
for power, for magic . . . and then suddenly this philistine little sextet
follows, in which the characters simply sing peacefully about the fact
that a rake has been punished, and good men will continue their ordinary,
perfectly peaceful lives thereafter. This was regarded as inartistic, shal-
low, bathetic and disgusting, and therefore eliminated" (123). A's account
of *Don Giovanni* is, perhaps, inadequate in proportion as it is unable to
accommodate the qualities of comic irony in the opera with which the
final sextet connects.

9   Kierkegaard, *Either/Or*, part I, 64–65.
10 Thomas Mann, *Doctor Faustus: The Life of the German Composer Adrian
    Leverkühn as Told by a Friend*, trans. H. T. Lowe-Porter (Harmondsworth:
    Penguin, 1968), 235, slightly altered.
11 Mann, *Faustus*, 230.
12 John Berger, *G.* (London: Chatto & Windus, 1985), 133.
13 Mann, *Faustus*, 150.
14 Mann, *Faustus*, 235–36, slightly altered.
15 Mann, *Faustus*, 222.
16 Mann, *Faustus*, 158.
17 Mann, *Faustus*, 131–12 (emphasis in original).
18 Mann, *Faustus*, 231–32. The first phrase is altered.
19 Mann, *Faustus*, 232.
20 Mann, *Faustus*, 235.
21 Mann, *Faustus*, 231, slightly altered. This draws on a passage in *Ecce Homo*,
    where Nietzsche describes the state of inspiration in which *Zarathustra*
    was composed. In an essay on Nietzsche, Mann praises the passage as a
    stylistic masterpiece, while also seeing in it the overstimulation of syphilis
    and commenting that Nietzsche overestimated the merits of *Zarathustra*.
    Thomas Mann, "Nietzsche's Philosophy in the Light of Recent History,"
    in *Last Essays*, trans. R. Winston and C. Winston (London: Secker & War-
    burg, 1959), 147–48.

22 Mann, *Faustus*, 61, slightly altered.

23 Mann, *Faustus*, 359.

24 Mann, *Faustus*, 361.

25 Mann, *Faustus*, 359.

26 Mann, *Faustus*, 364.

27 Mann, *Faustus*, 364, slightly altered.

28 Mann's late essay "Nietzsche's Philosophy" recounts the brothel anecdote and Nietzsche's subsequent contraction—"some say deliberately"—of syphilis, the disease which is another name for Nietzsche's "genius" (144–45). The essay is full of the themes of the novel. "Culture for Nietzsche is the aristocracy of life; and linked with it, as its sources and prerequisites, are art and instinct, whereas the mortal enemies and destroyers of culture and life are consciousness and cognition, science, and finally morality" (151). In the essay, Mann identifies two great errors in Nietzsche's thinking. One is his academic's supposition that the forces of instinct needed defending against the danger of oppression by the intellect; "recent history," i.e., the rise of fascism, refutes that fallacy. The second is "the utterly false relationship into which he puts life and morality when he treats them as antagonists. The truth is that they belong together. Ethics is the prop of life, and the moral man a true citizen of life's realm—perhaps a somewhat boring fellow, but highly useful. The real dichotomy lies between ethics and aesthetics" (162). With this critical revision of Nietzsche's insight we are at the heart of *Doctor Faustus*.

29 Mann, "Nietzsche's Philosophy," 156, 172. For a reading of Nietzsche which holds to this emphasis, see Alexander Nehamas, *Nietzsche: Life as Literature* (Cambridge, Mass.: Harvard University Press, 1985).

30 Mann, *Faustus*, 467.

31 Mann, *Faustus*, 467, 468.

32 Mann, *Faustus*, 240, slightly altered.

33 *The History of Doctor Johann Faustus*, trans. H. G. Haile (Urbana: University of Illinois Press, 1965), 131.

34 Mann, *Faustus*, 482, slightly altered.

35 Mann, *Faustus*, 488.

36 Mann, *Faustus*, 234, slightly altered.

37 Theodor W. Adorno, "Cultural Criticism and Society," in *The Adorno Reader*, ed. Brian O'Connor (Oxford: Blackwell, 2000), 210; Theodor W. Adorno, *Negative Dialectics*, trans. E. B. Ashton (New York: Seabury Press, 1973), 367. Mann drew directly on Adorno's writings and conversation for his treatment of music in the novel.

38 This is discussed further in the final chapter of this work.

39 Heinrich von Kleist, *Selected Writings*, trans. David Constantine (London: J. M. Dent, 1997), 414.

40 Mann, *Faustus*, 298.

41 Mann, *Faustus*, 182, slightly altered.

42 Mann, *Faustus*, 238, slightly altered.

43 Mann, *Faustus*, 255.

Chapter 2

1 Samuel Taylor Coleridge, *The Collected Works of Samuel Taylor Coleridge: Volume 16.1.1. Poems (Reading Text)*, ed. J. C. C. Mays (Princeton: Princeton University Press, 2001), 514.

2 *Blake: The Complete Poems*, ed. W. H. Stevenson, 3rd ed. (Harlow: Pearson/ Longman, 2007), 129, 124.

3 Derek Attridge, *The Singularity of Literature* (London: Routledge, 2004), 60.

4 Attridge, *Singularity of Literature*, 28.

5 Ezra Pound, *ABC of Reading* (London: Faber & Faber, 1961), 29 (emphasis in original).

6 Attridge, *Singularity of Literature*, 28.

7 Attridge, *Singularity of Literature*, 60, 124.

8 Henry Ansgar Kelly, *Satan: A Biography* (Cambridge: Cambridge University Press, 2006).

9 Jeffrey Burton Russell, *The Devil: Perceptions of Evil from Antiquity to Primitive Christianity* (Ithaca: Cornell University Press, 1977), 174.

10 John Holland, *The Smoke Out of the Bottomlesse Pit* (London, 1650), 5; quoted in Nathan Johnstone, *The Devil and Demonism in Early Modern England* (Cambridge: Cambridge University Press, 2006), 268. Insofar as Ranter beliefs were the projection of their opponents, they are no less significant for that, but versions of the view attributed in the quotation can be found in Jacob Bauthumley, *The Light and Dark Sides of God*; Raunce Burthall, *An Old Bridle for a Wilde Asse-Colt*; and Laurence Clarkson, *A Single Eye All Light, No Darkness: Or Light and Darkness One*, all published in London in 1650.

11 Neil Forsyth, *The Satanic Epic* (Princeton: Princeton University Press, 2003), carefully analyzes many passages in which *Paradise Lost* "loosens the relation between Milton's Satan and the firm place given the Devil by the Church Fathers" (80), permitting a much fuller engagement with Satan than the received theology would seem to allow. His account of Satan's relevant prehistory differs, however, from mine; Forsyth sees in him the antagonist of archaic combat myth, opponent of the myth's hero,

but not otherwise or essentially evil. In the Bible, Forsyth concedes, "the myth is nowhere spelled out in full. To find out what it said we need to turn to its sources"—Canaanite, Greek, and gnostic myth—rather than to the pre-New Testament *satan*, where "we soon lose touch with the combat myth" (28, 37).

12 Goethe, *Faust*, ed. Erich Trunz (Munich: C. H. Beck, 1972), lines 1331–38 (my translation).

13 Thomas Mann, *Doctor Faustus: The Life of the German Composer Adrian Leverkühn as Told by a Friend*, trans. H. T. Lowe-Porter (Harmondsworth: Penguin, 1968), 219.

14 John Milton, *Paradise Lost*, ed. Gordon Teskey (New York: Norton, 2005), v.658–60.

15 This "so called" formula recurs in the references to Lucifer at v.760 and x.425. For full discussion, see John Leonard, *Naming in Paradise: Milton and the Language of Adam and Eve* (Oxford: Clarendon, 1990), chap. 2, esp. 86–101, 140–46.

16 Forsyth intriguingly suggests that the early Christian promotion of this identification was intended to counter "a Gnostic heresy that identified the serpent with Christ, the bringer of wisdom" (*Satanic Epic*, 46). See Elaine Pagels, *Adam, Eve, and the Serpent* (London: Weidenfeld & Nicolson, 1988); and A. D. Nuttall, *The Alternative Trinity: Gnostic Heresy in Marlowe, Milton, and Blake* (Oxford: Clarendon, 1998), 10–21.

17 When in the *De Doctrina Christiana* Milton cites Isaiah 45:7, where God describes himself as *"making peace and creating evil,"* he adds this dubious clarification: "that is, what afterwards became and is now evil, for whatever God created was originally good, as he himself testifies, Gen. i." *Complete Prose Works of John Milton*, ed. Don M. Wolfe et al., 8 vols. (New Haven: Yale University Press, 1953–1982), 6:330. This flinches from the plain import of the verse in Isaiah, but it also suggests how attention to the process of *becoming*—to *genesis*, precisely—might make possible apprehension of what is otherwise contradiction.

18 Elaine Pagels, *The Origin of Satan* (Penguin: London, 1996), 49.

19 Pagels, *Satan*, 8.

20 Pagels, *Satan*, 49 (emphasis in original).

21 *Byron: The Complete Poetical Works*, ed. Jerome McGann, 7 vols. (Oxford: Oxford University Press, 1980–1993), 6:228.

22 For contemporary responses, see T. G. Steffan, *Lord Byron's Cain* (Austin: University of Texas Press, 1968).

23 *The Complete Works of Percy Bysshe Shelley*, ed. Roger Ingpen and Walter E. Peck, 10 vols. (New York: Gordian Press, 1965), 7:104, 89, 87.

24 Charles Baudelaire, *The Poems in Prose*, trans. Francis Scarfe (London: Anvil Press Poetry, 1989), 128–29.

25 *His Very Self and Voice: Collected Conversations of Lord Byron*, ed. Ernest J. Lovell (New York: Macmillan, 1954), 569.

26 Keats to Woodhouse, 27 October 1818, in *The Letters of John Keats 1814–1821*, ed. H. E. Rollins, 2 vols. (Cambridge, Mass.: Harvard University Press, 1958), 1:386–87.

27 Thomas Mann, *Lotte in Weimar*, trans. H. T. Lowe-Porter (Harmondsworth: Penguin, 1968), 69–70.

28 Mann, *Lotte in Weimar*, 72.

29 Mann, *Lotte in Weimar*, 74.

30 Mann, *Lotte in Weimar*, 75.

31 Blake, *Poems*, 112, but without the editorial punctuation which somewhat reduces the ambiguity of Blake's phrasing: following the facsimile in *The Illuminated Blake*, ed. David V. Erdman (London: Oxford University Press, 1975), 103.

32 Ivan Turgenev, *Faust*, trans. Hugh Aplin (London: Hesperus, 2003), 11 (emphasis in original).

33 Turgenev, *Faust*, 38.

34 Turgenev, *Faust*, 45. Turgenev takes Faust's bitter "You must renounce, renounce" (Goethe, *Faust*, line 1549) as his epigraph.

35 Turgenev, *Faust*, 26.

36 Turgenev, *Faust*, 5.

37 Søren Kierkegaard, *Either/Or*, ed. and trans. H. V. Hong and E. H. Hong, 2 vols. (Princeton: Princeton University Press, 1987), part I, 226.

38 *The Selected Poetry of Rainer Maria Rilke*, trans. Stephen Mitchell (London: Pan Books, 1987), 193–97 (emphasis in original), substituting "unsupervised" for Mitchell's "unseparated" (*das Unüberwachte*).

39 T. S. Eliot, *On Poetry and Poets* (London: Faber & Faber, 1957), 143.

40 Lucy Newlyn's excellent study *Paradise Lost and the Romantic Reader* (Oxford: Clarendon, 1993) finely brings out the responsiveness of Romantic writers to the "double" or "equivocal" aspects of Milton's poem; she relates the "double perspective" often generated through their allusions to Milton to "the growth of consciousness that comes with falling" (220–21).

41 Blake, *Poems*, 111.

Chapter 3

1 *Blake: The Complete Poems*, ed. W. H. Stevenson, 3rd ed. (Harlow: Pearson/ Longman, 2007), 111–12.

2 Blake, *Poems*, 112.

3 Blake, *Poems*, 124.

4   *The Complete Poetry and Prose of William Blake*, ed. David V. Erdman, rev. ed. (Berkeley: University of California Press, 1982), 592; John Milton, *Paradise Lost*, ed. Gordon Teskey (New York: Norton, 2005), iv.110.

5   Blake, *Poems*, 127.

6   Blake, *Poems*, 75–78.

7   Blake, *Poems*, 225.

8   See, e.g., Ben Wilson, *Decency and Disorder: The Age of Cant 1789–1837* (London: Faber, 2007), 51–223.

9   Blake, *Poems*, 74.

10 Blake, *Poems*, 127–29.

11 "One such gnostic Christian, the author of the *Testimony of Truth* . . . dared to tell the story of Paradise from the serpent's point of view, and depicted the serpent as a teacher of divine wisdom who desperately tried to get Adam and Eve to open their eyes to their creator's true—and despicable—nature:
>   For the serpent was *wiser* than any of the animals that were in Paradise. . . . But the creator cursed the serpent, and called him devil."
Elaine Pagels, *Adam, Eve, and the Serpent* (London: Weidenfeld & Nicolson, 1988), 69. Pages 60–77 suggest several other points of striking affinity with Blake. For Blake and gnostic thought, especially in its tendency to denigrate God the Father, Creator and giver of the Law, see A. D. Nuttall, *The Alternative Trinity: Gnostic Heresy in Marlowe, Milton, and Blake* (Oxford: Clarendon, 1998), 192–272.

12 Blake, *Poems*, 366.

13 Blake, *Poems*, 365.

14 Blake, *Poems*, 386.

15 Blake, *Poems*, 388.

16 Blake, *Poems*, 389.

17 Blake, *Poems*, 404.

18 Northrop Frye, *Fearful Symmetry: A Study of William Blake* (Boston: Beacon Press, 1962), 219 and 187–226.

19 For fuller discussion of the evolving figure of Orc and "the heroic ambiguity of energy" (82), see Morton D. Paley, *Energy and the Imagination: A Study of the Development of Blake's Thought* (Oxford: Clarendon, 1970), esp. 61–88.

20 Urizen "saw the secret terror | Flame high in pride, & laugh to scorn the source of his deceit, | Nor knew the source of his own, but thought himself the sole author | Of all his wandering experiments in the horrible abyss": Blake, *Poems*, 388–89. Blake is remembering Satan's confidence in his own self-authorship: Milton, *Paradise Lost* v.853–63.

21 These replace the "german-forged links" of an earlier draft (Blake, *Poems*, 161n). The inhabitants of London are restrained not so much by the

Hanoverian establishment as by the processes of their own minds—which rebellion or revolution can scarcely hope to undo.

22 The role of contemporary political events in this ambivalence has its analogue in *Paradise Lost*. Milton also passionately identified with a rebellion in the cause of liberty that he saw to fail not because it was put down by monarchy, but under the pressure of its own internal contradictions. Satan's Cromwellian associations are an important factor in the complexity of feeling he arouses, contributing to the interplay of multiple perspectives that so involves the reader.

23 Blake, *Poems*, 127.

24 William Godwin, *An Enquiry Concerning Political Justice, 1793*, 2 vols. (New York: Woodstock Books, 1992), 1:261–62.

25 Blake, *Poems*, 113–16, 127 (italics in original).

26 Blake, *Poems*, 114.

27 Blake, *Poems*, 218.

28 Alexander Pope, *Poetical Works*, ed. Herbert Davis (London: Oxford University Press, 1966), 267.

29 Lorraine Clark refers to this poem in particular in discussing how the absence of an authoritative personal voice in Blake "threatens to dissolve the authority of the text into radical perspectivism or unmastered irony"; *Blake, Kierkegaard, and the Spectre of Dialectic* (Cambridge: Cambridge University Press, 1991), 130. She argues that Blake overcomes this danger by moving, especially in the later poems, away from "both/and" to the decisiveness (as she reads Kierkegaard) of a Kierkegaardian "either/or." She applauds this as a piece of ethical thinking; insofar as I agree with her account, I want to deplore its consequences for the poetry.

30 T. S. Eliot, *Selected Essays*, 3rd ed. (London: Faber & Faber, 1951), 303.

31 Blake, *Poems*, 221–22.

32 Blake, *Poems*, 117, 119.

33 Voltaire, *Philosophical Dictionary*, trans. Peter Gay (New York: Harcourt, Brace, & World, 1962), 197.

34 Blake, *Complete Poetry and Prose*, 565–66.

35 Pope, *Poetical Works*, 92.

36 Entry in Crabb Robinson's diary, 24 July 1811, in *William Blake: The Critical Heritage*, ed. G. E. Bentley (London: Routledge & Kegan Paul, 1975), 69.

37 Entry in Crabb Robinson's diary, 24 July 1811, in *Blake: The Critical Heritage*, 69.

38 *Jubilate Agno*, B.89, in Christopher Smart, *The Poetical Works of Christopher Smart. Volume I*, ed. Karina Williamson (Oxford: Clarendon, 1980), 26.

39 Blake, *Poems*, 219.

40 Thomas Mann, *Doctor Faustus: The Life of the German Composer Adrian Leverkühn as Told by a Friend*, trans. H. T. Lowe-Porter (Harmondsworth: Penguin, 1968), 161.

41 See Mann, *Faustus*, 161, 255.

42 Blake, *Poems*, 152–53.

43 Mann, *Faustus*, 161.

44 See A. D. Nuttall, *The Alternative Trinity: Gnostic Heresy in Marlowe, Milton, and Blake* (Oxford: Clarendon, 1998), 243–52.

45 Mann, *Faustus*, 221, altered. "Engel des Giftes" is rendered by Lowe-Porter as "angel of death."

46 "London," in Blake, *Poems*, 220.

47 *Diary, Reminiscences, and Correspondence of Henry Crabb Robinson*, ed. Thomas Sadler, 3 vols. (London: Macmillan, 1869), 2:310.

48 Blake, *Poems*, 169.

49 Blake, *Poems*, 174.

50 See, e.g., *Milton*, 41:25–33; *Jerusalem*, 44:33 (Blake, *Poems*, 599, 755).

51 *Milton*, 33:17–19 (Blake, *Poems*, 579). The Divine Voice, be it noted, is lecturing his own jealous wife on the subject! The same fantasy appears in *Jerusalem*, 69:15 (Blake, *Poems*, 821).

52 Blake, *Poems*, 223, but with the "R" in Rose capitalized as in the plate.

53 Blake, *Poems*, 565; *Milton*, 27:37–39.

54 *The Literary Works of Matthew Prior*, ed. H. Bunker Wright and Monroe K. Spears, 2 vols. (Oxford: Clarendon, 1959), 1:455 (spelling modernized).

55 F. J. Lelièvre, "The Basis of Ancient Parody," *Greece and Rome* 1 (1954): 66–81, 66, with Greek transliterated.

56 Margaret Rose, *Parody: Ancient, Modern, and Post-Modern* (Cambridge: Cambridge University Press, 1993), 45–47.

57 Dorothy Van Ghent, *The English Novel: Form and Function* (New York: Rinehart, 1953), 13 (emphasis in original).

58 See *Milton*, 40:32–36; *Jerusalem*, 10:7–16, 17:32–35 (Blake, *Poems*, 597–98, 676, 693).

59 Mikhail Bakhtin, *Problems of Dostoevsky's Poetics*, ed. and trans. Caryl Emerson (Manchester: Manchester University Press, 1984), 193. See also 181–237 and Rose's discusssion of Bakhtin in *Parody*, 125–70.

60 Linda Hutcheon, *A Theory of Parody: The Teachings of Twentieth-Century Art Forms* (Urbana: University of Illinois Press, 2000), 6.

61 Hutcheon, *Parody*, 26.

62 One example: the design "I want! I want!" in Blake's 1793 emblem book, *For Children: The Gates of Paradise*, reworks Gillray's political cartoon, "The Straight Gate or the way to the Patriot's Paradise." In Gillray's picture

the deluded radical struggles toward the flag of Liberty, where stands a ladder pointing vainly toward the moon in the sky. In Blake's design, there is no apparent political reference, but an immensely extended (if fragile) ladder successfully connects the earth with the moon, and a youthful figure is about to climb it. For discussion, see David Erdman, *Blake: Prophet against Empire*, 3rd ed. (Princeton: Princeton University Press, 1977), 202–4.

63 See Elaine Pagels, *The Gnostic Gospels* (London: Weidenfeld & Nicolson, 1979), 29, 58. E.g., "he boasted continually, saying . . . 'I am God, and no other one exists except me.' But when he said these things, he sinned against all of the immortal ones . . . when Faith saw the impiety of the chief ruler, she was angry . . . she said, 'You err, Samael (i.e., 'blind god'). An enlightened, immortal humanity [*anthropos*] exists before you!'" in *The Nag Hammadi Library in English*, ed. J. M. Robinson (New York: Harper, 1979), 165; quoted in Pagels, 29.

64 Blake, *Poems*, 112.

65 William Hazlitt, "Letter to William Gifford," in *The Complete Works of William Hazlitt*, ed. P. P. Howe, 21 vols. (London: J. M. Dent, 1930–1934), 9:37.

66 Paley, *Energy*, 87.

Chapter 4

Parts of the argument in this chapter have appeared in a different form in *Cambridge Quarterly*, 30.1, and in *International Faust Studies*, ed. Lorna Fitzsimmons (New York: Continuum, 2008).

1 *Byron: The Critical Heritage*, ed. Andrew Rutherford (London: Routledge & Kegan Paul, 1970), 180–81.

2 Journal entry, 27 November 1813, in *Byron's Letters and Journals*, ed. Leslie A. Marchand, 12 vols. (London: John Murray, 1973–1982), 3:225.

3 Caroline Lamb's prescient description in her journal of 1812, quoted in Fiona MacCarthy, *Byron: Life and Legend* (London: John Murray, 2002), 164.

4 *His Very Self and Voice: Collected Conversations of Lord Byron*, ed. Ernest J. Lovell (New York: Macmillan, 1954), 106.

5 Byron, *Critical Heritage*, 39.

6 Byron, *Critical Heritage*, 38–39.

7 Byron, *Critical Heritage*, 53–54.

8 Byron, *Critical Heritage*, 98, 100.

9 Byron, *Critical Heritage*, 115.

10 *Byron: The Complete Poetical Works*, ed. Jerome McGann, 7 vols. (Oxford: Oxford University Press, 1980–1993), vol. 5: *Don Juan*, xiii.5.

11 Germaine de Staël, *Germany*, 3 vols. (London: John Murray, 1813), 1:268; Germaine de Staël, *De l'Allemagne*, ed. S. Balayé, 2 vols. (Paris: Garnier-Flammarion, 1968), 1:190.

12   Line-references to Goethe's *Faust*, given parenthetically in the text, are to the edition by Erich Trunz (Munich: C. H. Beck, 1972).

13   Satan in *Paradise Lost*, i.249–50.

14   Søren Kierkegaard, *Either/Or*, ed. and trans. H. V. Hong and E. H. Hong, 2 vols. (Princeton: Princeton University Press, 1987), part I, 106–8.

15   Kierkegaard, *Either/Or*, part I, 70.

16   *Byron: Poetical Works*, 6:15.

17   George Finlay to Leicester Stanhope, June 1824; *His Very Self and Voice*, 458.

18   Quoted in *Faustus: From the German of Goethe*, ed. Frederick Burwick and James C. McKusick (Oxford: Clarendon, 2007), 123.

19   Byron, *Letters and Journals*, 7:113.

20   Goethe himself recognized this when he referred to the child of Faust and Helen, who appears in *Faust: Part Two*—a youth of enchanting loveliness, springing from Faust's encounter with the spirit of an idealized Greece, who climbs too high to live long—as a portrait of Byron.

21   *Life And Writings of Joseph Mazzini*, 6 vols. (London: Smith, Elder, 1870), 6:79.

22   J. W. Goethe, *Essays on Art and Literature*, ed. J. Gearey (Princeton: Princeton University Press, 1994), 175.

23   Byron, *Letters and Journals*, 5:144; also 11:172; and in Byron's note to line 380 in *Hints from Horace*, *Poetical Works*, 1:437.

24   *The Complete Works of Percy Bysshe Shelley*, ed. Roger Ingpen and Walter E. Peck, 10 vols. (New York: Gordian Press, 1965), 7:104.

25   From the prose scene "Dreary Day. Field," after line 4398.

26   One might compare Goya's depictions of witchcraft—satirical, yet nonetheless haunting—in, e.g., the later plates of *Los Caprichos*, before these turn into the nightmare of the late "black" paintings.

27   *Complete Works of Shelley*, 10:378.

28   J. P. Eckermann, *Gespräche mit Goethe in den letzten Jahren seines Lebens*, ed. E. Beutler (Munich: Deutscher Taschenbuch Verlag, 1976), 251.

29   Goethe to Schiller, 6 April 1801, in *Goethe: Briefe*, ed. Philipp Stein, 8 vols. (Berlin: Wertbuchhandel, 1924), 5:29 (my translation).

30   *Medwin's Conversations of Lord Byron*, ed. Ernest J. Lovell (Princeton: Princeton University Press, 1966), 130 (emphasis in original).

31   Percy Bysshe Shelley, *Posthumous Poems* (London: John & Henry Hunt, 1824), 398.

32   When Crabb Robinson visited Goethe in 1829, he found Goethe overflowing with admiration for the *Vision*, in which "Byron has surpassed himself." *Diary, Reminiscences, and Correspondence of Henry Crabb Robinson*, ed. Thomas Sadler, 3 vols. (London: Macmillan, 1869), 2:436.

33 See Jerome J. McGann, *Towards a Literature of Knowledge* (Oxford: Oxford University Press, 1989), 38–64. McGann sees Byron's way of maintaining oppositions as calling into question Romantic ideals of self-integrity and identity, since these depend, by the Hegelian analysis, on the negation of "Otherness, that which is not the subject . . . in the process of knowledge we call consciousness" (41).

34 Shelley, *Posthumous Poems*, 398.

35 All the versions of *Faust* published in Byron's lifetime omit the prologue. Anster explains in *Blackwood's* that it "is written in a light and irreverent tone, and possesses, we think, very little merit of any kind." The introduction to the 1821 translation, which Burwick and McKusick attribute to Coleridge, declares it "repugnant to notions of propriety such as are entertained in this country" (*Faustus*, ed. Burwick and McKusick, 230, 7).

36 *Critical Heritage*, 162–63 (emphasis in original). *Don Juan* indeed became a book for the "vulgar"; as Byron's sales dropped among the fashionable classes, its cheap and pirate editions found a new and much larger popular readership. Piquantly, it was "probably read by thousands who read no other book of any kind except the Bible." William St. Clair, "The Impact of Byron's Writings: An Evaluative Approach," in *Byron: Augustan and Romantic*, ed. Andrew Rutherford (London: Macmillan, 1990), 13–19 (18).

37 As reported by Severn. Byron, *Critical Heritage*, 163.

38 Byron, *Critical Heritage*, 161.

39 *Lord Byron: The Complete Miscellaneous Prose*, ed. Andrew Nicholson (Oxford: Clarendon, 1991), 128.

40 de Staël, *De l'Allemagne*, 1:355, 190.

41 On John Johnson I am much indebted to Anne Barton's discussion in *Byron: Don Juan* (Cambridge: Cambridge University Press, 1992), 47–49, 56–58.

42 We recall the "riddle" whereby the Devil speaks of himself as one who, willing evil, produces good. Negation is—perhaps—creative beyond and despite its own purposes. But in the lovers' relationship Gretchen uncovers the same riddle in an inverted form: "But everything that brought me to sin—O God!—it was so good, so lovely!" (3585–86).

43 Byron, *Critical Heritage*, 203.

44 Thomas Mann, *Doctor Faustus: The Life of the German Composer Adrian Leverkühn as Told by a Friend*, trans. H. T. Lowe-Porter (Harmondsworth: Penguin, 1968), 238.

45 Eckermann, *Gespräche mit Goethe*, 313; Kierkegaard, *Either/Or*, part I, 205, and see also 90–91.

46 Bernard Beatty has written well about this aspect of the poem in *Byron's Don Juan* (London: Croom Helm, 1985). He argues that when the poem

breaks off it is preparing its own deliverance through the figure of Aurora Raby, who brings with her values beyond the reach of the narrator's negativity, and whose connection with Juan will redeem him from the nullity of London life. If this is right, then Aurora would take approximately the same place in *Don Juan* that Gretchen has in *Faust*: a crucial third center of consciousness that stands altogether clear of the rhythm of aspiration (or lament) and bathos.

47 No one, in fact, has the last word; the last line is given to an unexplained "*Voice: from inside*: Heinrich! Heinrich!" eerily echoing Gretchen's cry. Even without knowing that Goethe was already drafting passages for a second part, we feel the lack of closure in what we have. The imaginative effect mirrors the actual trajectory of composition: the final scene is substantially already there in the earliest draft of *Faust*, without those unattributed "voices," but it proved to be only the beginning of a project that extended over more than fifty years.

48 Beatty, *Byron's Don Juan*, 46.

49 Jerome McGann, *Don Juan in Context* (London: John Murray, 1976), 95.

50 Charles Baudelaire, "Of the Essence of Laughter, and generally of the Comic in the Plastic Arts," in *Selected Writings on Art and Artists*, trans. P. E. Charvet (Cambridge: Cambridge University Press, 1972), 160.

51 Baudelaire, "Of Laughter," 145, 148.

52 Baudelaire, "Of Laughter," 148.

53 See further Anne Barton's wonderfully suggestive discussion of *The Deformed Transformed* as itself "the dark twin" of *Don Juan*: "*Don Juan* Transformed," in *Byron: Augustan and Romantic*, 191–220 (200).

54 Byron, *Letters and Journals*, 11:172.

55 Baudelaire, "Of Laughter," 143.

Chapter 5

1 Thomas Mann, *Doctor Faustus: The Life of the German Composer Adrian Leverkühn as Told by a Friend*, trans. H. T. Lowe-Porter (Harmondsworth: Penguin, 1968), 11, 9, 9.

2 Mann, *Faustus*, 10–11, slightly altered.

3 Mann, *Faustus*, 10.

4 Mann, *Faustus*, 15.

5 Mann, *Faustus*, 10.

6 Mann, *Faustus*, 14, slightly altered.

7 Mann, *Faustus*, 14, slightly altered.

8 Mann, *Faustus*, 490.

9 Mann, *Faustus*, 297.

10 Mann, *Faustus*, 330.

11 Mann, *Faustus*, 298.

12 Mann, *Faustus*, 485.

13 Love and parody are connected by Mann elsewhere, in the mouth of Goethe: "culture is parody—love and parody." Thomas Mann, *Lotte in Weimar*, trans. H. T. Lowe-Porter (Harmondsworth: Penguin, 1968), 215.

14 Mann, *Faustus*, 11.

15 Mann, *Faustus*, 11–12, slightly altered.

16 Mann, *Faustus*, 182, slightly altered.

17 Mann, *Faustus*, 399.

18 Erich Heller, *Thomas Mann: The Ironic German*, 2nd ed. (Cambridge: Cambridge University Press, 1981), 259–60.

19 Thomas Mann, *The Genesis of a Novel*, trans. Richard Winston and Clara Winston (London: Secker & Warburg, 1961), 33, 74.

20 Mann, *Genesis*, 18, 13.

21 Mann, *Genesis*, 30, 37, 55, 107.

22 Mann, *Genesis*, 126.

23 Mann, *Genesis*, 37.

24 Mann, *Genesis*, 83.

25 Mann, *Genesis*, 144.

26 Mann, *Genesis*, 124.

27 Mann, *Genesis*, 34.

28 Mann, *Faustus*, 235.

29 Mann, *Faustus*, 469. These passages constitute something of a crux in discussions of parody in *Doctor Faustus*. Erich Heller, in *Thomas Mann: The Ironic German*, sees the novel as endorsing the Devil's dismissiveness. "It is the hero of the novel, not the novelist, who has produced an authentically great work. Without the Devil's help the artist is condemned to the sphere of higher parody, the only thing that is still left when the 'real thing' has become impossible" (274). That Mann himself has written the whole novel in the spirit of parody, through the voice of Zeitblom, is a tribute to his understanding of what has become impossible; it is "the novelist's offer of abdication, the *nom de plume* of silence" (279). Bond Johnson's excellent study in *The Mode of Parody* (Frankfurt: Peter Lang, 2000), on the other hand, distinguishes the Devil's negativity (seen as the projection of Leverkühn's premature despair) from a more positive sense of the renewing and rejuvenating powers of parody which *Doctor Faustus* exemplifies, not least in this very dialogue with the Devil. Given that the *Lamentation* is a masterpiece, Heller supposes Zeitblom must be essentially right in describing it as being without parody; apart from only "a

faint echo of the old cynically-parodistic manner," this music is so "pure" that it can suggest "the hope beyond hopelessness, the transcendence of despair" (278). Johnson, however, disputes Zeitblom's judgment that the *Lamentation* is composed without parody; through invoking the *Faustbook*, baroque forms, and the expressive model of Monteverdi, the *Lamentation* is surely still parodic, but in a sense beyond the Devil's cynicism. "It is through parody that he achieves the breakthrough to expression. . . . His failure to reject parody totally from his creative process is in part responsible for the hope beyond hopelessness at the conclusion of his final work" (116). This difference between two fine critical discussions illustrates the ambiguousness of parody's relation to negativity.

30 Mann, *Faustus*, 471, slightly altered.

31 Mann, *Faustus*, 471.

32 Mann, *Faustus*, 215.

33 Mann, *Faustus*, 214, slightly altered.

34 Goethe, *Faust*, ed. Erich Trunz (Munich: C. H. Beck, 1972), lines 1335–36 (my translation).

35 Mikhail Bulgakov, *The Master and Margarita*, trans. Diana Burgin and Katherine Tiernan O'Connor (London: Picador, 1997), 12.

36 Bulgakov, *Master and Margarita*, 245.

37 Bulgakov, *Master and Margarita*, 112.

38 It is notable that Jesus makes a *request* of the Devil, who assents and gives commands. "Nothing is difficult for me to do" (305). All *power* in this book lies with the Devil—which is not to say that it is always used for evil.

39 Bulgakov, *Master and Margarita*, 325.

40 Bulgakov, *Master and Margarita*, 16.

41 Bulgakov, *Master and Margarita*, 22.

42 Bulgakov, *Master and Margarita*, 26.

43 Bulgakov, *Master and Margarita*, 323–24.

44 Bulgakov, *Master and Margarita*, 324.

45 Bulgakov, *Master and Margarita*, 334.

46 Bulgakov, *Master and Margarita*, 335.

47 The variations on this phrase are helpfully set out for the English reader in Simon Franklin's introduction to Michael Glenny's translation (London: Everyman's Library, 1992).

48 Bulgakov, *Master and Margarita*, 8.

49 Bulgakov, *Master and Margarita*, 97.

50 Bulgakov, *Master and Margarita*, 125.

51 Bulgakov, *Master and Margarita*, 74, 285.

52 Bulgakov, *Master and Margarita*, 95.

53 Bulgakov, *Master and Margarita*, 112.
54 Bulgakov, *Master and Margarita*, 316.
55 Bulgakov, *Master and Margarita*, 216, 243.
56 Bulgakov, *Master and Margarita*, 244.

INDEX